Blond's
LAW GUIDES

Civil Procedure

Fifth Edition

RPR Publishing, Inc.

blondslaw.com

Blond's Law Guides: Civil Procedure, *Fifth Edition*
by Neil C. Blond, John Marafino, Mark Monack, Mark D. Pellis, & Louis Petrillo

Published by RPR Publishing, Inc.

For more Blond's Law Guides, please visit *www.blondslaw.com*

ISBN: 0-9760351-2-X

Civil Procedure

Fifth Edition

Neil C. Blond
John Marafino
Mark Monack
Mark D. Pellis
Louis Petrillo

RPR Publishing, Inc.

blondslaw.com

How To Use This Book

Law school is very different from your previous educational experiences. In the past, course material was presented in a straightforward manner both in lectures and texts. You did well by memorizing and regurgitating. In law school, your fat casebooks are stuffed with material, most of which will be useless when finals arrive. Your professors ask a lot of questions but don't seem to be teaching you either the law or how to think. Sifting through voluminous material seeking out the important concepts is a hard, time-consuming chore. We've done that job for you. This book will help you study effectively. We hope to teach you the law and how to think.

Preparing for class

Most students start their first year by reading and briefing all their cases. They spend too much time copying unimportant details. After finals they realize they wasted time on facts that were useless on the exam.

Case Clips

Case Clips help you focus on what your professor wants you to get out of your cases. Facts, Issues, and Rules are carefully and succinctly stated. Left out are details irrelevant to what you need to learn from the case. In general, we skip procedural matters in lower courts. We don't care which party is the appellant or petitioner because the trivia is not relevant to the law. Case Clips should be read before you read the actual case. You will have a good idea what to look for in the case, and appreciate the significance of what you are reading. Inevitably you will not have time to read all your cases before class. Case Clips allow you to prepare for class in about five minutes. You will be able to follow the discussion and listen without fear of being called upon.

"Should I read all the cases even if they aren't from my casebook?"

Yes, if you feel you have the time. Most major cases from other texts will be covered at least as a note case in your book. The principles of these cases are universal and the fact patterns should help your understanding. The Case Clips are written in a way that should provide a tremendous amount of understanding in a relatively short period of time.

EasyFlow™ Charts

A very common complaint among law students is that they "can't put it all together." When you are reading 400 pages a week it is difficult to remember how the last case relates to the first and how November's readings relate to September's. It's hard to understand the relationship between different torts topics when you have read cases for three or four other classes in between. Our EasyFlow™ Charts will help you put the whole course together. They are designed to help you memorize fundamentals. They reinforce your learning by showing you the material from another perspective.

Outlines

More than one hundred lawyers and law students were interviewed as part of the development of this series. Most complained that their casebooks did not teach them the law and were far too voluminous to be useful before an exam. They also told us that the commercial outlines they purchased were excellent when used as hornbooks to explain the law, but were too wordy and redundant to be effective during the weeks before finals. Few students can read four 500-page outlines during the last month of classes. It is virtually impossible to memorize that much material and even harder to decide what is important. Almost every student interviewed said he or she studied from homemade outlines. We've written the outline you should use to study.

"But writing my own outline will be a learning experience."

True, but unfortunately many students spend so much time outlining they don't leave time to learn and memorize. Many students told us they spent six weeks outlining, and only one day studying before each final!

Mnemonics

Most law students spend too much time reading, and not enough time memorizing. Mnemonics are included to help you organize your essays and spot issues. They highlight what is important and which areas deserve your time.

TABLE OF CONTENTS

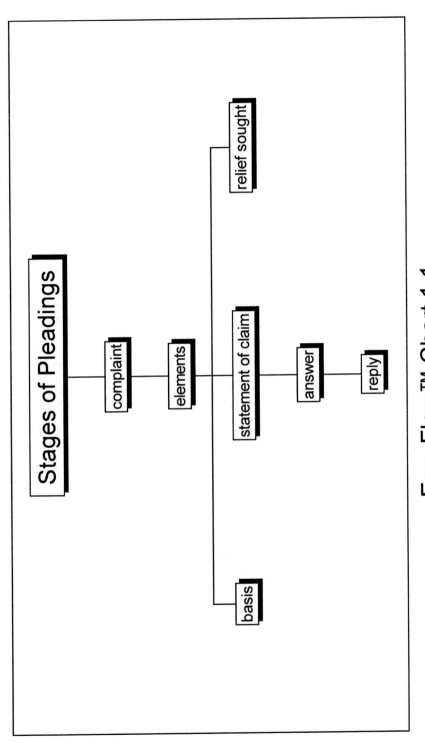

Stages of Pleadings

- complaint
  - elements
    - basis
    - statement of claim
    - relief sought
- answer
- reply

EasyFlow™ Chart 1.1

The Civil Action

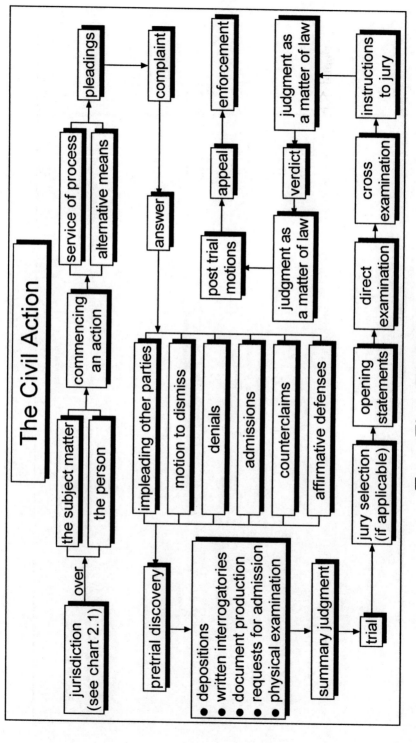

jurisdiction (see chart 2.1) — over — the subject matter / the person — commencing an action — service of process / alternative means — pleadings → complaint

complaint → answer → impleading other parties
- motion to dismiss
- denials
- admissions
- counterclaims
- affirmative defenses

impleading other parties → pretrial discovery
- depositions
- written interrogatories
- document production
- requests for admission
- physical examination

pretrial discovery → summary judgment → trial → jury selection (if applicable) → opening statements → direct examination → cross examination → instructions to jury → judgment as a matter of law → verdict → judgment as a matter of law → post trial motions → appeal → enforcement

EasyFlow™ Chart 1.2

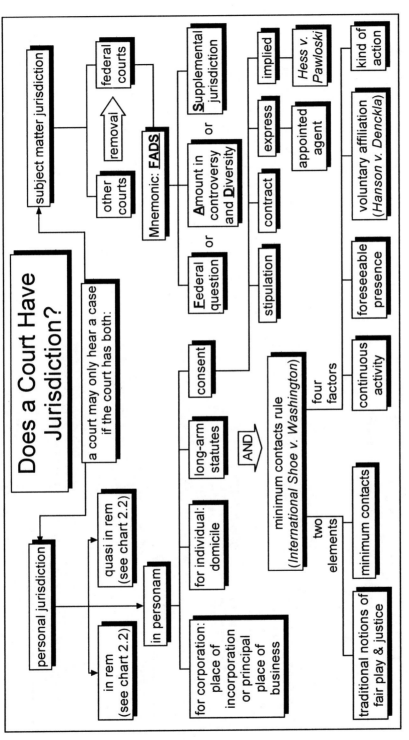

Does a Court Have Jurisdiction?

a court may only hear a case if the court has both:

subject matter jurisdiction

- federal courts
- other courts

removal

Mnemonic: **FADS**

- **F**ederal question
- or
- **A**mount in controversy and **D**iversity
- or
- **S**upplemental jurisdiction

- stipulation
- contract
- express
- implied

- appointed agent
- *Hess v. Pawloski*

personal jurisdiction

- in rem (see chart 2.2)
- quasi in rem (see chart 2.2)
- in personam
  - for individual: domicile
  - for corporation: place of incorporation or principal place of business

- long-arm statutes

AND

- consent

minimum contacts rule (*International Shoe v. Washington*)

four factors
- kind of action
- voluntary affiliation (*Hanson v. Denckla*)
- foreseeable presence
- continuous activity

two elements
- minimum contacts
- traditional notions of fair play & justice

EasyFlow™ Chart 2.1

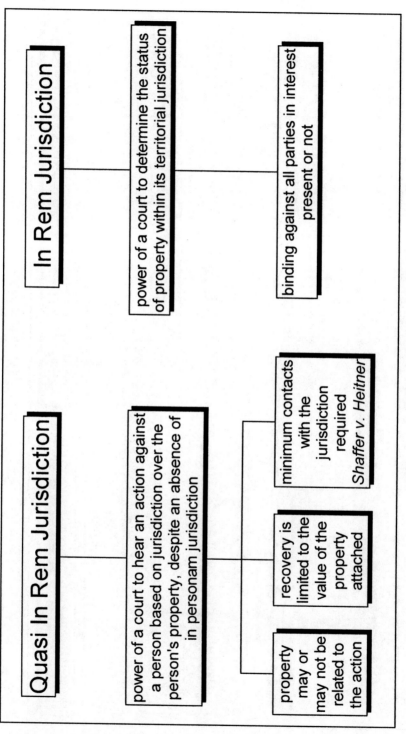

In Rem Jurisdiction

power of a court to determine the status of property within its territorial jurisdiction

binding against all parties in interest present or not

Quasi In Rem Jurisdiction

power of a court to hear an action against a person based on jurisdiction over the person's property, despite an absence of in personam jurisdiction

property may or may not be related to the action

recovery is limited to the value of the property attached

minimum contacts with the jurisdiction required *Shaffer v. Heitner*

EasyFlow™ Chart 2.2

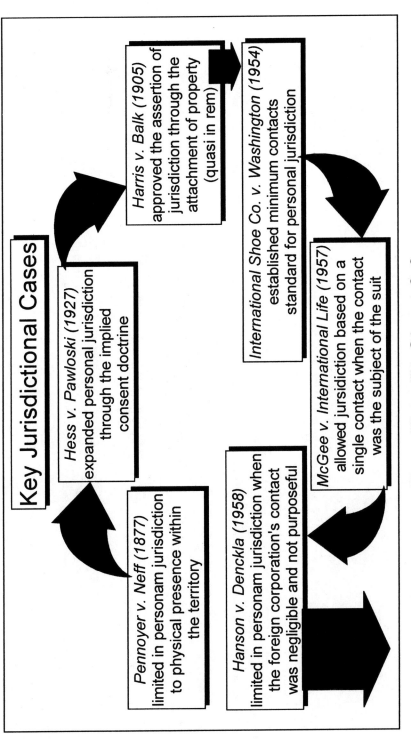

Key Jurisdictional Cases

Hess v. Pawloski (1927) expanded personal jurisdiction through the implied consent doctrine

Harris v. Balk (1905) approved the assertion of jurisdiction through the attachment of property (quasi in rem)

International Shoe Co. v. Washington (1954) established minimum contacts standard for personal jurisdiction

Pennoyer v. Neff (1877) limited in personam jurisdiction to physical presence within the territory

Hanson v. Denckla (1958) limited in personam jursidiction when the foreign corporation's contact was negligible and not purposeful

McGee v. International Life (1957) allowed jurisdiction based on a single contact when the contact was the subject of the suit

EasyFlow™ Chart 2.3

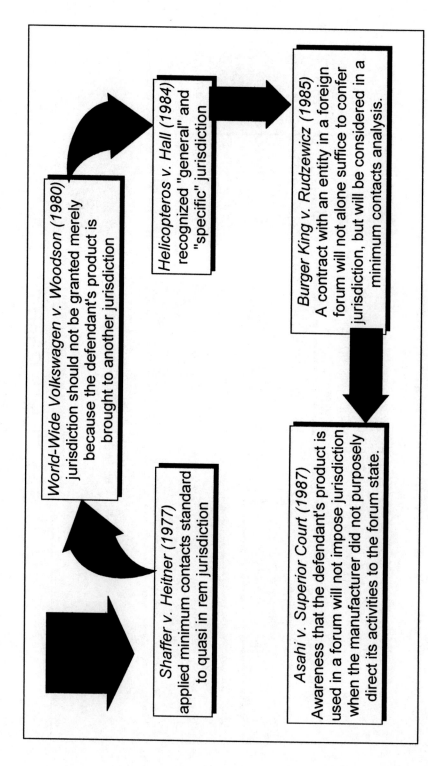

World-Wide Volkswagen v. Woodson (1980) jurisdiction should not be granted merely because the defendant's product is brought to another jurisdiction

Helicopteros v. Hall (1984) recognized "general" and "specific" jurisdiction

Burger King v. Rudzewicz (1985) A contract with an entity in a foreign forum will not alone suffice to confer jurisdiction, but will be considered in a minimum contacts analysis.

Shaffer v. Heitner (1977) applied minimum contacts standard to quasi in rem jurisdiction

Asahi v. Superior Court (1987) Awareness that the defendant's product is used in a forum will not impose jurisdiction when the manufacturer did not purposely direct its activities to the forum state.

EasyFlow™ Chart 2.4

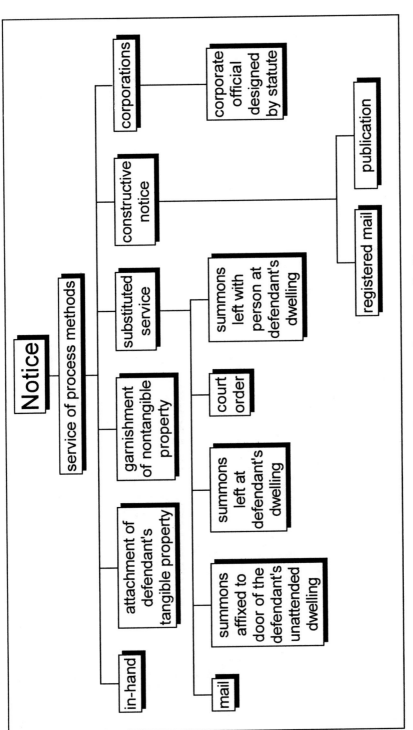

Notice

- service of process methods
  - in-hand
  - attachment of defendant's tangible property
    - mail
      - summons affixed to door of the defendant's unattended dwelling
  - garnishment of nontangible property
    - summons left at defendant's dwelling
    - court order
  - substituted service
    - summons left with person at defendant's dwelling
- constructive notice
  - registered mail
  - publication
- corporations
  - corporate official designed by statute

EasyFlow™ Chart 2.5

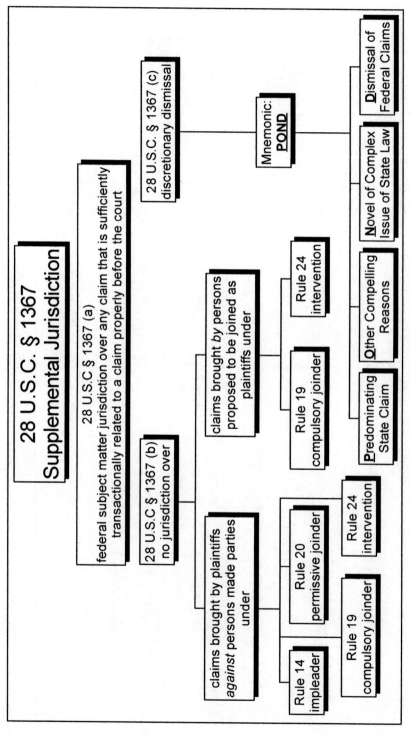

28 U.S.C. § 1367
Supplemental Jurisdiction

28 U.S.C § 1367 (a)
federal subject matter jurisdiction over any claim that is sufficiently transactionally related to a claim properly before the court

28 U.S.C § 1367 (b)
no jurisdiction over

claims brought by plaintiffs *against* persons made parties under

Rule 14 impleader

Rule 19 compulsory joinder

Rule 20 permissive joinder

Rule 24 intervention

claims brought *by* persons proposed to be joined as plaintiffs under

Rule 19 compulsory joinder

Rule 24 intervention

28 U.S.C. § 1367 (c)
discretionary dismissal

Mnemonic: **POND**

Predominating State Claim

Other Compelling Reasons

Novel of Complex Issue of State Law

Dismissal of Federal Claims

EasyFlow™ Chart 2.6

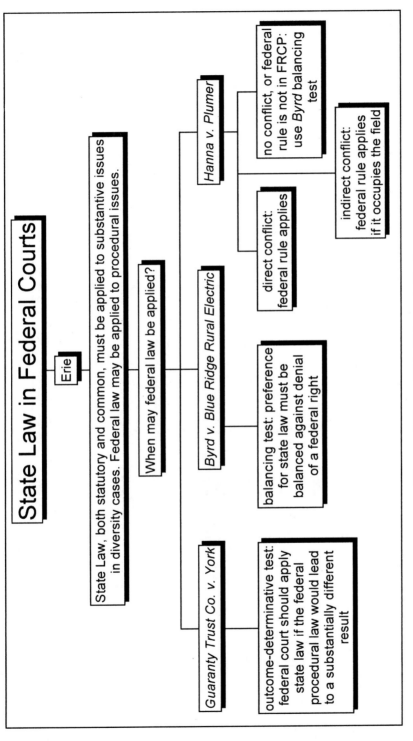

State Law in Federal Courts

Erie

State Law, both statutory and common, must be applied to substantive issues in diversity cases. Federal law may be applied to procedural issues.

When may federal law be applied?

Guaranty Trust Co. v. York

outcome-determinative test: federal court should apply state law if the federal procedural law would lead to a substantially different result

Byrd v. Blue Ridge Rural Electric

balancing test: preference for state law must be balanced against denial of a federal right

Hanna v. Plumer

direct conflict: federal rule applies

no conflict, or federal rule is not in FRCP: use *Byrd* balancing test

indirect conflict: federal rule applies if it occupies the field

EasyFlow™ Chart 3.1

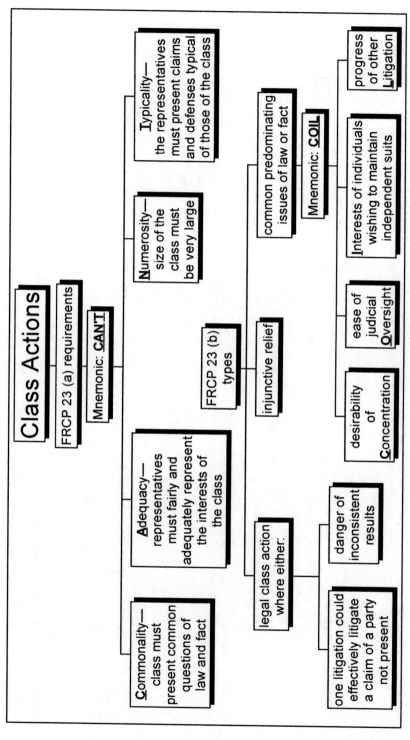

Class Actions

FRCP 23 (a) requirements

Mnemonic: **CAN'T**

- **C**ommonality—class must present common questions of law and fact
- **A**dequacy—representatives must fairly and adequately represent the interests of the class
- **N**umerosity—size of the class must be very large
- **T**ypicality—the representatives must present claims and defenses typical of those of the class

FRCP 23 (b) types

- legal class action where either:
  - one litigation could effectively litigate a claim of a party not present
  - danger of inconsistent results
- injunctive relief
- common predominating issues of law or fact

Mnemonic: **COIL**

- desirability of **C**oncentration
- ease of judicial **O**versight
- **I**nterests of individuals wishing to maintain independent suits
- progress of other **L**itigation

EasyFlow™ Chart 6.1

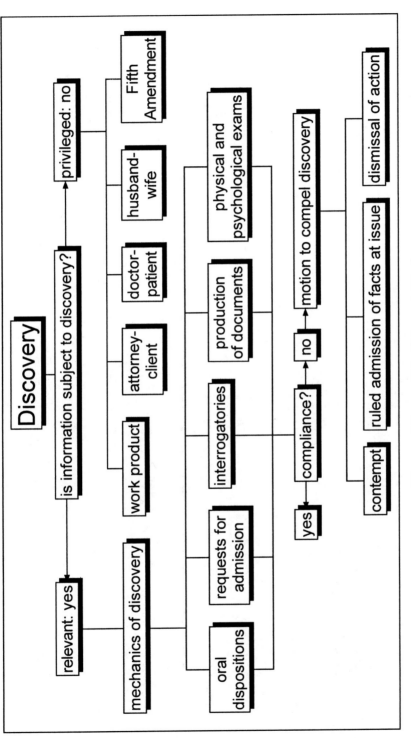

EasyFlow™ Chart 7.1

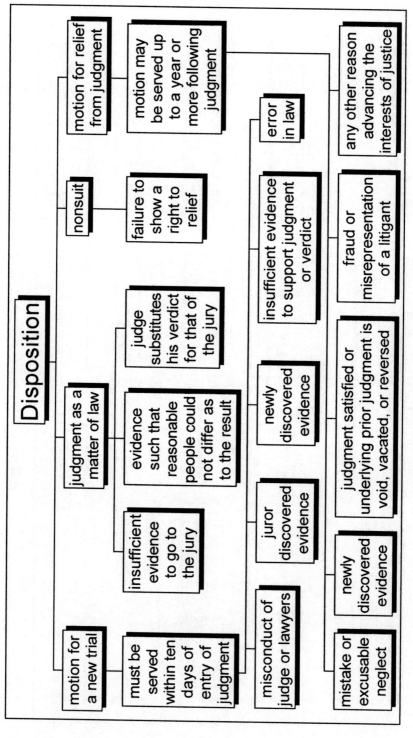

Disposition

- **motion for a new trial**
  - must be served within ten days of entry of judgment
    - misconduct of judge or lawyers
    - juror discovered evidence
    - newly discovered evidence
  - insufficient evidence to go to the jury
- **judgment as a matter of law**
  - evidence such that reasonable people could not differ as to the result
  - judge substitutes his verdict for that of the jury
- **nonsuit**
  - failure to show a right to relief
- **motion for relief from judgment**
  - motion may be served up to a year or more following judgment
    - insufficient evidence to support judgment or verdict
      - newly discovered evidence
      - judgment satisfied or underlying prior judgment is void, vacated, or reversed
      - mistake or excusable neglect
    - fraud or misrepresentation of a litigant
    - error in law
    - any other reason advancing the interests of justice

EasyFlow™ Chart 9.1

Claim Preclusion (Res Judicata)

After a valid and final judgment, a transactionally related claim may not be relitigated between the parties of the original suit.

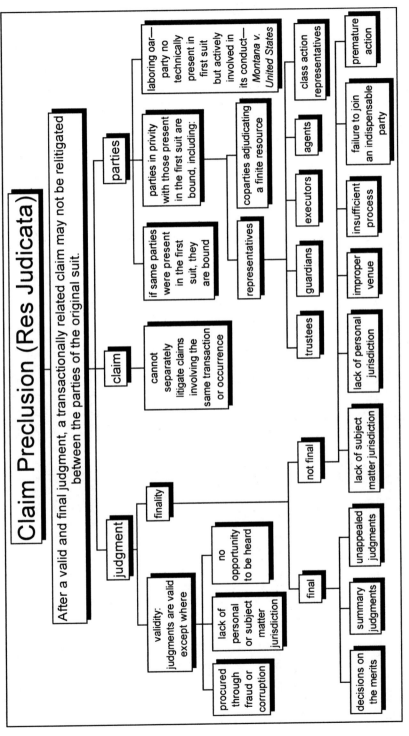

judgment

- **finality**
  - **not final**
    - lack of personal jurisdiction
    - lack of subject matter jurisdiction
  - **final**
    - decisions on the merits
    - summary judgments
    - unappealed judgments
- **validity: judgments are valid except where**
  - procured through fraud or corruption
  - lack of personal or subject matter jurisdiction
  - no opportunity to be heard

claim

- cannot separately litigate claims involving the same transaction or occurrence

parties

- if same parties were present in the first suit, they are bound
- parties in privity with those present in the first suit are bound, including:
  - representatives
    - trustees
    - guardians
    - executors
    - agents
  - coparties adjudicating a finite resource
  - class action representatives
- laboring oar—party no technically present in first suit but actively involved in its conduct—*Montana v. United States*

- lack of personal jurisdiction
- improper venue
- insufficient process
- failure to join an indispensable party
- premature action

EasyFlow™ Chart 11.1

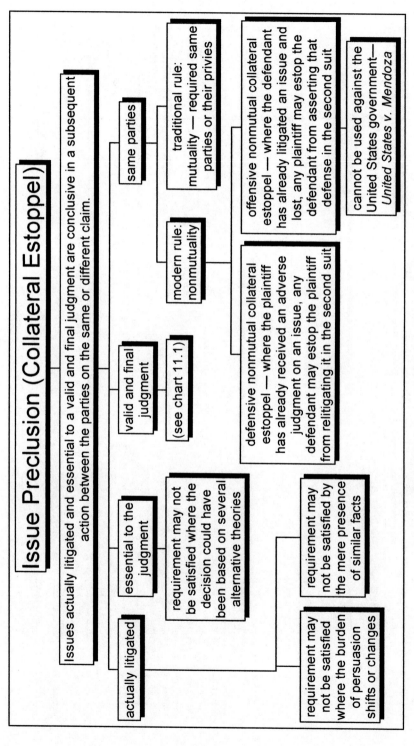

Issue Preclusion (Collateral Estoppel)

Issues actually litigated and essential to a valid and final judgment are conclusive in a subsequent action between the parties on the same or different claim.

actually litigated

- requirement may not be satisfied where the burden of persuasion shifts or changes
- requirement may not be satisfied by the mere presence of similar facts

essential to the judgment

- requirement may not be satisfied where the decision could have been based on several alternative theories

valid and final judgment

(see chart 11.1)

same parties

- traditional rule: mutuality — required same parties or their privies

modern rule: nonmutuality

- defensive nonmutual collateral estoppel — where the plaintiff has already received an adverse judgment on an issue, any defendant may estop the plaintiff from relitigating it in the second suit

- offensive nonmutual collateral estoppel — where the defendant has already litigated an issue and lost, any plaintiff may estop the defendant from asserting that defense in the second suit

- cannot be used against the United States government— *United States v. Mendoza*

EasyFlow™ Chart 11.2

CHAPTER 1

INTRODUCTION

As an introduction to civil procedure, it is sometimes helpful to look at the process of a civil action, both the procedures and issues involved.

I. COMMENCING THE ACTION
    The plaintiff must notify the defendant of the suit being brought, what court is asserting jurisdiction over the case, and something of the nature of the case (although exactly what is needed is unclear and will be discussed in greater detail elsewhere in the book).
    There are various methods of commencing the action, but the most common is service of process.

II. PLEADINGS

A. Filing the Complaint
    The plaintiff must also notify the court of the impending case. This is done by filing a complaint.

    1. Benefits of Being a Plaintiff
       As plaintiff, a party has great leeway in framing the structure of the case:

       a. The plaintiff gets to choose (at least initially) whether federal or state courts will be used.

       b. The plaintiff chooses (also initially) the state or district in which the suit is brought.

       c. The plaintiff initially defines the issues involved, including what parties to join as defendants, what relief is sought (injunctive, monetary or both), and how much.

    2. Burdens of Being a Plaintiff

       a. To the Court
           The plaintiff must also carefully frame the nature of the case, for if the plaintiff fails to set forth certain very

specific requirements (which will be discussed in detail in Chapter 2), the case may be dismissed.

    b.   To the Defendant
The plaintiff must also set forth in the complaint enough information such that the defendant may identify and respond to the allegations.

B.   Responsive Pleadings
What follows from the initial pleadings are a series of responses by both parties.

1. Purpose
The pleadings are designed to identify the precise issues disputed by the parties, thereby saving both the courts and parties' time and money that may have been wasted arguing irrelevant or undisputed issues.

However, the pleadings may also be used to harass parties or delay the action.

2. Content
In the pleadings, a party may:

    a.   Amend the Complaint

    b.   Assert an Affirmative Defense

    c.   Assert a Counterclaim

    d.   Implead a Third Party

    e.   Make a Motion to Dismiss

    f.   Admit and Deny Factual Allegations

III.   DISCOVERY
After the pleadings, parties then use various pretrial procedures in order to unearth knowledge in the other party's possession, or in the possession of witnesses. Discovery, however, is not designed to allow a party to discover their opponent's legal strategy, and there are several safeguards and sanctions available to courts and parties to ensure proper discovery.

Some discovery tools available to the litigator are:

A. Depositions
    Used to orally interview witnesses.

B. Written Interrogatories
    Used to compel written answers to submitted questionnaires.

C. Subpoenas Duces Tecum
    Used to compel production of documents in a witness's possession.

D. Medical Examinations
    Either physical or psychological, it must be for a specific and necessary purpose, such as determining the extent of injuries, or determining mental capacity.

IV. TRIAL

A. Jury Trials

    1. Trial by jury is a right in certain actions (criminal trial, most federal court suits).

    2. Jurors are usually selected by the judge.

    3. Peremptory challenges (challenge for no reason) to jury selection are allowed.

B. Trial Procedure

    1. Order of Parties
       The plaintiff always goes first.

    2. Opening Statements
       The parties briefly explain their positions and what they hope to prove.

    3. Questioning of Witnesses

    a.   Direct Examination
Witness' initial questioning. Evidence may be introduced through a witness' reference to it. The evidence must comply with the appropriate rules of evidence (state law or the Federal Rules of Evidence).

    b.   Cross-Examination
Witness' answers to direct examination may be probed, or additional information known to the witness may be brought out.

    c.   Redirect
After cross-examination the party who called the witness may question them about matters brought out in cross-examination.

4. Motion for Summary Judgment
If a party has not produced enough evidence to sustain its claim, and the judge feels that no reasonable jury could find otherwise, the judge may summarily dismiss the claim or issue of law involved or, alternatively, direct the jury that the issue involved cannot be decided otherwise.

5. Closing Arguments
Parties summarize their version of the case.

6. Jury Instruction
Judge tells jury the relevant law, and instructs them as to the relevant burdens of persuasion, as well as any presumptions they may be entitled to make. If there is to be a general verdict with interrogatories or a special verdict, the judge will also instruct the jury on these issues.

7. Verdict

    a.   General Verdict
Jury decides which party prevails.

    b.   General Verdict With Interrogatories
In complicated cases, a judge may require a jury to answer a questionnaire in order to ensure that the jury fully understood the issues involved.

    c. Special Verdict
The jury only decides limited factual issues that the judge uses to reach a final decision.

V.   APPEAL

A.   Reversing the Jury
A jury may only be overturned where no evidence submitted could have resulted in a jury deciding as it did.

B.   Reversing the Judge

1. Factual Findings
A judge's findings of fact may be reversed only where "clearly erroneous." This standard is supposed to be very high.

2. Procedural Findings
A case may be successfully appealed where a judge's procedural conclusions constitute an "abuse of discretion."

3. Legal Findings
Generally, courts will reverse a trial judge who has misapplied the applicable law.

CASE CLIPS

Capron v. Van Noorden (S.Ct. 1804)

Facts: Capron brought an action in federal court without either raising a federal question, or alleging diversity of citizenship.

Issue: May an action in federal court be successfully challenged on appeal on the grounds that neither diversity of citizenship nor a federal question exist?

Rule: Where federal questions are not at issue and diversity of citizenship does not exist, a federal court does not have jurisdiction to hear a case and a judgment of the federal court must be reversed on appeal.

Tickle v. Barton (1956)

Facts: In order to assert jurisdiction over Barton, Tickle's attorney phoned Barton and deceitfully induced him to attend a banquet in the county where Tickle had brought his action.

Issue: Is service of process valid when a party was originally brought within the jurisdiction of the court by deceit?

Rule: Where a party is brought within the jurisdiction of the court by deceit, the courts will deem the service of process invalid and refuse jurisdiction.

Case v. State Mutual Automobile Insurance Co. (1961)

Facts: Three insurance companies had appointed Case to act as their agent pursuant to a written contract that allowed any party to terminate the contract without cause. Case brought an action after the contract was terminated, alleging malicious and wrongful termination of the contract. The complaint did not set forth an independent claim in tort alleging interference by the insurance companies in Case's performance of the contract, although the facts would have supported such a claim had it been asserted.

Issue: When the plaintiff presents facts upon which a valid claim might be asserted but does not raise that claim in the pleadings, should the court create the claim?

Rule: It is the court's duty to adjudicate cases based solely on the pleadings before it. Courts should not create claims that the parties have not raised.

Temple v. Synthes Corp. (S.Ct. 1990)

Facts: Temple underwent surgery to have a plate-and-screw device implanted in his spine. After surgery, the screws broke. Synthes manufactured the device. Temple filed a federal suit against Synthes and a separate state action against the doctor and hospital. Synthes filed a motion to dismiss Temple's federal suit for failure to join necessary parties (the doctor and the hospital) pursuant to FRCP 19.

Issue: Are joint tortfeasors indispensable parties under FRCP 19?

Rule: Although there is a public interest in avoiding multiple lawsuits, it is not necessary for all joint tortfeasors to be named as defendants in a single lawsuit. Therefore, joint tortfeasors are not indispensable parties under FRCP 19 and failure to join them is not grounds for dismissal.

DiMichel v. South Buffalo Railway Co. (1992)

Facts: DiMichel commenced action against his former employer, South Buffalo, for injuries sustained while falling at work. DiMichel asked for the disclosure of any video or surveillance films that South Buffalo may have taken of him. South Buffalo refused on the grounds that such material was undiscoverable.

Issue: Are surveillance films prepared by a defendant in a personal injury action discoverable by the plaintiff before trial?

Rule: Surveillance films should be treated as material prepared in anticipation of litigation, and are therefore subject to a qualified privilege. This can be overcome by a factual showing of substantial need and undue hardship by the plaintiff.

Alderman v. Baltimore & Ohio R. Co. (1953)

Facts: While traveling on the defendant's train with a free pass that contained a waiver of liability, Alderman was injured in a derailment caused by a sudden break in a rail. In light of the legal effect of the waiver, she charged the railroad with willful or wanton conduct, although she could offer no proof of such willfulness.

Issue: May a court properly grant summary judgment where the undenied facts of the parties' affidavits show that plaintiff cannot substantiate the charge?

Rule: A court must grant summary judgment for defendant where the facts are undisputed and it is in the nature of the case that plaintiff will be unable to prove the elements of the case at trial.

Alexander v. Kramer Bros. Freight Lines, Inc. (1959)

Facts: A trial judge erroneously placed the burden of proof of contributory negligence on the defendant trucking company, who had taken exception during an off-the-record discussion with the judge at the close of Alexander's case, but failed to object at all during the trial.

Issue: May a judgment be reversed because a trial court placed the burden of proof on the wrong party, where the party did not object on the record at trial?

Rule: A party who fails to object to a jury charge at trial waives that issue on appeal.

Diniero v. United States Lines Co. (1961)

Facts: A jury found one of the judge's interrogatories so ambiguous as to be unanswerable. The judge then withdrew all written interrogatories and instructed the jury to bring in a general verdict for the personal injury action. The jury returned a verdict for the plaintiff.

Issue: May a judge withdraw written interrogatories from jury consideration for the purpose of eliminating confusion?

Rule: Withdrawing written interrogatories is not an abuse of a trial judge's discretion where the defendant is not thereby prejudiced.

Note: Distinguish this case from one in which the jury simply delays in returning answers to interrogatories, and the trial judge withdraws the interrogatories. That is prejudicial to the defendant, and reversible error.

Texas Employers' Insurance Association. v. Price (1960)

Facts: During jury deliberations in a personal injury action, one of the jurors related his personal experiences in an effort to persuade the jury.

Issue: Is a juror's effort to persuade a jury by relating his personal experiences reversible error?

Rule: It is misconduct and reversible error for a juror to relate to other jurors his own personal experience as original evidence of material facts to be considered in their deliberations.

Lavender v. Kurn (S.Ct. 1946)

Facts: In an action under the Federal Employers Liability Act, the administrator of the decedent's estate alleged that decedent had been killed by a mail hook protruding from the side of defendant's railway car in the dark. The court of appeals reversed the jury's verdict for the decedent's estate, asserting that the jury's decision was based on speculation.

Issue: When may an appellate court reverse a jury's decision on the grounds that the jury must have used speculation and conjecture in reaching its decision?

Rule: (Murphy, J.) An appellate court may reverse a jury's decision only where there is a complete absence of probative facts to support the jury's verdict.

Hicks v. United States (1966)

Facts: In an action tried under the Federal Tort Claims Act, the administrator of the decedent's estate alleged negligence, based on failure of "ordinary care" on the part of the Navy doctor. The doctor had examined decedent in the emergency room, told her she had an intestinal "bug," and sent her home, where she died of an obstruction. The district court relied upon the testimony of the government's expert witness in determining that the doctor had exercised "average judgment," and entered judgment for the government.

Issue: When may a court of appeals reverse a trial judge's finding of negligence, as opposed to a finding of fact, which may only be set aside where "clearly erroneous"?

Rule: An appellate court may freely review a trial judge's ruling on the issue of negligence, as it is not a question of fact.

Des Moines Navigation & R. Co. v. Iowa Homestead Co. (S.Ct. 1887)

Facts: The Homestead Company removed an action from state court to federal court, and a verdict was rendered there despite a lack of diversity of jurisdiction. The railroad company subsequently instituted a new action on the same claim in state court, claiming that the federal court's judgment had been void for lack of subject matter jurisdiction.

Issue: Is the judgment of a court fully binding on the parties, even if the court had no jurisdiction to hear the case?

Rule: (Waite, C. J.) Federal jurisdiction must be challenged in the course of federal court proceedings. Unless so challenged, decisions of the federal court are binding on the parties.

Georgia High School Association v. Waddell (1981)

Facts: Parents of players on a football team challenged a referee's decision made in a high school football game.

Issue: May state courts review decisions of high school football referees?

Rule: State courts are without authority to review decisions of high school referees, since decisions of referees do not present judicial controversies.

Cudahy Junior Chamber of Commerce v. Quirk (1969)

Facts: In a brochure regarding an upcoming referendum on water fluoridation, Quirk offered $1,000 to the Cudahy Junior Chamber of Commerce if they could prove that fluoridation was safe. They claimed to have done so, and demanded their $1,000.

Issue: May courts decide the accuracy of statements made in public debates concerning public referenda?

Rule: The courts will not decide the accuracy of statements made regarding a public referendum when such issues are not relevant to a pending case or controversy, such as slander or libel.

Note: The court also concluded that wagers are unenforceable as they are against public policy.

Frummer v. Hilton Hotels International, Inc. (1969)

Facts: Frummer, staying in a Hilton Hotel in London, England, injured himself in the shower. He sued Hilton in New York and lost. On appeal, Frummer demanded that the court set aside a jury verdict for the defendant because the court had improperly charged the jury with New York instead of British law.

Issue: May a jury verdict be set aside on the grounds that the jury was charged with law of the wrong jurisdiction, although such issue was not raised at trial?

Rule: Although a court is not required to know the applicable law of a foreign country unless raised at trial, a new trial may be ordered in the interests of justice.

Sibbach v. Wilson & Co. (1941)

Facts: Sibbach, having asserted a personal injury action, refused to submit to a physical examination and was found guilty of contempt.

Issue: Does the Supreme Court have the authority to enact the Federal Rules of Civil Procedure, which include the right to request physical examinations and exempt the arrest of parties who fail to undertake such examinations?

Rule: (Roberts, J.) Congress has validly authorized the Supreme Court to enact rules governing procedural rights, such as the right to request a litigant to undergo a physical examination as well as the consequences for failure to undergo such an exam.

Gordon v. Steele (1974)

Facts: Gordon left her parents home in Pennsylvania to attend college in Idaho. She had an apartment in Idaho and intended to remain there indefinitely, although she returned to Pennsylvania during vacations and maintained a Pennsylvania Driver's License. At age 19, Gordon brought a malpractice action in federal court against two doctors who were Pennsylvania citizens. The defendants moved to dismiss for lack of diversity.

Issue: Where are students who attend out-of-state colleges domiciled?

Rule: In light of the modern trend to treat 18-year-olds as emancipated, a factfinder should determine whether a student has established a new domicile by looking to such circumstances as declarations of intent, exercise of political rights, payment of personal taxes, house of residence, and place of business. In this case, the court found that Gordon was domiciled in Idaho, primarily because she rented an apartment there and had no intent to return to Pennsylvania.

Smith v. Egger (1985)

Facts: Smith filed an action requesting damages and seeking a restraining order against IRS officials who had attempted to levy on Smith's property for past due taxes. The defendants requested reimbursement for their attorneys' fees on grounds that the action was frivolous and without any merit because, inter alia, the claim was barred by statute.

Issue: May defendants recover attorneys' fees expended to defend against frivolous claims?

Rule: Under FRCP 11, parties and/or their attorneys can be held liable for reasonable expenses incurred in defending against signed papers (i.e., pleadings, motions, etc.) that are clearly not grounded in fact, warranted by existing law, or a good faith argument for extension of the law. Here, the plaintiff's original claim was clearly without merit because it was barred by a statute, such that it appeared that the complaints were filed solely to harass and delay tax collection. Therefore, they were liable for the attorneys' fees reasonably incurred in defending against the claims.

Bell v. Novick Transfer Co. (1955)

Facts: In a negligence action arising out of an auto accident, the defendants moved to dismiss on the basis that the complaint did not allege specific acts of negligence, but only that "an accident occurred due to the negligence of the defendants as a result of which the plaintiffs were injured."

Issue: What information must a complaint contain?

Rule: Under FRCP 8, a complaint need only contain a short and plain statement of the claim snowing that the pleader is entitled to relief. The defendant may obtain more detailed information later through discovery procedures (e.g., interrogatories, depositions, etc.). Thus, the court held that Bell's complaint was sufficient and overruled Novick Transfer's motion to dismiss.

Note: This action was originally filed in Maryland State court and removed to federal court. Had the action remained in State court, Maryland rules of procedure would have applied under which the complaint may not have been sufficient.

Goldinger v. Boron (1973)

Facts: As part of a contract action, Goldinger alleged that the defendant's commission manager agreements were unconscionable. Goldinger filed a Motion to Compel (FRCP 37(a)) Boron to answer an interrogatory that asked whether Boron had entered into new agreements with commission managers and, if so, why changes were made to the agreements.

Issue 1: Can parties obtain discovery of information concerning acts and events that transpired after the cause of action arose?

Rule 1: Discovery of acts and events occurring after the cause of action arose is permitted where there is a possibility that the information sought may be relevant to the subject matter of the pending action, even if that information may not be admissible at trial.

Issue 2: Does attorney-client privilege protect information from discovery?

Rule 2: Information is protected from discovery by attorney-client privilege if it satisfies the four-part privilege test: (1) confidence that the communication will not be disclosed, (2) confidentiality of the disclosure, (3) an existing legal relationship between the parties, and (4) if the injury disclosure would cause to the client is greater than the benefit to the factfinder. Under this rule, Baron Oil's agreements are discoverable because they must be read and signed by someone other than the defendant and its attorney (i.e., they are not confidential). The rationale for any changes in the agreements, however, is privileged legal planning and is therefore not discoverable.

Houchins v. American Home Assurance Co. (1991)

Facts: Mr. Houchins was missing for over seven years and, by law, presumed dead. He had two life insurance policies, both of which required that the insured's death be accidental to be entitled to coverage. Mrs. Houchins sued for payment on the policies. American Home moved for summary judgment on the ground that Mrs. Houchins offered no evidence to establish that the death was accidental.

Issue: May a party defeat a motion for summary judgment by offering an inference as evidence of a material fact?

Rule: FRCP 56(c) provides that summary judgment must be granted against a party that fails to make a snowing sufficient to establish the existence of an element essential to that party's case. A presumption of a material fact, such as a legal presumption of death, is sufficient to defeat a summary judgment motion. However/an inference based on another inference (e.g., presuming death and then inferring that it was accidental) is too meager to provide evidence sufficient to defeat a summary judgment motion.

Norton v. Snapper Power Equipment (1987)

Facts: Norton was injured when the Snapper mower he was riding slid into a creek; the blade sliced off four of his fingers. The mower was found to be defective because it did not have a "dead-man" device to stop the blade. Norton did not know exactly how or when his hand got caught in the blade. After the jury rendered a verdict in favor of Norton, Snapper requested a directed verdict on the grounds that there was not sufficient evidence from which a jury could have found that a "dead-man" device would have reduced or prevented Norton's injuries.

Issue: What is the standard for granting a judgment notwithstanding the verdict?

Rule: A verdict cannot be based on speculation and conjecture. However, a jury can reach a verdict by reconstructing events by drawing inference upon inference. A court should grant judgment notwithstanding the verdict only where the evidence, when viewed in the light most favorable to the nonmoving party, so strongly points in favor of the moving party that reasonable people could not find otherwise.

Dunn v. Phoenix Newspapers (1984)

Facts: Newspaper home-delivery carriers brought an anti-trust suit against the publisher of two newspapers, alleging illegal price fixing. At a bench trial (i.e., no jury), the court decided in favor of the defendants. The plaintiffs appealed.

Issue: What is the standard for appellate review of a lower court decision?

Rule: On appeal, an appellate court reviews findings of law *de novo* (considers the issues anew). Findings of fact, however, must stand unless the findings are clearly erroneous.

CHAPTER 2

JURISDICTION

I. OVERVIEW
    A court may only hear a case if the court has both:

A. Subject Matter Jurisdiction
    Power to adjudicate that kind of case presented.

      i. Power to act.

      ii. The defendant must be provided with adequate notice and opportunity to be heard.

B. Personal Jurisdiction
    Power over the parties or property involved.

1. In personam jurisdiction
   The court has jurisdiction due to its power over the defendant himself.

2. In rem jurisdiction
   The court has jurisdiction due to its power over the property in question.

3. Quasi in rem jurisdiction
   The court has jurisdiction by seizing property that belongs to the defendant but that is not the property that is the subject of the litigation.

II. SUBJECT MATTER JURISDICTION

A. Defined
    Power of a court to decide the kind of action before it.
    Mnemonic: **FADES**

B. **F**ederal Question Cases

1. Federal courts have jurisdiction over "all civil actions arising under the Constitution, laws, or treaties of the United States."

2. Although cases to be decided under federal question jurisdiction have never been precisely defined, most cases will have federal law as the source of the cause of action.

3. Claims created by state law that require interpretation of a federal law do NOT fall within federal question jurisdiction.

C.   Diversity

1. <u>A</u>mount in Controversy

   a.   This rule does not apply to federal question cases.

   b.   The party seeking federal jurisdiction must show that his claim was made in good faith and that it is possible the amount in controversy is over $75,000. The party is not required to prove the actual value of the amount in controversy.

   c.   The party challenging the jurisdiction will only prevail if he shows with "legal certainty" that the claim will be adjudicated for less than $75,000.

   d.   The jurisdiction may not be challenged if the actual recovery turns out to be less than $75,000.

   e.   Under the majority rule, the amount at stake must be $75,000 to either the plaintiff or the defendant.

   f.   Multiple plaintiffs or defendants:

      i.   One plaintiff may aggregate several claims against a single defendant to reach the $75,000 minimum.

      ii.   One plaintiff may not aggregate several claims against several defendants nor may he join claims against other defendants when he has aggregated several claims against one defendant to reach the minimum.

      iii.   Multiple plaintiffs will qualify for federal jurisdiction when at least one plaintiffs claim is valued at $75,000.

        iv. Jurisdiction will not be allowed when several plaintiffs' claims total $75,000 but no single claim is $75,000. **Exception:** Two or more plaintiffs enforcing the same right or interest that they share or own.

        v. The same rules apply for class action suits.

        vi. A counterclaim may satisfy the $75,000 requirement.

  2. **D**iversity of Citizenship

      a. Complete Diversity
Each plaintiff must be from a different state than each defendant. However, co-plaintiffs and co-defendants may be citizens from the same state.

      b. Minimal Diversity
In federal interpleader cases, there is diversity where one or more plaintiffs are from a different state than one or more of the defendants.

      c. Citizenship is measured at the time the suit is brought, not at the time of the event in controversy.

D. **E**numerated Areas

  1. Constitution
The Constitution enumerates various areas where the federal courts have original jurisdiction, such as admiralty and cases involving ambassadors and public ministers. None of these cases require the amount in controversy.

  2. Statutes
Congress has also passed statutes granting federal courts exclusive and original jurisdiction over certain areas of the law, including patent and copyright law, antitrust law, and cases where the United States is a party. With the exception of cases where the United States is a defendant, no amount in controversy requirement need be met.

E.   Supplemental Jurisdiction

1. Traditional View
Prior to the passage of the Federal Judiciary Act of 1991, state claims and parties, which would otherwise have to be adjudicated in a state court due to lack of federal subject matter jurisdiction, might be joined with a valid federal claim by virtue of notions known as pendent and ancillary jurisdiction.

   a.   Pendent Jurisdiction
   By filing a state claim at the same time as a federal claim, and petitioning the federal court to hear both claims, a party is attempting to pend the state claim to the federal claim.

   b.   Ancillary Jurisdiction
   By petitioning a federal court presently hearing a valid federal claim to attach a state claim onto the federal proceeding, a party is requesting the court assert ancillary jurisdiction. The distinction between the two is largely academic because the rules governing both types of jurisdiction are identical, and in any event, they have both been rendered moot by the supplemental jurisdiction statute.

   c.   Rules for Pendent/Ancillary Jurisdiction
   As long as the state and federal claims derive from a "common nucleus of operative facts," the state and the federal claim may both be litigated in federal court, unless:

      i.   The federal claim is dismissed before trial, or

      ii. The federal claim is based solely on diversity, and diversity does not exist with regards to the state claim (*United States v. Finley*).

2. Supplemental Jurisdiction
To correct what many perceived as the Supreme Court's misinterpretation of pendent and ancillary jurisdiction, Congress in 1991 enacted 28 U.S.C. § 1367.

a. What is Covered? (28 U.S.C. § 1367(a))
Federal courts may now hear almost any claim that is transactionally related to a claim that is properly before the court. "Transactionally related" means that the supplemental claim arises out of the same transaction, occurrence or series of transactions or occurrences as the claim properly before the court.

b. What is not Covered? (28 U.S.C. § 1367(b))
Claims brought by impleaded parties (FRCP 14), necessary parties (FRCP 19), indispensable parties (FRCP 20) and intervenors (FRCP 24) may not be attached to an existing diversity claim unless there is independent satisfaction of the diversity and amount in controversy requirements.

c. Discretionary Dismissal (28 U.S.C. § 1367(c))
Even if a claim is not prohibited under § 1367(b), a court may still dismiss a supplemental claim at its discretion if:

Mnemonic: **POND**

i. **P**redominating State Claim
When the state claim predominates over the federal case it would be fairer to have a state court decide the case.

ii. **O**ther Compelling Reasons
The statute requires "exceptional circumstances," but it has yet to be seen how rigid this requirement will be.

iii. **N**ovel or Complex State Law
State courts are more qualified than federal courts to develop novel issues of state law.

iv. **D**ismissal of Federal Claims
The courts will be wary of using fraudulent diversity claims simply to get around federal jurisdiction requirements.

III. PERSONAL JURISDICTION

A. In Personam

1. Physical Presence

   a. *Pennoyer v. Neff* (S.Ct. 1877)
   A state court cannot assert in personam jurisdiction over a defendant unless the defendant was personally served with process in the state or the defendant voluntarily appeared before the court. But a state court may exercise jurisdiction over a defendant's property, even if the property is not related to the action at hand, if the property is located within the court's jurisdiction.

   b. Kinds of jurisdiction:

      i. In Personam
      Personal service on the defendant within the state.

      ii. In Rem
      Attachment of defendant's in-state property when the defendant is out of state.

   c. Momentary Presence

   d. Jurisdiction may be asserted over any person entering the state for even a brief moment such as persons passing through by car or flying over in a plane.

2. Domicile

   a. Defined
   A court has in personam jurisdiction over an individual though the person is not physically within the jurisdiction if that person was domiciled within the court's jurisdiction.

b. Determination
Domicile is determined by:

   i. Party's intent to permanently locate there, and

   ii. An affirmative act expressing such intent.

c. Limitation
A person may only have one domicile, even though he has more than one residence.

3. Jurisdiction Based On Consent

a. A court may render a binding enforceable judgment against a party who consents to the jurisdiction of the court even if the court would not have had jurisdiction over the individual absent his consent.

b. Kinds of Consent

   i. Express Consent

     (1) Defendant stipulates court's jurisdiction in advance of litigation.

     (2) Parties to a contract may specify jurisdiction in case of a dispute.

     (3) Parties to a contract appoint an in-state agent to accept process.

     (4) An appearance or filing of a motion will constitute express consent.

   ii. Implied Consent
State statutes may specify that persons engaging in certain activities will impliedly consent to that state's jurisdiction.

   iii. Motorist Statutes
In *Hess v. Pawloski* (1927), the Supreme Court validated a state statute conferring implied consent

to jurisdiction upon any motorist operating a vehicle within the state.

4. Jurisdiction Over Corporations

a. A corporation is subject to the jurisdiction of the state in which it is incorporated.

b. Fine Line Distinction
For in personam jurisdiction, a corporation is resident in the state in which it is incorporated. For federal diversity purposes, a corporation is considered resident in both its state of incorporation and the state where it maintains its principal place of business.

c. Unlike an individual, a corporation will not fall under a state's jurisdiction by the mere presence within the state of a corporate employee or officer.

5. Minimum Contacts Rule

a. *International Shoe Co. v. Washington*
In order to subject a defendant to in personam jurisdiction in a state where the defendant is neither domiciled nor present, there must be certain minimum contacts between the defendant and the forum such that maintenance of the suit does not offend traditional notions of fair play and substantial justice.

b. Two-Step Analysis

i. Does the defendant have minimum contacts with the forum? If so,

ii. Will asserting jurisdiction comply with traditional notions of fair play and justice?

c. *Hanson v. Denckla*
Jurisdiction may not be invoked when a defendant's contact with a forum is negligible and not purposeful.

d. *McGee v. International Life Insurance Co.*
    A defendant's activities in the forum may subject the defendant to personal jurisdiction, even if sporadic or a single act, as long as the action arises from that single act.

e. *Helicopteros Nacionales de Colombia, SA. v. Hall*
    The Court recognized a distinction made by some courts between "general" and "specific" jurisdiction.

    i.   Specific jurisdiction
         Defendant's presence in the forum jurisdiction is sporadic but the cause of action arose from a contact.

    ii. General jurisdiction
         Regular activity that will subject a party to a forum's jurisdiction even if the action did not arise from in-state activity. General jurisdiction may only be asserted when the defendant had substantial forum-related activity.

f. *Kulko v. Superior Court*
    A parent does not have minimum contacts with a state because he allowed a child to live with the other parent in the forum state.

g. *World-Wide Volkswagen v. Woodson*
    Conduct in a forum, not expectation of revenue, is how jurisdiction is determined. The fact that the defendant derived revenue from use of its product in the forum state was not sufficient to confer jurisdiction.

h. *Asahi Metal Industry v. Superior Court*
    Actions that are not purposefully directed toward the forum state do not confer jurisdiction.

i. *Burger King v. Rudzewicz*
    Jurisdiction is not conferred because one party to a contract resides in the forum.

B.   In Rem Jurisdiction

1. Definitions

    a. In Rem Jurisdiction
    Jurisdiction based on a court's power over a thing, not a person. The action is technically against the property, not a person. The subject of the litigation is related to the property.

    b. Quasi In Rem Jurisdiction
    Jurisdiction based on an action against a person. Since the court is unable to obtain jurisdiction against the defendant, jurisdiction is obtained by seizing the defendant's property. The property is NOT related to the action. The action is against the person not the property. Had the court been able to obtain jurisdiction against the defendant, the action would have been based upon in personam jurisdiction. Quasi in rem actions may force the sale of real property, garnishment of wages, or assignment of a debt.

2. *Rush v. Savchuk*
Quasi in rem jurisdiction over an insurer may not be based on its obligation to defend a policy holder.

3. *Shaffer v. Heitner*
Quasi in rem jurisdiction may only be asserted when the defendant has the "minimum contacts" with the forum state that would satisfy the requirements for in personam jurisdiction as defined by *International Shoe*. The effect of this case is to almost eliminate the availability of quasi in rem jurisdiction. *Shaffer* blurred the difference between in rem and quasi in rem jurisdiction.

IV.   NOTICE AND OPPORTUNITY TO BE HEARD

A.   Generally
A court that has proper jurisdiction over a case may only proceed when the defendant has proper notice of the proceedings against him. Proper notice usually entails service

of "process" consisting of a summons to appear and a copy of the complaint. The defendant need not necessarily receive actual notice of the suit but the procedures followed must be "reasonably likely" to provide notice. The defendant must have adequate time to prepare his defense.

B.   Methods of Service

    1. In Hand Service
    Defendant is physically handed a summons.

    2. Attachment
    Defendant receives notice by the attachment of his tangible property. Statutes typically require additional notice such as mailing the summons or publication.

    3. Garnishment
    Garnishment of a debt or other nontangible property will satisfy the notice requirement in quasi in rem cases. Statutes require that further notice be provided.

    4. Substituted Service
    Modern statutes often allow substituted service so that justice will reach a defendant avoiding "hand service." Some types of substituted service generally allowed:

      a.   Mail

      b.   Summons affixed to door of the defendant's unattended dwelling

      c.   Summons left at defendant's dwelling

      d.   Court order

      e.   Summons left with a person of "suitable age and discretion" residing in the same dwelling as the defendant

    5. Constructive Notice

      a.   Registered or certified mail

   b.   Publication

6. Corporations

   a.   Designated Corporate Official
        The statute will designate the official to receive process.

   b.   *Mullane* Rule
        Expense and availability of the names and addresses of
        the beneficiaries to numerous small trust funds should be
        taken into account in determining the sufficiency of
        notice by publication. Subsequent cases have required
        notice by mail to all parties.

V.   REMOVAL

A.   Generally
     A defendant may remove an action to a federal court when the
     action had original federal jurisdiction but was asserted in a
     state court.

B.   Exception
     A diversity action may only be removed when neither party is a
     citizen of the state in which the action was asserted.

C.   Defendant's Right
     The right of removal is a defendant's right, not a plaintiffs.

D.   Valid State Jurisdiction Necessary
     The state court's jurisdiction must be valid for removal
     jurisdiction to be valid.

VI.   CHALLENGES TO JURISDICTION

A.   Special Appearance

     1. Traditional View
        Since presence is one way of asserting jurisdiction over a
        party, without special appearance, any appearance in court,
        even to challenge jurisdiction, would invite a court to assert
        jurisdiction over the party. With special appearance a party
        appears only to challenge jurisdiction. If the challenge is
        successful, the case is dismissed, and the suit must be re-

filed with a new assertion of jurisdiction. If the challenge fails, the party is still present to challenge the merits of the case.

2. Modern View

Special appearance has been superseded by federal and other courts. In these courts, a defendant may now challenge jurisdiction by filing a motion to dismiss for lack of jurisdiction without being subject to jurisdiction for filing the motion. Many courts also allow a special appearance for in rem and quasi in rem actions.

B. Collateral Attack

A defendant defaulting on an action may collaterally attack a default judgment asserted in another jurisdiction on the grounds that the first action was asserted in a forum without proper jurisdiction. This often occurs where an award granted in one jurisdiction is to be enforced in a second jurisdiction.

VII. VENUE

A. Defined

The place within a jurisdiction where an action is brought.

B. State and Local Courts

Local rules establish venue. The location where the cause of action arose, residence, place of business of the defendant and plaintiff, and other factors are usually considered.

C. Federal Venue

Federal Venue shall be where defendants reside or where the claim arose. A corporation may be sued where incorporated, licensed to do business, or where it actually does business. An alien may be sued in any district.

D. Forum Non Conveniens

A court may decline jurisdiction over a case if it decides that the case should be tried elsewhere.

CASE CLIPS

Pennoyer v. Neff (S.Ct. 1877)

Facts: Mitchell brought an action against Neff in an Oregon court to recover legal fees. By publication he served Neff, a nonresident, and obtained judgment by default. Thereafter, Neff learned of the sale of his property in Oregon to satisfy the judgment. He sued Pennoyer, the purchaser, in Oregon to recover his property. Neff argued that the Oregon court had no jurisdiction over him.

Issue: Is service by publication sufficient to give a state court in personam jurisdiction over a nonresident?

Rule: (Field, J.) A personal judgment against a nonresident served only by publication is invalid. For personal jurisdiction (as opposed to in rem jurisdiction over property) the defendant must come within the court's jurisdiction by personal service within the state or by voluntarily submitting himself to service of process. In rem jurisdiction may be achieved by attaching the in-state property of an out-of-state defendant who otherwise could not be brought into the jurisdiction by in personam jurisdiction.

Dissent: (Hunt, J.) The states have the exclusive power to determine what notice is required to prospective defendants. As long as that notice is "reasonably likely" to communicate notice of the suit, is made in a good faith effort to notify him, and the defendant receives an opportunity to defend himself, the notice statute should be valid.

Hess v. Pawloski (S.Ct. 1927)

Facts: In a Massachusetts court, the plaintiff of Massachusetts sued the defendant of Pennsylvania for injuries arising from an auto accident in Massachusetts. Process was served in compliance with a state statute which appointed the state registrar of motor vehicles as a nonresident's agent for service of process.

Issue: May a state enact a statute which deems a state official to be appointed in advance as a nonresident's agent on whom process may be served for claims arising out of automobile accidents within the state?

Rule: (Butler, J.) Since a state has the right to regulate and promote safety on its highways, it may deem a nonresident motorist to have appointed one of its officials as his agent on whom process may be served in proceedings arising out of such highway use.

International Shoe Co. v. Washington (S.Ct. 1945)

Facts: The state of Washington brought suit to collect unemployment taxes from a company that did not have an office in Washington and that was incorporated in another state, but which did have a sales force of eleven to thirteen people in Washington who regularly solicited business.

Issue: What contacts are required for the courts of a state to exercise in personam jurisdiction over a nonresident defendant?

Rule: (Stone, C.J.) The courts of a state may exercise in personam jurisdiction over a nonresident defendant where that defendant has "the minimum contacts with the forum state such that maintenance of the suit does not offend traditional notions of fair play and substantial justice." It suffices that the defendant conducts systematic and continuous activities that relate to the obligation sued upon in the forum state.

Concurrence: (Black, J.) The Court should not be able to invalidate an otherwise valid state jurisdiction statute because of a foggy notion of "fair play."

Gray v. American Radiator & Standard Sanitary Corp. (1961)

Facts: Gray was injured in Illinois when a water heater exploded. She sued Titan, the manufacturer of a safety valve, a nonresident corporation which did not do business in Illinois. Gray obtained jurisdiction over Titan using Illinois' long-arm statute, the first one in the nation.

Issue: Do minimum contacts sufficient to satisfy the requirements of due process exist when a defendant's only physical contact with the forum state is the injury to the plaintiff?

Rule: Minimum contacts with a state exist, and will bring the defendant within the jurisdiction of the courts of that state, where the defendant's business may result in use and consumption of its products in the state, because the corporation therefore benefits from the laws of the state.

Note: The Illinois court noted that since Pennoyer v. Neff the concept of personal jurisdiction had developed, and no longer required personal service within the state. The fundamental requirements are reasonable notice and opportunity to be heard.

World-Wide Volkswagen Corp. v. Woodson (S.Ct. 1980)

Facts: The Woodsons of New York bought an Audi in New York. When they were injured in a crash while driving through Oklahoma, they brought an action in Oklahoma against the New York dealer and the New York distributor of the car for defective design. Jurisdiction was based on the Oklahoma long-arm statute.

Issue: May a state exercise personal jurisdiction over a nonresident corporation who places its products into a "stream of commerce" that happens to place some of those products in the state?

Rule: (White, J.) The forum state may not exercise personal jurisdiction over a nonresident corporation whose product is "fortuitously" in the forum state, and whose conduct and connection with the forum are so attenuated that it would not reasonably anticipate becoming subject to the forum state's jurisdiction.

Dissent 1: (Brennan, J.) Given the nature of the automobile business, it is foreseeable that a car sold in New York may pass through Oklahoma, so jurisdiction should not be denied.

Dissent 2: (Marshall, J.) If a product enters the forum state through the intended use of the purchaser, that state should be able to assert jurisdiction over the product's manufacturer.

Dissent 3: (Blackmun, J.) Since "we are a nation on wheels" it is not unreasonable for a manufacturer of automobiles to be brought to any state where an accident involving one of its automobiles occurs.

Burger King Corp. v. Rudzewicz (S.Ct. 1985)

Facts: Rudzewicz, a Michigan resident, entered an agreement with Burger King, a Florida corporation, to operate a franchise in Michigan. The contract stated that Florida law controlled and required monthly payments to be made to the corporation's headquarters in Florida. When Rudzewicz fell behind on his monthly obligations, Burger King brought suit in Florida.

Issue: May the forum state exercise in personam jurisdiction over a nonresident defendant who has entered into a contract with a corporation from the forum state?

Rule: (Brennan, J.) The forum state may exercise in personam jurisdiction over a nonresident defendant who has established a substantial and continuing relationship with a corporation from the forum state and received fair notice from the contract documents and the course of dealing that he might be subject to suit in the forum state.

Dissent: (Stevens, J.) A boilerplate contract should not be the basis for conferring jurisdiction over defendants with no contact with the forum state.

Asahi Metal Industry Co. v. Superior Court (S.Ct. 1987)

Facts: In a personal injury suit, Zurcher, a Californian, sued Cheng Shin, a tube-manufacturing company from Taiwan. The company, in turn, filed a cross-claim and sought indemnification from Asahi Metal, the Japanese manufacturer of the component part. Zurcher and Cheng Shin subsequently settled, leaving only the suit between Cheng Shin and Asahi.

Issue: Is the "minimum contacts" requirement for personal jurisdiction satisfied when a foreign corporation manufactures products outside the United States that end up in the forum state via the stream of commerce?

Rule: (O'Connor, J.) The "minimum contacts" test is not always satisfied when a component part manufactured outside the United States is later introduced into the stream of commerce. Assertion of jurisdiction must have been reasonably contemplated by the defending party, based on the defendant's interest in the forum state, the burden on the defendant to go to the forum, and the plaintiff's interest in obtaining relief.

Concurrence 1: (Brennan, J.) Although conferring jurisdiction over Asahi would not comport with "traditional notions of fair play and substantial justice," Asahi did have sufficient minimum contacts with the forum state. That a defendant may foresee that its products may enter the forum state via the stream of commerce should be sufficient. A stream of commerce is purposeful and directed, its outcome fairly predictable.

Concurrence 2: (Stevens, J.) Asahi certainly has minimum contacts with California, even if asserting jurisdiction in this case would be "unreasonable and unfair." Asahi, by dealing with Cheng Shin, knowing that a substantial portion of its business goes to California, has purposely availed itself of the forum state.

Helicopteros Nacionales de Colombia, S.A. v. Hall (S.Ct. 1984)

Facts: Hall brought a wrongful death action against Helicol, a foreign corporation engaged in transportation services outside the U.S. Although Helicol neither engaged in any business nor had any agents in the United States, it did negotiate a contract to purchase parts and to train personnel in Texas.

Issue: When a party purchases parts, trains personnel, and negotiates a contract in a state has it established the necessary contacts to subject itself to the state's in personam jurisdiction?

Rule: (Blackmun, J.) Due process requires that for a state to have in personam jurisdiction over a party, the party must engage in continuous and systematic general business contacts. Purchases and isolated trips are not continuous and systematic contacts. Furthermore, in this case, the cause of action here does not derive from the contacts.

Dissent: (Brennan, J.) The cause of action does arise out of those contacts that the defendant has with the forum state. Where the underlying cause of action relates to those contacts, a state should be able to assert jurisdiction, despite a lack of systematic and continuous contacts.

Shaffer v. Heitner (S.Ct. 1977)

Facts: Heitner brought a shareholder's derivative suit against Greyhound and 28 of its officers and directors in Delaware, where Greyhound was incorporate, alleging that the corporation and its officers and directors (including Shaffer) were the cause of Greyhound's loss in an antitrust action in Oregon. Jurisdiction was based on sequestration of Shaffer's Greyhound stock, which was deemed, pursuant to Delaware state law, to be located in Delaware.

Issue: Absent other contacts of a defendant with a state, will sequestration of property deemed to be located in the state provide a state court with a basis for quasi in rem jurisdiction over an individual?

Rule: (Marshall, J.) Property which is not itself the subject matter of the litigation does not alone provide a basis for jurisdiction. The exercise of jurisdiction over the interests of persons is consistent with the Due Process Clause only where the "minimum contacts" standard of International Shoe is met.

Concurrence 1: (Powell, J.) Some types of property may allow some quasi in rem cases to comport with "traditional notions of fair play and substantial justice."

Concurrence 2: (Stevens, J.) The majority goes too far in invalidating much of in rem and quasi in rem jurisdiction.

Dissent: (Brennan, J.) Jurisdiction over officers involved in a corporation subject to a shareholder derivative action should be able to be conferred via the traditional "minimum contacts" test. It is not unreasonable for an officer to believe that he may have to defend his actions as corporate officer in the state of incorporation. Minimum contacts is not best contacts.

Note: Shaffer extends the "minimum contacts" rule of International Shoe so as to overrule part of the implied holding of Pennoyer v. Neff regarding in rem actions.

Omni Capital International v. Rudolf Wolff & Co. Ltd.
(S.Ct. 1987)

Facts: Two New York corporations (collectively called "Omni"), marketed an investment program and employed a British corporation with London offices to manage trades on that Exchange. In an action in Louisiana, Omni impleaded both the British corporation and its representative arguing that their liability resulted from the representative's improprieties.

Issue: What are the prerequisites to a federal court's exercise of personal jurisdiction over a party?

Rule: (Blackmun, J.) A federal court can exercise personal jurisdiction over a party when there is a basis for the party's amenability to service of a summons, and if in addition, notice requirements and a nexus between the party and the forum state are established.

Mullane v. Central Hanover Bank & Trust Co. (S.Ct. 1950)

Facts: Known and unknown nonresident beneficiaries of a trust fund were given notice of the application for judicial settlement of the account by publication in a local newspaper.

Issue: Is notice by publication of the pendency of an action adequate when attempting to inform known parties who could be apprised more effectively by mail or other means?

Rule: (Jackson, J.) The fundamental requisite of due process is the opportunity to be heard. Due process requires that notice be reasonably calculated to apprise interested parties. Notice by publication to known nonresidents is inadequate because it is not reasonably calculated to reach those who could easily be informed by other means.

Dissent: (Burton, J.) The Constitution does not require more notice than that presently provided by statute here.

National Equipment Rental, Ltd. v. Szukhent (S.Ct. 1964)

Facts: Szukhent of Michigan leased farm equipment from National Equipment Rental, Ltd. of New York. The contract provided that attorney Florence Weinberg would accept service in New York for claims arising from the contract. When Szukhent defaulted on payment, Weinberg was served, and she mailed the complaint to Szukhent.

Issue: When may a party to a private contract appoint an agent to receive service of process?

Rule: (Stewart, J.) A party to a private contract may agree that any litigation under the contract shall be conducted in a particular state and may appoint an agent to receive service of process, even if the agent is not personally known to the party and the agent has not expressly undertaken to transmit notice to the party.

Dissent: (Black, J.) Service of process to an agent should not be valid, no matter how it is developed. Although there is no due process issue in this case because the defendant did receive actual notice of the summons and complaint, the possibility for abuse of such clauses exists where large companies may force customers to come to a forum state the seller prefers.

State ex rel. Sivnksty v. Duffield (1952)

Facts: Petitioner Sivnksty, a nonresident, was arrested on criminal charges of reckless driving following an accident involving respondent Duffield. While in jail awaiting trial, Sivnksty was served with process in the civil case.

Issue: When may a nonresident who is confined in jail on criminal charges be validly served with notice of a civil suit?

Rule: A nonresident party confined in jail on criminal charges can be served with process if he was voluntarily in the jurisdiction at the time of the arrest and confinement.

Note: A nonresident would be immune from civil process if he entered the jurisdiction only to take part in a criminal trial.

Wyman v. Newhouse (1937)

Facts: Newhouse of New York was induced by Wyman's fraud to enter Florida whereupon he was served with process.

Issue: May fraud be used to induce a party to enter the jurisdiction and be served with process?

Rule: When a defendant is fraudulently induced to enter the jurisdiction for service of process, the court lacks jurisdiction over him, and any judgment against him is null and void.

Fuentes v. Shevin (S.Ct. 1972)

Facts: Fuentes purchased a stove and other household goods from Firestone under an installment conditional sales contract. When a dispute arose over the servicing of the stove, the seller sued for repossession of all of the goods. Before the complaint had been served on Fuentes, Goodyear obtained a writ of replevin authorizing the sheriff to seize the disputed goods at once. Fuentes challenged the state statute authorizing prejudgment replevin, for which Fuentes was offered neither notice nor a hearing in advance of seizure.

Issue: Do prejudgment replevin procedures that allow property to be seized without notice or an opportunity to challenge violate due process where a hearing is granted after the property is taken?

Rule: (Stewart, J.) It is fundamental to due process that there be notice and an opportunity to be heard at a meaningful time and in a meaningful manner before there is a significant taking of property by a state.

Dissent: (White, J.) In these situations the importance to the creditor of being able to repossess the items while they are still able to be located may outweigh the danger of an erroneous repossession.

Note: There are "extraordinary situations" which may justify postponing notice and opportunity for a hearing. First, the seizure must be directly necessary to secure an important governmental or general public interest. *Gordon v. Steele.* Second, there must a special need for prompt action.

Connecticut v. Doehr (S.Ct. 1991)

Facts: DiGiovanni submitted an application to the Connecticut Supreme Court for an attachment on Doehr's home. The relevant prejudgment remedy statute provided that ex parte attachments of real property were allowable upon verification that there was probable cause to sustain the plaintiffs claim. The attachment was granted without giving Doehr prior notification, and Doehr filed a federal suit claiming that the statute was unconstitutional under the Fourteenth Amendment.

Issue: Does a state statute that allows prejudgment attachments of real estate without prior notice or hearing violate the Due Process Clause of the Fourteenth Amendment?

Rule: (White, J.) A prejudgment remedy statute which concerns deprivation of real property must satisfy a three part inquiry: consideration of the private interest affected by the measure, examination of the risk of error and value of providing additional safeguards, and the interest of the party seeking the remedy. Under this test, the relevant statute was found to violate the Due Process Clause.

Lacks v. Lacks (1976)

Facts: The court erroneously granted a divorce judgment in violation of a state law requiring residency.

Issue: Where a case lacks the elements of a cause of action, is the court's final judgment void for want of subject matter jurisdiction?

Rule: The rule that lack of subject matter jurisdiction makes a final judgment void only applies when the court lacked original jurisdiction. It does not apply when one of the elements of the cause of action is missing.

Mas v. Perry (1974)

Facts: Jean Paul Mas of France and Judy Mas of Mississippi settled in Louisiana after their marriage without intending to remain there permanently. They brought a suit in federal court against Perry, a Mississippi Resident, basing federal jurisdiction on diversity of citizenship.

Issue: Is mere "residence" in a state sufficient to establish state domicile so as to defeat or establish diversity?

Rule: For purpose of diversity, "domicile" is a permanent home, and requires intent to remain permanently in a state.

Note: In the instant case, neither Mas became a domiciliary of Louisiana, and there was complete diversity of citizenship.

A.F.A. Tours, Inc. v. Whitchurch (1991)

Facts: Whitchurch worked for AFA for seventeen years as a tour escort. Upon his resignation, Whitchurch attempted to organize his own tour business, using information he had misappropriated from AFA. AFA commenced action in district court for misappropriation of trade secrets, and sought an injunction against use of the information. AFA claimed damages "in an amount which is not presently ascertainable, but which is believed to exceed the sum of $50,000." The court raised the issue of whether the value of the claims exceeded the amount in controversy requirement.

Issue: What is the proper test for determining whether a plaintiff meets the minimum amount requirement for diversity jurisdiction set forth under 28 U.S.C. § 1332?

Rule: In a diversity suit, the proper test governing the amount in controversy is whether the sum claimed by the plaintiff is made in good faith. It must appear to a legal certainty that the claim is for less than the minimum amount to justify a dismissal. The court found just cause to believe AFA's submission of damages was made in good faith.

Note: The amount in controversy requirement for diversity jurisdiction was raised from $50,000 to $75,000 in 1996.

Louisville & Nashville R.R. v. Mottley (S.Ct. 1908)

Facts: Mottley brought an action in federal court alleging that the opposing party had breached a contract by revoking a pass for free transportation. Mottley asserted federal question jurisdiction based on the railroad company's anticipated defense that an act of Congress proscribed free passes.

Issue: Does the anticipated assertion of federal law as a defense to an action suffice to provide federal question jurisdiction?

Rule: (Moody, J.) Only when a plaintiffs own cause of action states a federal question do federal courts have federal question jurisdiction.

Merrell Dow Pharmaceuticals, Inc. v. Thompson (S.Ct. 1986)

Facts: Thompson brought a state tort action against Merrell Dow to recover damages for their child's birth defects allegedly caused by the mother's ingestion of Bendectin during her pregnancy. One element of the Thompson's case alleged Dow's violation of a federal statute. Dow removed the case to federal court on the ground that the action turned on an interpretation of federal law, and subsequently moved for dismissal of the case on the ground of forum non conveniens. The Thompsons appealed the removal.

Issue: Does pleading a violation of a federal statute as an element of a state cause of action create federal question jurisdiction under 28 U.S.C. § 1331?

Rule: (Stevens, J.) A claim that alleges a violation of a federal statute as an element of a state cause of action does not create federal question jurisdiction if Congress withheld a private right of action when enacting the statute. Generally, a "suit arises under the law that creates the cause of action." Because the statute in this case did not provide for a private right of action, federal question jurisdiction did not exist over the plaintiffs claim and removal to federal court was improper.

Dissent: (Brennan, J.) The fact that Congress withholds a private federal remedy when crafting a statute does not mean that Congress intends to withhold federal jurisdiction from a suit alleging a violation of that statute as an element of a state claim. Federal jurisdiction over such claims would further the important federal interest of uniformity in interpretation and application of the federal statute at issue.

T.B. Harms Co. v. Eliscu (1964)

Facts: There was a disagreement between the parties regarding ownership of a copyright. Harms brought an action in federal court seeking equitable and declaratory relief.

Issue: Does an action to determine ownership of a copyright "arise under" the laws of the United States, thereby conferring jurisdiction on the federal courts?

Rule: An action arises under federal copyright law only if it deals with (a) infringement; (b) royalties for reproduction; (c) a claim requiring construction of the Act; or (d) a distinctive policy of the Act requiring that federal principles should control. Issues of ownership are issues of state contract law and are insufficient to invoke jurisdiction in federal courts.

Sniadach v. Family Finance Corp. of Bay View (S.Ct. 1969)

Facts: Family Finance commenced a garnishment action against Sniadach and Miller Harris Instrument Company, her employer, alleging Sniadach defaulted on a promissory note. A state statute allowed Family Finance ten days to serve the summons and complaint on Sniadach after the garnishee was served. Pursuant to the garnishment action, Miller Harris, prior to judgment, held back

Sniadach's wages, stating it would pay half to Sniadach and hold the other half subject to the order of the court.

Issue: Does the freezing of a party's wages before a hearing violate procedural due process?

Rule: (Douglas, J.) Where the taking of one's property is so obvious, absent notice and a prior hearing, the prejudgment garnishment procedure violates the fundamental principles of due process.

Concurrence: (Harlan, J.) The property of which Sniadach has been deprived is not the wages, but the use of the wages. Since this loss is not de minimis, due process protection must be afforded.

Dissent: (Black, J.) The court is invalidating the garnishment law, not because of due process, but because they disapprove of garnishment. That is the job of the legislature, not the courts.

North Georgia Finishing, Inc. v. Di-Chem, Inc. (S.Ct. 1975)

Facts: Di-Chem brought a quasi in rem action to recover its debt against North Georgia Finishing and simultaneously filed a bond for the process of garnishing North Georgia Finishing's funds being held by a third-party bank.

Issue: Does the garnishment of a bank account pending litigation, without notice, an early hearing, or participation by a judicial officer violate due process?

Rule: (White, J.) Procedural due process requires that for any significant taking of property the property owner must be afforded some form of early hearing or at least a showing of probable cause. The length of deprivation and the existence of a bond are immaterial.

Concurrence 1: (Stewart, J.) "It is gratifying to note that my report of the demise of *Fuentes v. Shevin* seems to have been greatly exaggerated."

Concurrence 2: (Powell, J.) The majority does not give enough weight to the need of creditors to quickly attach property which may be put beyond the reach of the courts. There is no need to revive *Fuentes v. Shevin* to find this statute unconstitutional.

Dissent: (Blackmun, J.) North Georgia Finishing is not a helpless wage-earner like the defendant of garnishment proceedings in

Sniadach. It is a corporation amply protected by the fact that garnishment could only take place after the creditor has initiated proceedings, by the requisite double bond, and by the requirement of an affidavit of apprehension of loss. There is no hint of adhesion, imbalance, or inequality.

Carroll v. President and Commissioners of Princess Anne (S.Ct. 1968)

Facts: President and Commissioners of Princess Anne requested and obtained a restraining order against Carroll and other members of the National States Rights Party, a white supremacist organization. As a result, a scheduled rally was not held. The proceeding in which the order was granted was ex parte, and the National States Rights Party was not notified. In the subsequent trial, the court issued an injunction extending the earlier restraining order for an additional ten months. On appeal, the ten-day injunction was upheld, but the ten-month injunction was reversed. Carroll appealed to the Supreme Court, alleging that the case was not moot, because the ruling continued to have an adverse effect on their First Amendment rights.

Issue: Does the issuance of an ex parte injunction prohibiting a public meeting violate the First Amendment Right of free association?

Rule: (Fortas, J.) An ex parte order enjoining a party from holding a public meeting is an unconstitutional prior restraint on speech unless the applicant can show that reasonable efforts to notify the adverse party had been made and failed.

Franchise Tax Board of the State of California v. Construction Laborers Vacation Trust for Southern California (S.Ct. 1983)

Facts: The Franchise Tax Board of California brought suit against the Construction Laborers Vacation Trust for Southern California for failure to pay taxes. The Board also sought a declaratory judgment concerning the Trust's defense that the trust was subject to federal law (ERISA), thereby preempting the levy of state taxes.

Issue: Should removal to federal court be granted when a complaint asserts a state-law cause of action but seeks a declaratory judgment regarding a federal defense that the defendant may raise?

Rule: (Brennan, J.) Federal courts have jurisdiction to hear only those cases in which a "well-pleaded complaint" establishes either that federal law creates the cause of action or that the plaintiffs right to relief necessarily depends on resolution of a federal question. Jurisdiction may not be derived from an actual or potential claim of the defendants, even if it raises a valid federal question.

United Mine Workers of America v. Gibbs (S.Ct. 1966)

Facts: Gibbs brought an action in federal court, asserting both a federal claim, under the Management Relations Act, and a state claim, conspiracy to interfere with a contract.

Issue: Do federal courts have jurisdiction to hear state claims if they are brought together with federal claims?

Rule: (Brennan, J.) Federal courts have discretion to assume pendent jurisdiction of state claims if they are brought together with substantial federal claims and are derived from a common nucleus of operative facts.

Patterson Enterprises, Inc. v. Bridgestone/Firestone, Inc. (1993)

Facts: Plaintiffs Patterson Enterprises, Patterson Trucking and Jere Patterson brought a diversity suit against Firestone for negligence, strict liability, and breach of warranty. The suit stemmed from a tractor trailer accident which allegedly was caused by a failure of a Firestone tire on the vehicle. The plaintiffs all asserted different theories and amounts of recovery. Although Mr. Patterson's claim met the amount in controversy requirement, Firestone argued that Enterprises' and Trucking's claims failed to meet the requirement.

Issue: When does 28 U.S.C. § 1367 grant supplemental jurisdiction over claims which lack an independent basis of subject matter jurisdiction?

Rule: The test for whether supplemental jurisdiction should be applied is whether diverse parties' claims are "so related to claims in the action . . . that they derive from a common nucleus of operative fact." Since all the claims in this case arose from the same event, they need not have all met the amount in controversy requirement.

Roe v. Little Company of Mary Hospital (1992)

Facts: Roe underwent a surgical procedure which required that he receive multiple blood transfusions. Some of the blood received apparently was contaminated with HIV. Roe filed a negligence suit in state court against the hospital and the doctors, as well as the Red Cross. Red Cross removed the entire case to federal court, asserting that its creation by federal statute gave the federal court automatic subject matter jurisdiction. Roe claimed that the federal court had no jurisdiction over the non-Red Cross defendants and, therefore, the court should use its discretion to remand the entire case back to state court.

Issue 1: May a federal court use its discretion to remand previously removed claims that lack an independent basis for subject matter jurisdiction?

Rule 1: 28 U.S.C. § 1441(c) allows a federal court discretion in remanding claims that have been previously removed to federal court but which lack independent subject matter jurisdiction. Remand is generally proper if the claims are such that state law predominates.

Issue 2: May a federal court use its discretion to remand previously removed claims if the court derives its subject matter jurisdiction over the claim under a "separate and independent jurisdictional grant"?

Rule 2: The discretion conferred by 28 U.S.C. § 1441(c) to allow federal courts to remand previously removed cases does not apply to claims which derive jurisdiction from a "separate and independent jurisdictional grant." Since the Red Cross was created under a federal statute, and the court derives its jurisdiction from the same statute, the court lacks the ability to remand.

Finley v. United States (S.Ct. 1989)

Facts: Finley's husband died in a plane crash in which both die San Diego Gas and Electric Company (SDGEC) and the Federal Aviation Administration (FAA) were implicated. Finley and SDGEC were not diverse, so she could only sue in state court. But according to 28 U.S.C. § 1346(b) she could only sue the FAA for tort damage in federal court. Finley sued the FAA in federal court and tried to assert pendent jurisdiction over SDGEC.

Issue: May a nondiverse party be pended to a federal claim that shares a common nucleus of operative facts where no other forum exists to adjudicate the entire controversy?

Rule: (Scalia, J.) In order to pend a claim to another factually-related federal claim, there must be independent subject-matter jurisdiction.

Dissent 1: (Blackmun, J.) Congress never intended 28 U.S.C. § 1346 to be used to keep factually-related claims from being adjudicated together where one of the claims has valid federal subject matter jurisdiction.

Dissent 2: (Stevens, J.) The theory behind the court's reasoning contravenes the holdings in many prior cases, such as *Aldinger, Owen, Zahn v. International Paper Co.* Previously, the Court only refused to allow pending nondiverse claims to federal claims where Congress explicitly expresses such an intent. Now the Court will refuse pendent jurisdiction unless Congress expresses a contrary intent.

Note: The majority ruling has been legislatively overruled with the supplemental jurisdiction statute, 28 U.S.C. § 1367.

Reasor-Hill Corp. v. Harrison (1952)

Facts: Planters Flying Service sued Barton in an Arkansas court to collect money for spraying his Missouri crops. Barton cross-claimed against Reasor-Hill, the Arkansas manufacturer of the pesticide used.

Issue: May a state court entertain a suit for injuries to real property situated in another state?

Rule: In adjudicating disputes between citizens of different states, state courts should no longer distinguish between transitory and real property actions. Having jurisdiction over Reasor-Hill, the court may adjudicate cases regardless of where the injured real property is situated.

Note: The majority based its holding in part on the fact that application of the contrary common law rule may result in there being a wrong without a remedy.

Bates v. C & S Adjusters, Inc. (1992)

Facts: Bates, originally a resident of Pennsylvania, had incurred debts which were referred to C & S, a local collection agency. Bates subsequently moved to New York. C & S sent a collection notice to Bates at his former residence in Pennsylvania, and the letter was forwarded by the Post Office to his New York address. Bates commenced an action in the Western District of New York against C & S for violation of the Fair Debt Collection Practices Act. C & S subsequently filed a motion to dismiss for improper venue.

Issue: Is a district in which a debtor resides and to where a bill collector's payment notice has been forwarded a proper venue under 28 U.S.C. § 1391(b)(2)?

Rule: 28 U.S.C. § 1391(b)(2) allows an action to be brought in "a judicial district in which a substantial part of the events or omissions giving rise to the claim occurred." Since the receipt of a collection notice is a substantial part of the events giving rise to the claim of this type, it is irrelevant that the actions of the defendant did not voluntarily direct the notice into the forum.

Hoffman v. Blaski (S.Ct. 1960)

Facts: Blaski and other citizens of Illinois brought a patent infringement action against Hoffman and a Texas corporation controlled by Hoffman, in federal district court in Texas. Hoffman moved, under 28 U.S.C. § 1404(a), for a change of venue to the Northern District of Illinois. The court granted the motion despite the fact that the district court in Illinois would not have had jurisdiction over the defendants had the case originally been brought there.

Issue: May a federal district court in which a civil action is properly brought transfer the action under 28 U.S.C. § 1404(a) to a district in which the plaintiff did not have a right to bring the action in the first place?

Rule: (Whittaker, J.) The power to transfer an action to another district depends not upon the wish or waiver of the defendant but upon whether the transferee district was one in which the action "might have been brought" by plaintiff.

Piper Aircraft Co. v. Reyno (S.Ct. 1982)

Facts: Reyno sued in federal district court as administratrix on behalf of the estates of five Scottish passengers killed in a plane crash in Scotland. Both Piper Aircraft Co., manufacturer of the plane, and Hartzell Propeller, Inc., manufacturer of the propellers, were American corporations. Suits against the estate of the Scottish pilot and others were brought in Scotland. The district court dismissed on the grounds of forum non conveniens. The court of appeals reversed, principally because Scottish law was less favorable to plaintiffs.

Issue: In exercising its discretion on whether to dismiss a case for forum non conveniens, should the trial court consider which law will be more favorable to the plaintiff?

Rule: (Marshall, J.) Unless the other jurisdiction is so clearly inadequate or unsatisfactory as to fail to provide for any recovery at all, the possibility of application of less favorable law is not a factor in a decision on forum non conveniens. The court should consider the private interests involved, convenience to the parties and witnesses, location of the evidence, and where the event in controversy occurred.

Dissent: (Stevens, J.) The case should be remanded to the Pennsylvania court to determine whether the District Court correctly determined that Pennsylvania was not a convenient forum in which to litigate.

Strawbridge v. Curtiss (S.Ct. 1806)

Facts: Citizens of Massachusetts brought an action in federal court against other Massachusetts residents and one resident of Vermont.

Issue: Can federal diversity jurisdiction be established in a suit in which there is no diversity between the plaintiffs and one of the defendants?

Rule: (Marshall, C. J.) In order to establish diversity jurisdiction in federal courts, diversity must be "complete" (i.e., none of the plaintiffs can be a citizen of the same state as any of the defendants).

State Farm Fire & Casualty Co. v. Tashire (S.Ct. 1967)

Facts: In a federal proceeding, State Farm sought to interplead all prospective claimants involved in a multivehicle accident. Not all of the defendants were diverse in relation to State Farm.

Issue: In a federal interpleader action, must there be complete diversity?

Rule: (Fortas, J.) The federal interpleader statute requires only "minimum diversity" (one plaintiff need be diverse to any one defendant).

Deutsch v. Hewes Street Realty Corp. (1966)

Facts: Deutsch brought a diversity action in federal court against Hewes Street Realty for injuries she sustained when her kitchen sink fell on her foot. Plaintiff requested $25,000 in damages, comprised of special damages of $141.00, one month's disability of $1500, and loss of future earnings of $23,359.

Issue: When may a federal court dismiss a diversity suit because of inadequate amount in controversy, despite the fact that the amount claimed would fulfill the amount in controversy requirement?

Rule: For purposes of fulfilling the jurisdictional "amount in controversy," the sum claimed by the plaintiff in good faith controls. Dismissal will be justified only when it appears to be a "legal certainty" that the claim will be adjudicated for less than the minimum jurisdictional amount (i.e., $10,000 in this case).

Owen Equipment & Erection Co. v. Kroger (S.Ct. 1978)

Facts: Kroger brought a wrongful death action in federal court, based on diversity of citizenship. The original defendant impleaded Owen Equipment and Erection Co. as a third-party defendant. The original defendant was granted summary judgment, leaving Owen as the sole defendant. It was subsequently discovered that Kroger and Owen were citizens of the same state.

Issue: In an action in which federal jurisdiction rests solely on diversity of citizenship, may the court exercise ancillary jurisdiction under FRCP 14, of a claim against an impleaded third-party defendant whose citizenship is the same as the plaintiff's?

Rule: (Stewart, J.) Title 28 U.S.C. § 1332(a)(1) requires complete diversity of citizenship. The federal court in a diversity case may therefore not assume ancillary jurisdiction under FRCP 14 of an action against a third-party defendant whose citizenship is identical with the plaintiff's.

Dissent: (White, J.) Since Kroger's claims against Owen and OPPD arose from a common nucleus of operative facts, the federal court should be able to hear the claim against Owen, following the Court's previous holding in *Mine Workers v. Gibbs*. This Court reads the diversity jurisdiction statute too narrowly.

Cooper v. Wyman (1898)

Facts: Defendant, a nonresident, was served with a summons while he was attending a state court action in which he was acting as a witness in his own behalf. He was not in the state for any other purpose.

Issue: May a nonresident be served with process if he is within the boundaries of the state for the sole purpose of acting as a witness in a proceeding?

Rule: A summons or other civil process cannot be served on a nonresident who enters a state for the sole purpose of attending a litigation as suitor or witness.

Harkness v. Hyde (S.Ct. 1878)

Facts: Defendant was served with process on a Native American reservation. He moved, through special appearance, for a dismissal for want of jurisdiction. After losing the motion, the defendant answered the complaint. A judgment was entered for the plaintiff.

Issue: May a defendant object to service after judgment, even though he made a special appearance contesting service and later answered the complaint when his original motion was denied?

Rule: (Field, J.) The right of a defendant to object to illegality of service is not waived by special appearance contesting such service, nor is the objection waived when the defendant is thereby compelled to answer because a challenge was overruled.

Milliken v. Meyer, Administratrix (S.Ct. 1940)

Facts: Meyer brought an action in Colorado to set aside a judgment rendered in Wyoming on the grounds that the Wyoming court had no jurisdiction over her. The Colorado Supreme Court held the Wyoming judgment void on its merits after a lower Colorado court had determined that Wyoming did have jurisdiction over the initial suit.

Issue 1: May a state court review the merits of a suit litigated in another jurisdiction after it has been established that the previous court had proper jurisdiction?

Rule 1: (Douglas, J.) A court's finding of personal jurisdiction over a defendant is presumed valid unless disproved by extrinsic evidence or by the record. Where jurisdiction is not disproved, the Full Faith and Credit clause precludes inquiry by a court of another jurisdiction into the merits of the suit.

Issue 2: May substituted service be used to bring an absent domiciliary within the reach of a state's jurisdiction?

Rule 2: Domicile in a state is alone sufficient to bring an absent defendant within the reach of a state's jurisdiction for purposes of a personal judgment, even by means of a substituted service.

McGee v. International Life Insurance Co. (S.Ct. 1957)

Facts: McGee of California, a beneficiary of an insurance policy carried by International Life Insurance Co., a Texas corporation, recovered a favorable judgment in a California state court. International Life had been served by registered mail in Texas. McGee later filed suit in Texas to recover the judgment made in California.

Issue: Does a state court have jurisdiction over a nonresident corporation that has no contact with the state beyond a contract that has a substantial connection to a citizen of that state?

Rule: (Black, J.) Due process requires that a nonresident defendant have "minimum contacts" with the state in order for the state to have in personam jurisdiction. An action based on a contract that had substantial connections to a citizen of that state will satisfy the requirements of "minimum contacts."

Hanson v. Denckla (S.Ct. 1958)

Facts: A Pennsylvania resident created a trust, naming a Delaware bank as trustee. After moving to Florida, the Pennsylvania resident executed a will and separately exercised her power of appointment under the trust. The beneficiaries of her will sued in Florida asking for a judgment declaring that title passed under the will. The Florida plaintiffs were not able to get jurisdiction over a trustee domiciled in Delaware.

Issue: Where all other relevant parties are domiciled in a state, may that state assert jurisdiction over the one party not located within the state?

Rule: (Warren, CJ.) It is essential that a nonresident defendant do some act to avail himself of the privilege of conducting activities within the forum state. The "center of gravity" of a controversy as well as the most convenient location for litigation are irrelevant considerations for determining in personam jurisdiction over a nonresident defendant.

Dissent 1: (Black, J.) Where a transaction has a strong relationship to the forum state, courts of that state should have the power to adjudicate controversies arising out of that transaction unless litigation there would impose such a heavy burden on the nonresident defendant as to offend "traditional notions of fair play and substantial justice."

Dissent 2: (Douglas, J.) Florida has such a plain and compelling relation to the matter, and the relationship between the matter and the nonresident are so close that Florida should have the ability to adjudicate the matter even without personal jurisdiction over all the nonresidents.

Combs v. Combs (1933)

Facts: The plaintiff initiated an action in Kentucky to recover a loan from an Arkansas resident. The defendant, who had a lien on his Arkansas property, brought an equity action in Arkansas fixing the amount due by him to the plaintiff and allowing him to pay that amount in exchange for a decree canceling the lien. The defendant then answered the complaint relying upon the Arkansas judgment to bar recovery in the Kentucky action.

Issue: Can a quasi in rem action to determine the status of a lien, established pursuant to a loan, later be used in another jurisdiction to bar an in personam action concerning the debt?

Rule: A quasi in rem action to determine the amount of a lien or to determine whether a loan has already been paid has a binding affect upon title to the land. Such actions do not affect personal obligations of the parties, nor do they operate as res judicata estoppel in future actions.

Harris v. Balk (S.Ct. 1905)

Facts: Harris owed a debt to Balk, both of whom were residents of North Carolina. While Harris was visiting Maryland he was served with a writ of attachment by Epstein who had an outstanding claim against Balk. Epstein wanted to secure the money Balk owed him by getting the money Harris owed Balk.

Issue: Does a state have jurisdiction to award a judgment of condemnation, even though the garnishee was a nonresident of that state and was only temporarily within its boundaries?

Rule: (Peckham, J.) Where a state law provides for attachment of a debt, and a garnishee is in the state and process is personally served upon him, the court acquires jurisdiction, and can both garnish and condemn his debt to the original creditor, provided the garnishee could himself be sued by his creditor in that state.

New York Life Insurance Co. v. Dunlevy (S.Ct. 1916)

Facts: A judgment creditor of Dunlevy brought a garnishment proceeding in Pennsylvania on money due to Dunlevy from a fund set up by Gould, Dunlevy's father, through New York Life. New York Life admitted its indebtedness, but both Dunlevy and Gould had claims to the fund. New York Life interpleaded Dunlevy. Dunlevy was given notice in California but never appeared. After the Pennsylvania court awarded the insurance claim to Gould, Dunlevy brought an action in California against New York Life to recover the value of the policy. She claimed that the Pennsylvania court had no jurisdiction over her as she was a resident of California and had no contacts with Pennsylvania.

Issue: Where a party is interpleaded to determine his interest in property, must the court have personal jurisdiction over the interpleaded party?

Rule: (McReynolds, J.) Interpleader actions bring about a final and conclusive adjudication of personal rights; consequently, a court must have personal jurisdiction over the parties.

Rush v. Savchuk (S.Ct. 1980)

Facts: Savchuk and Rush, both Indiana residents, were injured in a car accident in Indiana. Savchuk moved to Minnesota after the accident and then sued Rush in Minnesota state court for injuries he sustained in the Indiana accident. Rush's only connection to the state was that he was insured by a resident insurance company.

Issue: Can a state constitutionally exercise quasi in rem jurisdiction over a defendant by attaching the contractual obligation of an insurer licensed to do business in the state to defend and indemnify him?

Rule: (Marshall, J.) The ownership of either property or an interest in an insurance obligation is insufficient to establish "minimum contacts" necessary for quasi in rem jurisdiction. A defendant must engage in purposeful activity related to the forum so that jurisdiction is fair, just, and reasonable.

Atkinson v. The Superior Court of Los Angeles County (1957)

Facts: California members of the American Federation of Musicians brought a class action suit in a California trial court seeking to invalidate a bargaining agreement made between the Federation and an employer stipulating that royalties be paid to a New York trustee with no contacts with California. Plaintiffs sought to intercept delivery of payments to the trustee by appointment of a receiver to collect payments and a preliminary injunction to prevent their employers from making payments to the trustees. The trustee, though interpleaded and served, did not appear.

Issue: May intangible personal property (i.e., royalties) be treated as being within a forum for purposes of exercising in rem or quasi in rem jurisdiction?

Rule: Where intangible property arises from contact(s) with the forum, quasi in rem jurisdiction over the intangible is proper.

Coleman v. American Export Isbrandtsen Lines, Inc. (1968)

Facts: Coleman brought a personal injury action against American Export in a New York federal district court. American Export filed a third-party complaint against Atlantic & Gulf Stevedores, a Philadelphia-based corporation that had not engaged in any business in New York.

Issue: May a nonresident third party be served with process in a federal court action if such party, though not personally within a district, resides within 100 miles of the courthouse?

Rule: FRCP 4(f) allows service to be made on third-party defendants residing within 100 miles of the courthouse, providing the state in which he is served has jurisdiction over him.

Volkswagenwerk Aktiengesellschaft v. Schlunk (S.Ct. 1988)

Facts: Schlunk's parents were killed in a car accident while driving a Volkswagen. Schlunk sued Volkswagen of America, an American subsidiary of Volkswagenwerk Aktiengesellschaft (a German corporation), in a federal court in Illinois. Schlunk tried to join Volkswagenwerk as a party by serving its American subsidiary.

Issue: Has a court properly asserted jurisdiction over a foreign corporation by serving its American subsidiary?

Rule: (O'Connor, J.) As long as a state statute authorizes service on a subsidiary to serve the parent corporation, that service neither violates due process, nor the Hague Convention regulating legal service sent abroad.

In Re Union Carbide Corp. Gas Plant Disaster at Bhopal, India in December, 1984 (1987)

Facts: More than 2,000 people were killed after lethal gas escaped a chemical plant in India operated by Union Carbide, an American corporation. A month later, the government of India passed a law designating itself the sole representative of the victims. India then sued Union Carbide in federal court in New York. Union Carbide moved to dismiss to India on the ground of forum non conveniens. The district court granted the motion on the grounds that Union Carbide consent to Indian jurisdiction, agree to pay any decision that comports with minimal requirements of due process, and makes itself available to federal discovery rules.

Issue: May a court dismiss a suit on the ground of forum non conveniens subject to conditions?

Rule: A court may dismiss on the ground of forum non conveniens subject to a party consenting to jurisdiction, but may not put additional burdens that impugn the integrity of a foreign court's ability to conduct a fair trial (such as the latter two conditions).

Baker v. Keck (1936)

Facts: As a citizen of Illinois, Baker was attacked by Keck and others, also citizens of Illinois. Baker then moved to Oklahoma so that, among other reasons, he could establish diversity of jurisdiction to enable him to bring a federal suit.

Issue: May one establish residency in a state in order to establish diversity of citizenship?

Rule: One may change citizenship for the purposes of establishing diversity jurisdiction, as long as an actual legal change occurs.

Bell v. Hood (S.Ct. 1946)

Facts: Petitioners brought suit in federal district court alleging that respondents, agents of the Federal Bureau of Investigation, conspired to act beyond their authority and violated petitioners' rights under the Fourth and Fifth Amendments to the Constitution, by unlawfully searching petitioners' homes, seizing their property, and imprisoning them, in some cases, without warrants. Respondents moved to dismiss, asserting that they had acted within their authority, incident to a lawful arrest. The district court dismissed for want of federal jurisdiction, on the ground that the case did not "arise under" the Constitution or laws of the United States.

Issue: Does federal jurisdiction depend upon whether the law provides for relief, or upon whether the claimant in his complaint asserts a right to recover under the Constitution and laws of the United States?

Rule: (Black, J.) A federal district court has jurisdiction of a case asserting deprivation of rights under the Constitution. Only after the court assumes jurisdiction may it decide whether the complaint states a cause of action upon which relief can be granted.

Revere Copper & Brass, Inc. v. Aetna Casualty & Surety Co. (1970)

Facts: Revere Copper brought a federal diversity action against Aetna for breach of contract. Aetna impleaded a third party named Fuller who made a compulsory counterclaim against Revere Copper. There was no diversity between Revere Copper and Fuller.

Issue: May a federal court take ancillary jurisdiction over a third party defendant's counterclaim against the plaintiff where no diversity exists between the plaintiff and the third party defendant?

Rule: Ancillary jurisdiction will allow federal courts to adjudicate a third party's compulsory counterclaim against a plaintiff even though no diversity exists if such claim arises out of the same aggregate of operative facts as the original claim.

Note: The Supplemental Jurisdiction statute of 1991 has superseded this case, although the law is essentially the same.

Kramer v. Caribbean Mills, Inc. (S.Ct. 1969)

Facts: In a dispute between Panama and Venezuela Finance Company, a Panamanian corporation, and Caribbean Mills, a Haitian corporation, the Panamanian corporation assigned 95 percent of its interest to Kramer of Texas, who had no other connection with the matter, and who agreed to return the recovery, if any, to the assignor. The sole purpose of the assignment was to create diversity jurisdiction, so that the dispute could be heard in a federal court.

Issue: When is a party "improperly or collusively" made a party in order to invoke the jurisdiction of the federal court within the meaning of 28 U.S.C. § 1359?

Rule: (Harlan, J.) Where an assignee lacks previous connection with a suit and simultaneously reassigns most of the interest back to the original owner it is evident that such party was improperly and collusively joined to manufacture federal jurisdiction. (See 28 U.S.C. § 1359.)

Nelson v. Keefer (S.Ct. 1971)

Facts: The court dismissed a personal injury diversity action at pretrial as it appeared "to a legal certainty" that the claims were "really for less than the jurisdictional amount."

Issue: May a court exercise discretion prior to trial and adjudicate a challenge to the jurisdictional amount requirement?

Rule: (Black, J.) Based on pretrial discovery, comprehensive pretrial narrative statements, and medical reports, courts may determine with legal certainty the upper limit of a possible award and decide whether the minimum jurisdictional amount has been satisfied.

Snyder v. Harris
Gas Service Co. v. Coburn (S.Ct. 1969)

Facts: In two separate cases class action plaintiffs filed claims whose individual amounts in controversy were under the jurisdictional limit. In *Snyder v. Harris*, Snyder filed a class action against the Board of Directors of the Missouri Fidelity Union Trust Life Insurance, in which her claim fell just short of the jurisdictional amount, but the aggregate claims would satisfy the amount in controversy requirement. In *Gas Service Co. v. Coburn*, Coburn filed a class action charging illegal collection of a tax against people exempt from the law. The individual claims equaled less than ten dollars, but the aggregate claims easily surpassed the jurisdictional amount.

Issue: May plaintiffs in a class action aggregate their claims to satisfy the jurisdictional amount?

Rule: (Black, J.) The "amount in controversy" means the total claims of one plaintiff or the interest of two or more plaintiffs in a single right, not the aggregate claims of several plaintiffs.

American Fire & Casualty Co. v. Finn (S.Ct. 1951)

Facts: Fire damaged Finn's Texas home. She sought recovery in a Texas court against her Texas insurance broker and two nonresident insurance companies. One of the insurance companies had the entire case removed to federal district court under 28 U.S.C. § 1441(c), which states that where a separate cause of action may be removed under diversity, the court has discretion to remove otherwise nonremovable matters joined with it, or to remand all matters not within its original jurisdiction to the state court. After losing its case in federal court, the insurance company claimed that removal jurisdiction was improper because of a lack of complete diversity.

Issue: May a federal court asserting removal jurisdiction over a diverse claim assert removal jurisdiction over the entire case even if some of the claims in the entire case are not diverse?

Rule: (Reed, J.) Where there are multiple defendants, but only a single wrong is sued upon, removal is proper only if diversity is complete. The court must remand the whole case to state court, or dismiss the nondiverse claims if they are separable.

Dissent: (Douglas, J.) Having, by its own request, sued in federal court and lost on the merits, the defendant should not be able to relitigate the issues.

United States v. United Mine Workers (S.Ct. 1947)

Facts: To prevent labor disputes, the United States government in 1946 operated the nation's coal mines. A dispute arose between the United Mine Workers and the government. Lewis, president of the union, terminated the union-government agreement. The government received a temporary restraining order enjoining the union from striking until a trial could be held on the validity, of a preliminary injunction in light of the Norris-La Guardia Act's prohibition of injunctive court action in labor disputes. Nonetheless, the miners struck. The court held the union in contempt of court. The union challenged the "jurisdiction" of the court on the grounds that the Norris-La Guardia Act prohibited the granting of injunctive relief.

Issue: Does a federal court have jurisdiction to preserve conditions while it determines its own jurisdiction to grant injunctive relief?

Rule: (Vinson, CJ.) A court which has both subject matter and personal jurisdiction over the parties can compel the parties to obey a temporary order while it determines its own authority to grant injunctive relief, and can punish violations of its orders by civil and criminal contempt.

Walker v. City of Birmingham (S.Ct. 1967)

Facts: A state court issued injunctions to prevent Martin Luther King, Jr., and others from conducting a protest march. The marchers violated the injunction and marched anyway. At the trial for violation of the injunction, the state court considered only whether it had jurisdiction to issue the injunction and whether the marchers had violated the injunction. The state court refused to consider either its constitutionality or the manner in which it had been administered.

Issue: When punishing violation of an injunction, may the court review the constitutionality of the law that authorized the injunction?

Rule: (Stewart, J.) Where the parties have sought neither judicial review of an injunction issued pursuant to state law nor judicial review of the constitutionality of that law, the state court properly has jurisdiction to hold the parties in contempt and to punish them for contempt.

Dissent: (Warren, CJ.) It shows no disrespect for law to violate a statute on the ground that it is unconstitutional and then submit one's case to the courts with the willingness to accept the penalty if the statute is held to be valid. That someone has violated a law does not show such disregard for the legislature that the violator must always be punished even if the statute is unconstitutional.

Tyler v. Judges of the Court of Registration (1900)

Facts: Tyler challenged the constitutionality of a land registration proceeding that required notice by mail to all known claimants as well as publication notice for unknown claimants. Tyler alleged that the unknown claimants were deprived of property without due process.

Issue: Does a land registration proceeding that provides publication as notice to unknown claimants violate the due process right of nonregistered interest holders?

Rule: An action that involves the status of a parcel of land may be adjudicated by a state court although notice by personal service was not made on the unknown claimants as long as the court had jurisdiction over the property.

Garfein v. McInnis (1928)

Facts: Garfein, a resident of New York, contracted to purchase real estate from McInnis, a resident of Connecticut. Garfein brought an action for specific performance and served process on McInnis in Connecticut.

Issue: Does an action for specific performance involving the sale of land require personal service within the state upon the defendant?

Rule: Specific performance actions are generally actions in personam and require personal service within the state. However, where statute allows, specific performance actions affecting title or interest to property situated in the state will be adjudicated without service of process within the state.

Campbell v. Murdock (1950)

Facts: Murdock made a special appearance for the purpose of challenging the court's jurisdiction over a foreclosure action to enforce a mechanic's lien. 28 U.S.C. § 1655 authorized actions to enforce liens on property within the district on nonresident defendants.

Issue: Can a court issue personal judgments when jurisdiction is based solely on the fact that the property in controversy is located in the district?

Rule: If a defendant does not appear and the action is in rem (i.e., concerns title to land), final judgment can only affect the property when the personal relief requested is closely related to the in rem action. The court can issue personal judgments if the defendant makes an appearance, even if only a special appearance to challenge jurisdiction.

Perkins v. Benguet Consolidated Mining Co. (S.Ct. 1952)

Facts: Perkins, who is not a resident of Ohio served Benguet, a Philippine corporation, with process in Ohio. Benguet maintained "continuous and systematic," but limited, business in Ohio. The suit did not arise in Ohio, nor was it related to corporate activities in Ohio.

Issue: May a state court assert in personam jurisdiction over a foreign corporation regarding a cause of action not arising in the state, nor related to the activities of the corporation in that state?

Rule: (Burton, J.) When a foreign corporation has sufficient and substantial business in a state, a state may entertain a cause of action against such corporation, even where the cause of action arises from activities entirely distinct from its activities in the forum state.

Cook Associates v. Lexington United Corp. (1981)

Facts: Cook Associates, an Illinois employment agency, brought a breach of contract action in Illinois state court against Lexington United, a Missouri corporate manufacturer. Lexington's only contacts with Illinois included an initial meeting with a candidate and trade shows where Lexington did a small amount of business.

Issue: Will a party be subject to a state's jurisdiction when its only contact with the state was a meeting that did not result in a transaction and a series of trade shows where some business was generated?

Rule: A party is not amenable to service of process under a state's long-arm statute unless the cause of action arose from the transaction of business in the state. A corporation is only deemed to be "doing business" in a state if its business is of such character and extent that the corporation has subjected itself to the jurisdiction of the state.

DeJames v. Magnificence Carriers (1980)

Facts: DeJames brought an admiralty suit in federal district court in New Jersey against Magnificence Carriers and Hitachi for injuries sustained while working aboard Magnificence's vessel as it was moored in New Jersey. Hitachi, a Japanese corporation, had worked on the vessel in Japan but conducted no other business in New Jersey.

Issue: Where a defendant is sued under admiralty jurisdiction, can a federal court consider the defendant's overall national contacts in order to satisfy due process requirements of jurisdiction?

Rule: Though an action arises under federal law, the "national contacts" of a nonresident defendant are insufficient to establish personal jurisdiction in federal court if service is made pursuant to a state statute.

Arrowsmith v. United Press International (1963)

Facts: Arrowsmith of Maryland brought an action for libel in federal court in Vermont against United Press International of New York, basing federal jurisdiction on diversity of citizenship. Service of process was obtained through FRCP 4(d)(3).

Issue: What standard should be used to determine whether a federal court has personal jurisdiction over a nonresident defendant in a suit founded on diversity?

Rule: Federal courts sitting in diversity should apply the standard of the state in which it sits when establishing personal jurisdiction.

Livingston v. Jefferson (1811)

Facts: Edward Livingston of New York brought an action in Virginia against Thomas Jefferson of Virginia for trespassing on Livingston's Louisiana land.

Issue: Can a court adjudicate a claim of trespass on lands located outside of the state where the trespasser is a resident of the state?

Rule: Since "local actions" may require investigations of title, boundaries, and surveys, they should be brought in the jurisdiction wherein they are situated.

D.H. Overmeyer Co. v. Frick Co. (S.Ct. 1972)

Facts: After an installment contract had been renegotiated, the parties consented to a new agreement. The new agreement included a cognovit whereby the debtor consented in advance to the holder's obtaining a judgment without notice or hearing.

Issue: May a party waive their right to object to the taking of property without notice or an initial hearing?

Rule: (Blackmun, J.) In a contract where there is equal bargaining power, a party may voluntarily, intelligently, and knowingly waive its due process right to notice and hearing.

Kulko v. Superior Court (S.Ct. 1978)

Facts: After a divorce, Sharon sued Ezra in California court for custody of their two children. Ezra was a New York resident, and had never been to California, except for three days during which he and Sharon had been married, and for one day during a stopover on a military tour of duty. Ezra had never directed any other activity at California, except for purchasing a one-way ticket to the state for his daughter when Ezra had agreed to let the daughter live with Sharon a few years earlier. Ezra appeared specially to challenge the California court's personal jurisdiction over him.

Issue: In an action for custody and child support, may a state exercise personal jurisdiction over a nonresident, nondomiciliary parent?

Rule: (Marshall, J.) A court may not exercise personal jurisdiction over a defendant unless the defendant has sufficient minimum contacts with state to indicate that he has "purposefully availed" himself of the forum. In this case, the contacts were not sufficient to support personal jurisdiction over the defendant.

Dissent: (Brennan, J.) The defendant's connections with California were not so attenuated that requiring him to conduct his defense in the California courts would be unreasonable or unfair.

American Eutectic Welding Alloys Sales Co. v. Dytron Alloys Corp. (1971)

Facts: Eutectic, a New York corporation, brought an equitable relief action in New York against two former nonresident employees and their new nonresident employer, Dytron, for both unfair competition and for disclosure of confidential information. Dytron resided out of state and had no activities in the forum. The former employees were trained in, and signed a contract with Eutectic in the forum state.

Issue 1: Do employment training and instructions as well as the signing of a contract in a forum state by a resident suffice to establish "minimum contacts"?

Rule 1: Purposeful acts preliminary to a contract together with the signing of a contract by a defendant in the forum state are sufficient to establish "minimum contacts."

Issue 2: Can a court establish personal jurisdiction over a nonresident party whose activities outside the forum caused a resident corporation to suffer economic loss?

Rule 2: Personal jurisdiction can be established over a nonresident party for activities outside the forum only if such activities resulted in injury within the state. Loss of profits in state is but a "consequence" of "injury" caused out of state.

Burnham v. Superior Court of California

Facts: Mr. and Mrs. Burnham lived in New Jersey. Mrs. Burnham moved to California with their children. When Mr. Burnham went to California to conduct business and visit the children, he was served with a California summons and a copy of Mrs. Burnham's divorce petition. He moved to quash the service of process on the grounds that the court lacked personal jurisdiction over him because his only contacts with California were a few short visits.

Issue: May a court exert jurisdiction over a non-resident who is personally served with process while temporarily in a state, in a suit unrelated to his activities in that state?

Rule: (Scalia, J.) Physical presence alone is sufficient for a state to exercise jurisdiction over a person; Due Process requirements are satisfied. Continuous and systematic contacts with the forum are not necessary. The litigation need not arise out of activities within the state.

Dissent: (Brennan, J.) The Due Process clause generally permits state courts to exercise jurisdiction over a defendant while he is voluntarily present in a state.

Carnival Cruise Lines, Inc. v. Shute (S.Ct. 1991)

Facts: The Shutes (both Washington residents) purchased tickets for a cruise with Carnival (a Miami corporation) through a Washington travel agent. Each ticket included a clause in fine print that named Florida as the forum state for any and all disputes arising from the cruise. A passenger's use of a ticket was deemed an acceptance of all the terms of the ticket. During the cruise, Eulala Shute slipped and fell on a deck mat. The Shutes sued Carnival in the U.S. District Court in Washington. Carnival argued that the Washington suit was invalid because the Shutes had implicitly agreed to the forum-selection clause by taking the cruise. The Shutes argued that the forum-selection clause was unenforceable because the clause was not a product of negotiation and that enforcement of the clause would deprive the Shutes of their day in court because they could not afford to sue in Florida.

Issue: Is a forum consent clause that is included in an adhesion contract for passage on a cruise enforceable?

Rule: (Blackmun, J.) A forum consent clause is generally enforceable, particularly where the clause is a vital part of the agreement entering into the parties' practical and economic calculations. A party claiming that such a clause is unfair bears "a heavy burden of proof." The forum selection clause in this case was reasonable because the cruise line had a high efficiency interest in conducting all litigation in a single forum. The passengers, too, derived an important benefit from the clause in the form of a reduced fare. The passengers in this case also failed to satisfy their "heavy burden of proof" with respect to their alleged financial hardship in litigating in Florida.

Dissent: (Stevens, J.) Forum selection clauses in passenger tickets are unenforceable because the parties do not have equal bargaining power.

Insurance Corp. of Ireland, Ltd. v. Compagnie des Bauxites de Guinee (S.Ct. 1982)

Facts: The Compagnie des Bauxites de Guinee of Delaware sued Insurance Corp. of Ireland and several other foreign "excess insurers" in a diversity action in Pennsylvania, alleging breach of an insurance contract guaranteed by Insurance Corp. and the excess investors. During discovery, Insurance Corp. failed to produce requested documents that might prove sufficient contact with Pennsylvania as to allow the court to assert federal jurisdiction. Pursuant to FRCP 37(b)(2)(A), the court issued an order compelling production of the requested documents, warning that failure to produce documents would result in the court presuming valid in personam jurisdiction.

Issue: May a court presume a valid assertion of jurisdiction pursuant to FRCP 37(b)(2)(A) due to a party's failure to produce requested documents during discovery?

Rule: (White, J.) Imposing a sanction pursuant to FRCP 37(b)(2)(A) for a party's failure to comply with discovery requests that a "finding" of personal jurisdiction over the party exists will not violate due process. The party's failure to produce requested documents in such situations allows the court to presume jurisdiction.

Concurrence: (Powell, J.) Rule 37(b) does not create a broader standard for jurisdiction. A court may not issue Rule 37(b) sanctions without first establishing that "minimum contacts" exist, even if the sanctions relate to that establishment of "minimum contacts."

Phillips Petroleum Co. v. Shutts (S.Ct. 1985)

Facts: Phillips Petroleum Company was a Delaware corporation. Shutts was one of over 28,000 royalty owners of leases with Phillips regarding the drilling of natural gas. These owners brought a class action suit in Kansas to recover interest on royalty payments which had been delayed by Phillips.

Issue: Can a class action be brought in a state where many of the absent plaintiffs do not have minimum contacts?

Rule: (Rehnquist, J.) The concerns of *International Shoe* in protecting the interests of defendants are not as strong where the absent party is a plaintiff, legally represented by similarly situated class members, who does not have to travel in order to recover a portion of an award which they may not have had the resources to pursue without the benefit of the multistate class action. Although not relevant here, a multistate class action may require a state to apply the different laws of several states to different subclasses of plaintiffs.

Concurrence: (Stevens, J.) It is not a defect of either the Due Process Clause or the Full Faith and Credit Clause for a state to apply its own law to matters that occur primarily outside the forum state.

Nelson v. Iowa-Illinois Gas & Elec. Co. (1966)

Facts: Nelson's estate brought a wrongful death action in federal court against Iowa-Illinois Gas and Electric Company (IIG&EC), Nelson's employer. Recovery was available under state law only if the decedent was an employee, not an independent contractor. The estate alleged that the injury occurred while Nelson was either an employee or an independent contractor for IIG&EC. IIG&EC asserted that Nelson was an independent contractor, and tried to use the estate's pleadings as an admission of that fact to prevent the court from asserting subject matter jurisdiction over the case.

Issue: Can a party be estopped from denying a question of fact because of statements made in the pleadings?

Rule: Subject matter jurisdiction can only be established by law and not by pleadings of a party.

Nuernberger v. State (1976)

Facts: Nuernberger was convicted in a New York county court of assault with intent to commit incest and impairment of minors. His conviction was reversed on grounds that exclusive original jurisdiction over the assault charge rested in family court.

Issue: Is the decision by a court that did not have proper subject matter jurisdiction over a fully litigated case null and void?

Rule: A party convicted in a court which lacked original jurisdiction can appeal the legality of the sentence.

Caterpillar Inc. v. Williams (S.Ct. 1987)

Facts: Caterpillar hired the plaintiffs under a collective bargaining agreement. During the course of their employment, the plaintiffs were promoted out of their collective bargaining positions and promised job security. Subsequently, Caterpillar laid them off. The plaintiffs brought suit in state court for breach of contract. Caterpillar had the case removed to federal court, on the ground that the plaintiffs' claims were "merged" into, and preempted by, their original collective bargaining contracts and were therefore subject to the exclusive jurisdiction of the federal courts under the Labor Management Relations Act.

Issue: When may a defendant remove an action to federal court based on federal question jurisdiction (28 U.S.C. § 1331)?

Rule: (Brennan, J.) If a federal question appears on the face of the plaintiffs "well-pleaded" complaint, a defendant may remove the action to federal court. If a plaintiff chooses to plead a complaint based purely on a state law cause of action, a defendant may not create federal question jurisdiction by asserting a defense that includes a federal question. In this case, the plaintiffs chose to plead based purely on state causes of action, and Caterpillar could not, therefore, remove.

Ferens v. John Deere Co. (S.Ct. 1990)

Facts: Ferens (of Pennsylvania) wanted to sue Deere (of Delaware) in federal court for damages after losing his right hand while operating a Deere combine harvester in Pennsylvania. Ferens could not bring the action in Pennsylvania, because the statute of limitations had run out on the claim, so he brought the tort claim in federal court in Mississippi. The federal court, employing Mississippi's choice of law rules, applied Pennsylvania substantive law to the tort claim, but applied Mississippi's statute of limitations, which had not expired. Ferens then successfully moved to have the suit transferred to Pennsylvania due to improper venue under 28 U.S.C. § 1404(a), but the Pennsylvania federal court ruled that the Pennsylvania statute of limitations barred the claim.

Issue: In a transfer initiated by the plaintiff under 28 U.S.C. § 1404(a), what choice of law rules must the transferee court apply?

Rule: (Kennedy, J.) If a plaintiff initiates a transfer under 28 U.S.C. § 1404(a), the transferee court must apply the choice of law rules of the transferor court. Decisions to transfer under 28 U.S.C. § 1404(a) are based on considerations of convenience only. Section 1404(a) should not be interpreted in such a way as to create forum shopping or substantive changes in applicable law.

Dissent: (Scalia, J.) A plaintiff who initiates a transfer under 28 U.S.C. § 1404(a) should not be able to rely on the choice of law rule of the transferor court, as it would create a lack of uniformity in the law applied within a state. Such a rule also infringes the interest that federal court deference to the law of a forum state is supposed to protect: uniformity in the application of state law by state courts and federal courts sitting in diversity.

Willy v. Coastal Corp. (1988)

Facts: Willy filed suit against Coastal for wrongful discharge, alleging that they fired him because he refused to act in violation of state and federal environmental and securities laws. Coastal removed the case to federal court on the ground that some of the statutes Willy was asked to violate were federal. The federal statutes had a "whistleblower" provision that created an administrative Remedy to protect informants from retributory firing. They were not intended to preempt state employment law.

Issue: May a defendant remove an action to federal court on the basis of federal question jurisdiction if there is a State cause of action that relies in part upon federal law?

Rule: A case may be removed to federal court if federal law completely preempts a state cause of action. A case may also be removed if federal law creates the cause of action or if the action requires resolution of a substantial question of federal law. The court found that Willy's suit could not be removed because: (1) federal environmental and security laws are not meant to preempt wrongful discharge claims; (2) federal law created a cause of action only for "whistleblowers," which is not applicable to Willy; (3) federal courts, at any rate, could not hear a "whistleblower" claim because federal law only provides an administrative remedy; and (4) the federal element of Willy's claim is not substantial enough to confer federal question jurisdiction.

CHAPTER 3

ERIE DOCTRINE

I. **INTRODUCTION**

A. Explanation
    A common conflict arising from the federal system is determining what procedures to use when a state claim is asserted in federal courts, and when federal claims are asserted in state courts. Further complicating matters is the fuzzy line between procedure and substance. The *Erie* doctrine sets forth a framework, however convoluted, for determining which law to apply.

B. Policy Considerations

    1. Forum Shopping
       Insofar as one procedural law might be more favorable to litigants than another, courts attempt to prevent litigants from using the federal courts as a method of finding the most favorable jurisdiction.

    2. Uniformity
       Having two sets of laws may create confusion amongst citizens, especially where one law may direct a citizen to do that which another law discourages.

    3. Federalism
       Despite the Supremacy Clause, federal courts are wary of treading too harshly on state autonomy in drafting their own substantive remedies.

    4. States as Laboratories
       State legislatures often take the initiative on various legislation that Congress may later incorporate into its own laws. Forcing uniformity may impede such inventiveness.

II. **STATE LAW IN FEDERAL COURTS**

A. History

1. Rules of Decision Act
Located in § 34 of the Judiciary Act of 1789, the Rules of Decisions Act directed federal courts to apply "the laws of the several states, except where the Constitution, treaties, or statutes of the United States shall otherwise require or provide . . . ."

2. *Swift v. Tyson* (1842)
Justice Story's decision held that:

   a. State law should be applied in federal court only when ruling on matters of purely local concern (e.g. real estate).

   b. Federal courts were free to evolve their own "general" common law regarding state laws.

3. The Advent of Forum Shopping
The creation of federal common law encouraged forum-shopping. Since litigants could choose between two distinct bodies of common law, the party would choose the forum with the most favorable law. This unsatisfactory state of affairs lasted for nearly a century.

B. *Erie Railroad Co. v. Tompkins* (1938)

1. The Holding
Justice Brandeis' decision ended the *Swift v. Tyson* era in its tracks. There the court:

   a. Held that state law, including both statutory and common law, must be applied to substantive issues in cases based on diversity jurisdiction.

   b. Expressly overruled *Swift v. Tyson* as "an unconstitutional assumption of powers by the Courts of the United States."

   c. Eradicated federal general common law.

2. Underlying Policies

   a. Elimination of uncontrolled forum-shopping, and

   b. Avoidance of inequitable administration of laws.

3. What *Erie* Did Not Change
   Federal law still applies in diversity cases when a federal statute or federal question is involved.

C. Federal Procedural Laws

   1. The Conformity Act (1872)
      Federal courts must follow the procedure of the courts of the state in which it is located. This law has been replaced by the Enabling Act of 1934.

   2. Enabling Act (1934)
      The Supreme Court may now formulate general rules of procedure for the federal courts. The Act stated that the procedural rules were not to "abridge, enlarge, nor modify the substantive rights of any litigant." However, substance and procedure are not easy to distinguish.

   3. Federal Rules of Civil Procedure (1938 – same year as *Erie*) provided general rules of procedure in accordance with the Enabling Act.

D. Scope of the *Erie* Decision
   Following *Erie*, the Supreme Court formulated a series of tests to help the federal courts decide whether a given state law is substantive or procedural.

   1. *York* Outcome-Determinative Test
      In *Guaranty Trust Co. v. York* (1945), a federal court in a diversity case should apply state law if the federal procedural rule would lead to a substantially different result. The court in *Guaranty* applied the state statute of limitations, finding it substantive for *Erie* purposes.

   2. *Byrd* Balancing Test
      In *Byrd v. Blue Ridge Rural Electric Cooperative, Inc.* (1958), Justice Brennan's decision held that the preference for state law must be balanced against denial of the federal right. If a state law in a diversity action would deny a party a strongly-protected federal right, the federal rule or policy

should be followed even if it would lead to a substantially different outcome.

3. *Hanna* "Smart Person" Test

In *Hanna v. Plumer* (1965), Chief Justice Warren set out what is currently the definitive test for ascertaining the applicable law.

a. Presumption of Procedure

State laws are presumed to be procedural. Thus, federal rules must be followed to the exclusion of a state law if the federal rule is sanctioned by the Rules Enabling Act.

  i. It does not "abridge, enlarge, nor modify the substantive rights of any litigant."

  ii. Note that no federal rule has yet been held to infringe on a litigant's rights. This is due in part to Chief Justice Warren's assertion that the FRCP were enacted by "smart people" who would know better.

b. Conflict With the State Law

  i. Direct Conflict

  If the federal rule is in direct Conflict with the law of the state, the federal rule must still be followed.

  ii. Indirect Conflict

  Even if there is no direct conflict with state procedural law, the federal rule will preclude the use of a state statute if it occupies the field of operation of the state statute (see *Burlington Northern Railroad Co. v. Woods*).

  iii. No Conflict

  If there is no conflict at all, or if the rule in question is not in the FRCP, *Hanna* does not apply.

    (1) Some courts employ the analysis of *Erie* and the balancing test of *Byrd*.

(2) Justice Scalia, dissenting in *Stewart Organization Inc. v. Ricoh*, would prefer to apply the *York* outcome determinative test, but his approach does not yet command a majority of the court. Several lower courts have applied *York*, however.

(3) Some courts have held that *Hanna* has overruled *Byrd*, and that unless a rule is in the FRCP, state law must apply, and if it is in the FRCP, the federal and state rules will be applied simultaneously.

(4) The Harlan Concurrence
Justice Harlan's concurrence in *Hanna v. Plumer* provided a stricter test. In deciding whether to apply a state or federal rule, a court must determine if the choice of rule would substantially affect those primary decisions respecting human conduct that our constitutional system leaves to state regulation. So far, this test has had no impact on the law, although it has been supported by several scholars.

E.   The Problem of Ascertaining State Law
Federal courts adjudicating a state claim must predict how the highest court of the state would decide the claim.

1. State Authority
Statutes and Constitutions of the state must be applied as interpreted by the state's highest court. If there is no holding in the highest court, lower court decisions should be consulted as persuasive authority.

2. Certification
The question may be certified to the state's highest court.

3. Analogy
If the issue has not been undertaken by the state before, other authorities may be consulted to help discern how the highest court would rule. Federal courts can also consider analogous

rulings and policies if the most recent case law on point is outdated or unclear.

4. Conflicts of Law

Federal courts must also apply the conflicts of laws rules of the state in which it is sitting (see *Klaxon v. Stentor Elec. Mfg. Co.*).

F.   Residual Federal Common Law

Even though Erie declares "there is no federal general common law," there are situations where federal common law is employed to avoid subjecting strong federal interests to the inconsistencies of the laws of the several states.

1. Federal common law is followed in most federal question cases:

2. Mnemonic: **FLUID**

a.   **F**oreign relations matters.

b.   Federal statute of **L**imitations applied where analogous state statutes of limitations either do not exist, or do not adequately protect the interests Congress wished to protect.

c.   **U**nited States is a party.

d.   **I**nterpreting federal statutes, treaties, or the Constitution.

e.   **D**isputes between the states.

3. Federal common law is also followed in some diversity cases:

a.   Federal defense is raised, or

b.   Federal interests outweigh state interests. Incidental federal concerns are not sufficient to compel the use of federal common law in a purely private litigation (see *Bank of America Nat. Trust & Sav. Ass'n v. Parnell*).

III.   FEDERAL LAW IN STATE COURTS (REVERSE *ERIE*)

A.   Supremacy Clause
When a federal claim is brought in a state court, the Supremacy Clause of the Constitution (Art. VI) compels the application of federal law.

B.   Federal Defense
A federal right may be relevant to a state action if it is interposed as a defense to a state action.

C.   Superseding State Law
State rules of procedure must not be followed if they impose unnecessary burdens on federal rights of recovery (see *Brown v. Western Ry. of Alabama*).

CASE CLIPS

Erie Railroad Co. v. Tompkins (S.Ct. 1938)

Facts: As Tompkins walked on Erie Railroad Company's land, a freight train injured him. While Pennsylvania common law would have denied Tompkins relief as a trespasser, federal common law did not regard Tompkins a trespasser. No Pennsylvania statute applied to the issue of trespassing. In *Swift v. Tyson* (S.Ct. 1842), Justice Story held that the Federal Judiciary Act required federal courts to apply state statutes, but not state common law, in diversity cases. Accordingly, the District Court applied federal common law in this diversity case and awarded damages to Tompkins.

Issue: Which law, federal or state, must be applied to substantive issues arising in a diversity case?

Rule: (Brandeis, J.) Under the Constitution, only state law, both common law and statutory law, may be applied to substantive issues arising in a diversity case. There is no federal general common law.

Concurrence: (Reed, J.) This case need only be decided by expanding the word "law" in § 34 of the Federal Judiciary Act to include common law as well as statutes. Absent the Federal Judiciary Act, it is unclear whether federal courts may, under the Constitution, develop their own common law.

Dissent: (Butler, J.) Since no finding of the railroad's negligence was ever made, the case should be retried. Furthermore, by forcing courts to adhere to state law, the majority infringes on Congress' ability to regulate the federal court system.

Guaranty Trust Co. v. York (S.Ct. 1945)

Facts: York, who could not sue in state court because the statute of limitations had run, brought suit in federal district court against the Guaranty Trust Company, alleging a breach of fiduciary duty. York claimed that the statute of limitations was a procedural matter to be governed by federal law. The court of appeals ruled that the fact that the action was brought in equity meant that the federal court could disregard the state rule.

Issue: When is a federal court hearing a state claim in a diversity case bound by state law?

Rule: (Frankfurter, J.) A federal court in a diversity case should follow the state rule if not following state law would lead to a substantially different result than if the suit had been brought in state court. Using this "outcome-determinative" test, the Court applied the state statute of limitations, finding it substantive for *Erie* purposes.

Dissent: (Rutledge, J.) Whether or not the action may be barred depends not upon the law of the state which creates the substantive right, but upon the law of the state where suit may be brought.

Byrd v. Blue Ridge Rural Electric Cooperative, Inc. (S.Ct. 1958)

Facts: After being injured on the job, Byrd brought a federal diversity action against his employer, Blue Ridge Electric, alleging negligence. A state workmen's compensation statute gave certain employers immunity from suit. Under state law a judge, not the jury, decides whether an employer fits within the statute's immunity. In the federal action, the jury decided all the factual issues, including whether Blue Ridge fit within the statute's immunity.

Issue: When should a federal court sitting in diversity follow a federal rule or policy even though the suit would lead to a substantially different outcome had it been prosecuted in state court?

Rule: (Brennan, J.) A federal rule or policy should be applied to the exclusion of state law that would mandate a different result where the federal interest at stake outweighs any countervailing state interest, coupled with the desire for uniform application of the laws. Applying this "balancing test," the court found that the federal interest injury decisions outweighed the state's interest in uniform application of the law. But the court remanded the case to allow Blue Ridge to introduce evidence showing it fit within the statutory immunity.

Hanna v. Plumer (S.Ct. 1965)

Facts: Osgood and Hanna of Ohio were involved in an auto accident in South Carolina. Hanna of Ohio sued Plumer, executor of Osgood's estate, in a federal diversity action in Plumer's home district of Massachusetts. In compliance with FRCP 4(d)(1), copies of the summons and complaint were left with Plumer's wife at his residence. Plumer moved for summary judgment on the ground that service was not sufficient because the complaint was not personally served upon him, as required by Massachusetts state law.

Issue: When must a federal court sitting in diversity follow an applicable federal rule despite a conflicting state law, even if the outcome of the diversity suit will be altered thereby?

Rule: (Warren, C.J.) Where federal procedure and state law conflict, only the federal procedure will be applied in federal court. A federal law is procedural if it has been validly enacted under the Federal Enabling Act, and does not violate constitutional principles. Where they do not conflict, the *York* "outcome-determinative" test should be applied to determine whether the federal rule should be applied at all.

Concurrence: (Harlan, J.) State rules should be applied in lieu of a contrary federal rule where the state law directs a "private primary activity." This state law does not address any primary interest.

Walker v. Armco Steel Corp. (S.Ct. 1980)

Facts: Armco claimed that Walker's federal personal injury suit, brought in diversity, was time barred because the state statute of limitations had run. Walker argued that the suit should be allowed to proceed because FRCP 3 governs the tolling of the statute of limitations.

Issue: Should a federal court sitting in diversity follow state law or FRCP 3 in determining when an action commences for the purpose of tolling the state statute of limitations?

Rule: (Marshall, J.) In diversity actions FRCP 3 governs the date from which various timing requirements of the federal rules begin to run, but does not affect the state statute of limitations. *Hanna* does not apply because there is no direct conflict between the federal rule and the state law.

Stewart Organization, Inc. v. Ricoh Corp. (S.Ct. 1988)

Facts: Stewart, Inc., an Alabama corporation, entered into a dealership agreement with Ricoh Corp., a New Jersey corporation.

Stewart later sued Ricoh in a federal diversity suit in Alabama for breach of contract. Ricoh petitioned the court for a transfer of venue, under 28 U.S.C. § 1404, to the southern district of New York, as specified in the contract's forum selection clause. The district court denied the transfer because of Alabama's strong interest against transfers of venue.

Issue: Should a federal court sitting in diversity apply state or federal law in deciding whether to transfer venue?

Rule: (Marshall, J.) Since the federal venue transfer statute (mandating some consideration of the forum selection clause) and the state venue transfer statute (mandating no consideration of the forum selection clause) conflict, *Hanna v. Plumer* dictates that the federal statute controls.

Mason v. American Emery Wheel Works (1957)

Facts: Mason, a citizen of Mississippi, filed suit against American Emery, a Rhode Island corporation, in Rhode Island district court. Mason claimed American Emery negligently manufactured an emery wheel, which subsequently exploded while in use at Mason's workplace in Mississippi, causing injuries. American Emery asserted that there was no privity of contract, since the wheel was not purchased directly by Mason. The district court, correctly applying Mississippi law, was compelled to rely on a 30 year old Mississippi decision which declared that a manufacturer was not liable for negligence to parties lacking privity of contract, and granted a motion to dismiss.

Issue: Does a federal court sitting in diversity have the discretion to depart from another state's precedent, when the existing law of the other state is "contrary to the great weight of authority"?

Rule: A federal court instructed to apply the law of another state may apply a different law in its decision if the existing law is "contrary to the great weight of authority," and it can reasonably be inferred that the highest court of the other state would rule that way if faced with the same decision.

McKenna v. Ortho Pharmaceutical Corp. (1980)

Facts: McKenna used a contraceptive manufactured by Ortho Pharmaceutical Corp. In 1969 she was hospitalized for hypertension. In March 1972 she suffered a catastrophic cerebrovascular stroke. In November 1973 she sued Ortho in Pennsylvania. Ortho removed the case to federal district court. Since the cause of action arose in Ohio, the district court reasoned that the Pennsylvania conflict of laws statute borrowed not only Ohio's two-year statute of limitations, but also Ohio law ruling that the action arose on the date of the injury. However, Ohio law was unclear as to whether the injury occurred when McKenna suffered hypertension (more than two years from commencement of the action) or when she suffered her stroke (less than two years from commencement of the action).

Issue: How should a federal court sitting in diversity decide how a state court would rule on an issue?

Rule: The federal court sitting in a diversity action must predict how the highest court of the appropriate state would decide the present action. The court can consider analogous rulings and policies if the most recent case law on point is outdated or unclear.

Clearfield Trust Co. v. United States (S.Ct. 1943)

Facts: Clearfied Trust cashed a United States check that had been forged by an unknown third party. Clearfield Trust also guaranteed all prior endorsements on the check. The United States sued Clearfield Trust in Pennsylvania federal court for the value of the check. Pennsylvania law would bar recovery.

Issue: Must a federal court not sitting in diversity apply state law to a federal claim?

Rule: (Douglas, J.) Where strong federal interests are at stake (as here, where the United States is a party), the federal interest in preserving a national law mandates that the state law be inapplicable.

Miree v. DeKalb County (S.Ct. 1977)

Facts: In 1973 a Lear jet crashed at the DeKalb-Peachtree Airport. The survivors sued the county in a federal diversity action in the northern district of Georgia, based on the county's contract with the

Federal Aviation Administration (FAA). Although state law gave the survivors standing to sue based on the contract, federal common law regarding the FAA did not.

Issue: Should a federal court sitting in diversity apply federal common law in a suit in which no federal interest is at stake?

Rule: (Rehnquist, J.) Since only the rights of private litigants are at issue, there is no reason to apply federal common law. Thus, the state law should apply exclusively.

DelCostello v. International Brotherhood of Teamsters
(S.Ct. 1983)

Facts: Several employees brought an action alleging that their employer had breached a provision of the collective bargaining agreement and that their union had breached its duty of fair representation. Under a related state statute of limitations, the suit was time barred. But under a related federal statute of limitations, the suit could proceed.

Issue: Should a federal court apply an analogous federal statute of limitations or a related state statute of limitations?

Rule: (Brennan, J.) Although it is standard practice for a federal court to "borrow" a suitable state statute of limitations for a federal cause of action, if the state statute of limitations does not adequately protect federal policies, the court should apply an analogous federal statute of limitations instead.

Dissent: (Stevens, J.) The Rules of Decisions Act mandates federal courts to "borrow" the appropriate state statute of limitations, rather than the analogous federal statute. Nothing in the Constitution, statutes, or treaties mandates a different result.

Dice v. Akron, Canton & Youngstown Railroad Co. (S.Ct. 1952)

Facts: Dice brought a negligence action in state court under the Federal Employers Liability Act. Told that it was merely a receipt for back wages, Dice had signed a release of liability. Under Ohio law, issues of fraud are decided by the judge, not the jury. The court entered judgment for the defendants.

Issue: Where an action brought in a state court arises under a federal statute, may state law control?

Rule: (Black, J.) Where a state court action is based on a federal claim, state laws do not control. Here, the Seventh Amendment right to a jury trial on an issue under federal law must control.

Dissent: (Frankfurter, J.) Requiring a jury for state actions brought under a federal statute and a judicial factfinder for all other state actions disregards the settled distribution of judicial power between the states and the federal government where Congress authorizes concurrent enforcement of federally-created rights.

Burlington Northern Railroad Co. v. Woods (S.Ct. 1987)

Facts: Woods sued Burlington Railroad for negligence in Alabama state court. Burlington removed to federal court based on diversity. After losing the suit, Burlington stayed judgment and then unsuccessfully appealed the holding. Alabama state law imposed penalties on appellants who stay judgment pending an unsuccessful appeal. FRCP 38 authorizes penalties at the court's discretion only for frivolous appeals.

Issue: Should a federal court sitting in diversity apply a state statute or federal statute that authorizes penalties?

Rule: (Marshall, J.) Since the federal and state rules conflict, under *Hanna v. Plumer* the federal rule must control unless it is unconstitutional, or, if passed pursuant to the Rules Enabling Act, if it abridges, enlarges or modifies any substantive right. However, rules located in the FRCP are presumptively valid. The federal rule here is valid and should control.

In Re "Agent Orange" Product Liability Litigation (1980)

Facts: Veterans of the Vietnam War sued the producers of the defoliant "agent orange" for damage allegedly caused by the chemical. The federal suit was based on "federal question" jurisdiction. The producers contest the suit, claiming that since no federal statute exists to confer jurisdiction, federal courts may not assert federal common law jurisdiction.

Issue: When, if ever, may there exist a federal common law to adjudicate disputes?

Rule: There exists a federal common law cause of action where three factors are met: (1) the existence of a substantial federal interest in the outcome of the litigation, (2) the effect on this federal interest should state law be applied, and (3) the effect on state interests should state law be displaced by federal common law. Here, no federal rights hinge on the outcome of the case, so there is no general federal interest in the uniform application of its rights. Furthermore, the two federal interests present, the interest in the welfare of its veterans and the interest in the suppliers of its materiel, stand in contrast to each other. It is for Congress to determine which is the more relevant. Since Congress has not done so, no substantial federal interest in the outcome of the litigation exists.

Masino v. Outboard Marine Corp. (1981)

Facts: Masino brought a diversity action in federal district court for injuries caused by a defective lawn mower manufactured by Outboard Marine Corp. Masino sought application of a state rule that a verdict of five-sixths of the jury suffices for entry of judgment. Federal procedure requires a unanimous jury.

Issue: Should a federal court sitting in diversity implement the federal or state procedures regarding jury verdicts?

Rule: Using the *Byrd* balancing test, the strong federal policy in favor of unanimous juries, as embodied by the Seventh Amendment, outweighs any relevant state interests. Therefore, a federal court sitting in diversity must implement the federal procedural requirement of a unanimous jury verdict for entry of judgment, regardless of state law.

Felder v. Casey (S.Ct. 1988)

Facts: Felder brought a civil rights action under 42 U.S.C. § 1983 in Wisconsin state court against Milwaukee and some city police officers, alleging police brutality. Felder's suit did satisfy the Wisconsin statute of limitations for personal injury actions, but not Wisconsin's notice-of-claim statute. Federal common law regarding

42 U.S.C. § 1983 would allow the claim to go forward had it been brought in federal court.

Issue: When must state courts apply federal common law, despite applicable state laws prohibiting the claim?

Rule: (Brennan, J.) The Supremacy Clause requires state courts to apply federal common law to federal statutes, even in the face of contrary state law. State law may not interfere with or frustrate substantive rights created by Congress.

DeWeerth v. Baldinger (2d Cir. 1987)

Facts: DeWeerth owned a Monet painting, which was stolen in 1943. DeWeerth stopped searching for the painting after fourteen years. In 1982, after fortuitously discovering the whereabouts of the painting, DeWeerth demanded that Baldinger, who had purchased the painting in good faith, return the painting. Baldinger refused. DeWeerth sued in U.S. District Court in New York. Whether DeWeerth's claim was time-barred hinged on whether the New York Statute of Limitations required an owner of a stolen work of art to maintain reasonable diligence in searching for the property for the limitations period to be tolled. There was no New York authority on directly point.

Issue: How should federal courts sitting in diversity decide cases for which there is no applicable state law precedent?

Rule: Federal courts sitting in diversity sit only as "another court of the state." When confronted with an absence of controlling state authority, the court must make an estimate of what the state's highest court would rule to be its law. In this case, after examining the state's approach and rationales in related controversies, the court decided that the New York Court of Appeals would require reasonable diligence from the owner of stolen property and found DeWeerth's claim to be time barred.

Note: When permitted by state law and when appropriate, federal courts sitting in diversity may also certify the unresolved state law issue to the highest court of the state in which they are sitting. The court in this case declined to employ this option.

DeWeerth v. Baldinger (S.D.N.Y. 1992)

Facts: Following the New York Court of Appeals' decision in Solomon R. Guggenheim v. Lubell, DeWeerth moved for a relief from judgment under FRCP 60. DeWeerth asked that the trial court disposition, which required a stolen Monet painting be returned to DeWeerth, be reinstated.

Issue: If, while deciding a case, the highest court of a state finds that a federal court sitting in diversity has misapplied state law in another case, is relief from the federal court's judgment proper under FRCP 60?

Rule: If, while deciding a case, the highest court of a state finds that a federal court sitting in diversity has misapplied state law in another case, relief from the federal court's judgment is proper under FRCP 60.

CHAPTER 4

PLEADINGS

I. INTRODUCTION

A. Generally
The purpose of pleadings under the Federal Rules is to give each party sufficient notice about a lawsuit. Under the Federal Rules, pleading the facts that serve as the basis for the complaint are not needed; a claimant's verified impression of a fact will suffice.

B. Pleading Stages
There are three pleading stages under the Federal Rules:

1. Complaint
Informs the defendant of the charges against him.

2. Answer
Alerts the plaintiff to the allegations in the complaint the defendant will contest, as well as any existing counterclaims and affirmative defenses.

3. Reply
In the event of a counterclaim, serves the same function as the answer to the complaint.

II. THE DEVELOPMENT OF MODERN PLEADING

A. Historical Survey

1. At the time of the Norman Conquest (1066) and for a century afterward, suitors resorted not to royal courts but to local and feudal courts. Royal courts handled offenses against the King's laws and did not interfere with the other courts.

2. Increasingly, people would seek justice from the King.

   a. A writ issued by the King was required for this.

   b. At first, the King drew each writ to fit a particular case.

     c.   Patterns emerged and writs became standardized.

     d.   By the twelfth century, a party could have justice done by the King if his case fit within the fixed formula of an existing writ.

3. Each writ came to embody a form of action which controlled

     a.   The manner in which a suit was commenced.

     b.   The substantive requirements of the case.

     c.   The procedure of the trial.

     d.   The remedies available.

4. Forms of Action

     a.   Trespass
         A means of seeking damages from a party who had done violence to land, body, and/or property.

     b.   Case
         Some trespass actions did not involve the direct application of unlawful force and evolved into an action on the "case."

        i.   The law of negligence unfolded within this form of action.

        ii. Sometimes the line between trespass and case was not clear. One of the rules employed was that a trespass action was maintainable if an "immediate injury" resulted from the action.

     c.   Other forms of action included debt, detinue, replevin, covenant, account, assumpsit, and trover.

B.   Common Law Pleading

1. Objective
To present a single issue for trial.

2. Highly Technical System
   Required each pleading to be designed in accordance with a form of action that bound the party to one theory of substantive recovery.

3. No Amendments
   Therefore an error in the pleadings would prove fatal to a complainant's case.

4. Only Pretrial Procedure
   This necessitated the use of numerous pleadings and responses which wasted judicial time (now we have summary judgment, pretrial conferences, discovery, etc.).

C. Rise of Equity

1. The Chancellor at the head of the Chancery drew up the writs for common law actions.

2. By the fourteenth century, the Chancery was also granting remedies in equitable proceedings.

3. Equity courts were entirely distinct from the common law courts and developed their own procedural methods and remedies.

4. Equitable relief was available if there was no adequate remedy at law. The court would be reluctant to fashion an equitable remedy if it was difficult to enforce or if it required detailed supervision.

5. Specific relief was obtainable through equity.

6. Equity courts could allow defenses or actions based on fraud, grant injunctions, or require specific performance. This was different from the common law courts which usually granted money damages.

7. Equity acted against the person so that a failure to satisfy a judgment could be enforced by fines and imprisonment. Since common law did not act against the person, the

plaintiff would have to resort to additional measures if the defendant failed to satisfy a common law judgment.

D.   Code Pleading
Modern Pleading originated with the 1848 New York Code of Civil Procedure, referred to as the "Field Code." The Code altered the old pleading structure in many ways:

1. Abolished forms of action so that the plaintiff could recover under any legal theory.

2. Merged law and equity.

    a.   All civil courts could grant legal and equitable relief.

    b.   The same procedure was to be used in all civil actions.

3. Emphasized factual pleadings

    a.   The pleadings were to include only "ultimate facts" and not evidentiary facts or conclusions of law.

    b.   The difficulty in determining whether or not a pleading contained "ultimate facts" was the cause of much litigation.

4. Limited the pleadings to a complaint, answer, reply, and demurrers.

5. Required liberal construction of the pleadings so that cases would not be decided for technical reasons.

E.   Theory of Pleadings
Many judges in Code states were reluctant to pull away too far from the rigidity of forms of action.

1. Required the judge to determine the single legal theory upon which the party relied.

2. If the facts pleaded did not support the legal theory, the cause of action could not be maintained and the party usually could not shift reliance to another legal theory of recovery.

3. Therefore, even in Code states cases were still being decided for technical reasons.

F. Federal Rules of Civil Procedure

1. The Federal Rules of Civil Procedure were introduced in 1938.

2. The principal purpose of pleadings under the Federal Rules is to give notice to the other party of the nature of the lawsuit.

3. Formal pleading requirements have been eliminated. Much reliance is placed on pretrial discovery to develop the issues of the case.

4. Many states have modeled their codes after the Federal Rules.

III. THE COMPLAINT
The complaint, when filed by the plaintiff, commences a lawsuit.

A. Requirements
A valid complaint should include the proper:

1. Elements

   a. Jurisdictional basis for the claim.

   b. A statement of the claim.

   c. The relief sought.

2. Language
The complaint need not be overly specific but should contain plain language (i.e., plaintiff need not specify which codes or statutes defendant allegedly violated). Thus, the defendant cannot say that the allegations were not technical enough or that he could not understand certain allegations.

B. Code Requirements
To be valid, a complaint must allege the material and ultimate facts upon which plaintiffs rights of action is based.

C. Federal Rules Requirements
Under FRCP 8(a) a complaint must contain the following:

1. A short and plain statement of the grounds upon which the court's jurisdiction depends.

2. A short and plain statement of the claim showing the pleader is entitled to relief.

3. A demand for judgment for the relief the pleader seeks.

D. The Right to Relief
Under FRCP 8(a)(2), the pleader must show that he is entitled to relief. A complaint lacking a material element should not be dismissed if the plaintiff can prove the material element at trial.

E. Alternative and Inconsistent Allegations
FRCP 8(e)(2) permits alternate pleadings even when they are inconsistent. In the past, courts have held that pleadings containing inconsistent allegations are defective if they appear in a single cause of action or defense, but they have approved such inconsistent allegations when listed in separate causes of action or separate defenses. Most jurisdictions now permit inconsistent allegations whether or not separately stated. Several states have modified their pleading rules to permit inconsistent allegations.

F. Damages
FRCP 9(g) requires that special damages must be specifically stated. Moreover, special damages must be pleaded before evidence relating to such damages is introduced.

G. Relief
FRCP 8(a)(3) states that a complaint that claims a relief must contain a demand for judgment for the said relief. FRCP 54(c) states that a judgment by default shall not be different from or exceed the demand for the judgment. However, some courts have held that a claimant may be awarded damages in excess of

those demanded in his pleadings if he is entitled to those damages under the evidence.

IV.   RESPONSE TO THE COMPLAINT

A.   The Time to Respond
FRCP 12(a) requires that most defendants respond to a complaint within twenty days. The United States government has 60 days to respond, ten days for motions.

B.   Motions Against the Complaint
The following technicalities can invalidate a complaint and serve the function of alerting the plaintiff or the plaintiff's attorney drafting the complaint to write precisely. If a motion to dismiss under FRCP 12(b)(6) is granted by the court, the plaintiff can choose between two avenues: abandon the action or appeal (i.e., the plaintiff is not "locked-in" if a motion to dismiss is granted and can still appeal).

1. Lack of subject matter jurisdiction;

2. Lack of in personam jurisdiction;

3. Improper venue;

4. Insufficiency of process;

5. Insufficiency of service of process;

6. Failure to state a claim upon which relief can be granted; and

7. Failure to join a necessary party.

C.   Motion To Dismiss

1. Background
The motion to dismiss finds its roots in the common-law demurrer. Under the common law, a party could either answer the complaint or demur. If the defendant demurred, and the demurrer was overruled, he was not allowed to contest the facts of the complaint. Moreover, if the demurrer was sustained, the plaintiff had no right to replead or amend the complaint. These austere requirements were later

dropped, allowing a defendant to proceed to the merits if the demurrer was overruled and to allow the plaintiff to amend the complaint if the demurrer was sustained.

2. Motion To Dismiss For Failure To State A Claim
The federal system's counterpart to the common-law demurrer is FRCP 12(b)(6), motion to dismiss for failure to state a claim upon which relief can be granted. FRCP 12(b)(6) must be viewed in light of other rules, such as FRCP 8.

3. Motion For More Definite Statement
Under FRCP 12(b)(6) a cause of action does not fail if a plaintiff does not set forth the allegations of his complaint with particularity. Instead of moving to dismiss the complaint, the defendant should move for a more definite statement.

4. Motion To Strike
Under FRCP 12(f) a party may motion to strike his opponent's pleadings when they contain scandalous, impertinent, and irrelevant information. To strike material as scandalous it must be obviously false and unrelated to the subject matter of the action. Even when allegations are not related to the subject matter of the case, in most cases they will not be stricken from a complaint unless their presence will prejudice the adverse party. Prejudice to the adverse party turns on whether the contents of the pleadings will be disclosed to the jury.

5. Motion to Strike the Pleading.
This motion challenges the entire pleading because it was filed too late, necessary court approval had not been obtained, or other rules of order had not been satisfied.

V.   ANSWERING THE COMPLAINT

A.   Generally
The answer serves a notice function. The court has to know the defendant's reply to the complaint. Under FRCP 15, pleadings can be liberally amended. This rule serves as a consideration

both to the plaintiff and to the plaintiff's attorney (i.e., if the plaintiff misunderstood some fact and included this error in the pleading or the plaintiff's attorney failed to carefully and thoroughly research a point of law, the plaintiff will not suffer a loss as a result). Therefore, the rules favor a very liberal amendment policy.

B.   Requirements Of An Answer
Under FRCP 8 a defendant must do one of three things to the paragraphs of plaintiff's complaint:

1. Defendant may deny the allegations.

2. Defendant may admit the allegations.

3. Defendant may plead insufficient information in response to each allegation.

C.   Failure To Answer
If defendant fails to specifically respond to an averment he is deemed to have admitted it. As a safeguard against inadvertent admission, defendants usually add an all-inclusive paragraph denying each and every averment unless otherwise admitted.

D.   General Denials
General denials of the entire complaint are permitted under FRCP 8 and under most state rules. This is very risky. If a court rules that a general denial does not meet the substance of the denied averments, the defendant may be deemed to have admitted the plaintiff's specific averments. Moreover, general denials do not put into issue matters that under FRCP 9 must be specifically challenged.

E.   Affirmative Defenses
FRCP 8(c) enumerates nineteen affirmative defenses which must be specifically raised. Generally, defendants are required to raise such affirmative defenses that do not logically flow from plaintiff's complaint. In deciding whether a defense must be raised affirmatively, courts generally look to statutes in federal questions and to state practice in diversity actions.

VI. THE REPLY

FRCP 7(a) permits a reply to a counterclaim and allows courts to order plaintiff to reply to allegations other than counterclaims. According to FRCP 8(d), allegations to which a reply is neither required nor permitted are considered denied or avoided, and plaintiff may contest them at trial. Under FRCP 8(d) allegations requiring responsive pleadings are deemed admitted if not denied in the reply.

VII. AMENDMENTS

A. Generally

1. Before a Reply

FRCP 15(a) allows a party to amend its pleading once before a responsive pleading is served, or if no responsive pleading is permitted and the action has not been placed on the trial calendar, twenty days after service.

2. Three-Strike Rule

A party may otherwise amend its pleading with the written consent of the adverse party or by leave of court, which shall be freely given when justice so requires. Most courts follow an unofficial three-strike rule, which gives a party three chances to correct defects in its pleadings, after which the court will find that justice no longer requires another opportunity. A party must amend a pleading within the response time to the original pleading or ten days after service of the amended pleading, whichever period may be longer, unless the court orders otherwise.

B. Amendments to Conform to the Evidence

FRCP 15(b) states that issues not raised by the pleadings when tried by the consent of the parties shall be treated as if raised in the pleadings. This motion can be made at anytime, even after judgment.

C. Relating Back Amendments

FRCP 15(c) states that when a claim or defense asserted in an amended pleading arose out of the conduct, transaction, or occurrence set forth or attempted to be set forth in the original pleading, the amendment relates back to the date of the original pleading for purposes of statutes of limitations.

D. Supplemental Pleadings (FRCP 15(d))
    Where relevant activity occurs after the pleadings have been filed, the court has discretion to allow the parties to file supplemental pleadings to reflect the new circumstances.

CASE CLIPS

Veale v. Warner (1670)

Facts: Warner tricked Veale in the pleading by omitting part of the arbitration award.

Issue: May a party use deception when crafting the pleadings?

Rule: A party who uses a trick in the pleadings may not receive a favorable judgment even if the court agrees with his position.

Scott v. Shepherd (The Squib Case) (1773)

Facts: Scott brought a trespass action when his eye was put out by a lighted squib made of gunpowder that had originally been lighted by Shepherd. But in the moments between the lighting and the explosion, the squib had been thrown about by several others to avoid injury.

Issue: When is an action in trespass maintainable?

Rule: Two theories are advocated by the four judges: (1) A trespass action is maintainable if the injury is caused by an illegal act; and (2) A trespass action is maintainable if an injury is the immediate result of an action. There is difficulty in deciding whether an injury is "immediate" or "consequential."

Bushel v. Miller (1718)

Facts: The defendant had removed some of the plaintiff's goods that were blocking the path to his assigned area of a storage hut. The plaintiff brought trover against the defendant when the goods were lost.

Issue: May an action in trover be brought against a party who has lost goods but never owned them?

Rule: An action in trover may only be used when there has been a conversion (i.e., where an exchange takes place).

Gordon v. Harper (1796)

Facts: The plaintiff brought an action of trover when a sheriff seized goods that were in possession of the plaintiff's lessee in execution of a judgment against yet another party.

Issue: Will trover lie where the plaintiff had neither the actual possession of the goods taken nor the right of possession?

Rule: In order to recover the value of property in an action of trover, a party must have had both actual possession and a right to possession of the goods taken.

Slade's Case (1602)

Facts: Slade failed to pay for the goods he had purchased.

Issue: May a party's failure to perform duties under a mutual executory contract allow the injured party at his election to bring either an action of debt or an action on the case on assumpsit?

Rule: A party's failure to perform duties under a mutual executory contract allows the injured party at his election to bring either an action of debt or an action on the case on assumpsit. A mutual executory agreement imports in itself an assumpsit, for when one agrees to pay money or to deliver anything, he thereby promises to pay or deliver it.

Lamine v. Dorrell (1705)

Facts: The defendant, pretending to be J.S.'s administrator, sold debentures from the estate as one that claimed a title and interest in them. The rightful administrator brought an action on indebitatus assumpsit for money received by the defendant.

Issue: May a party maintain an action on indebitatus assumpsit if the defendant did not receive the money at issue for the use of the plaintiff?

Rule: Although an action may be maintained for detinue or trover, a party may bring an action on indebitatus assumpsit even if the defendant did not receive the money at issue for the use of the plaintiff.

Jones v. Winsor (1908)

Facts: The plaintiffs brought actions against their attorney both in assumpsit for money he wrongfully accepted from them and also for fraudulent conversion of that money. The South Dakota Code had abolished the common law pleadings, requiring only that the facts be established in a plain and concise manner.

Issue: Since the Code has abolished forms of pleading, may two theories of recovery be united in one cause of action?

Rule: Although the Code has abolished forms of pleading, two theories of recovery may not be united in one cause of action.

Garrity v. State Board of Administration (1917)

Facts: The State Board claimed that Garrity's petition, asserting that the State Board unlawfully converted Garrity's valuable fossil, was subject to a demurrer because the tort claim of conversion was barred by the statute of limitations. Garrity claimed the right to waive the tort claim and recover upon the implied promise to pay what the fossil was worth.

Issue: If a petition stated a cause of action, may a party waive the theory of recovery asserted in the petition and recover upon another theory?

Rule: If a petition stated a cause of action, it must be held that sufficient facts were stated to authorize the plaintiff to waive the theory of recovery asserted in the petition and recover upon another theory.

Gillispie v. Goodyear Service Stores (1963)

Facts: Gillispie alleged that she was assaulted and humiliated by Goodyear's employees when they trespassed upon her place of residence. Gillispie further alleged that the employees' actions were both malicious and intentional.

Issue: Is a complaint which alleges conclusions but not facts sufficient to constitute a proper cause of action?

Rule: To be valid, a complaint must allege the material and ultimate facts upon which plaintiff's right of action is based. In this manner, the defendants may ascertain the charges against them and react accordingly.

Dioguardi v. Durning (1944)

Facts: Dioguardi imported several cases of "tonics" from Italy to be auctioned off. Two of the cases disappeared in the auction house. The collector of customs, Mr. Durning, sold the remaining cases at an auction. Durning charged Dioguardi's bidding price ($110 per case) instead of the buyer's ($120 per case). Dioguardi sued for $5,000 damages, plus interest and costs. Durning moved to dismiss because the complaint did not state the legal theory against him.

Issue: Can a complaint which states facts but does not offer a legal basis for relief satisfy the requirements for admission to federal court?

Rule: A complaint must provide sufficient information to notify the adverse party of a cause of action against him. However, it need not contain an explanation of legal theory.

Garcia v. Hilton Hotels International, Inc.(1951)

Facts: Garcia alleged that Hilton falsely and slanderously accused Garcia of facilitating prostitution, and then fired Garcia from his job. Garcia's complaint did not allege publication, which is a necessary element of libel.

Issue: Is a complaint lacking a material element that may be proven at trial subject to dismissal?

Rule: A complaint lacking a material element should not be dismissed if the plaintiff can prove the material element at trial.

Denny v. Carey (1976)

Facts: The plaintiff alleged that the defendants violated state and federal securities laws by issuing false and misleading financial statements about First Pennsylvania Corp. The defendants moved to dismiss the complaint pursuant to FRCP 12(b)(6), alleging that the plaintiffs allegations failed to state the circumstances constituting the alleged fraud with sufficient particularity as required by FRCP 9(b).

Issue: Does a complaint that fails to state the particular circumstances constituting fraud, but that sufficiently identifies the circumstances of the alleged fraud, meet the requirements of FRCP 9(b)?

Rule: The requirements of FRCP 9(b) are satisfied when there is sufficient identification of the circumstances constituting fraud so that the defendant can answer the allegations.

Ziervogel v. Royal Packing Co. (1949)

Facts: Ziervogel was awarded $2,000 for injuries suffered in a collision with Royal Packing Co.'s truck. Royal Packing objected to introduction of evidence at trial showing that Ziervogel's blood pressure increased as a result of the accident.

Issue: Can a party plead general damages in her complaint, and then introduce evidence at trial to recover for special damages?

Rule: Special damages that include a specific personal injury must be pleaded before evidence relating to such damage is introduced.

Bail v. Cunningham Brothers, Inc. (1971)

Facts: Bail sued Cunningham Brothers, Inc. alleging damages of $100,000. At trial, Bail moved to amend the complaint, increasing the amount to $250,000. The court denied Bail's motion. After the jury returned a verdict for $150,000, Bail was granted leave to amend his complaint to $150,000 in a post-trial motion.

Issue: Can a claimant be awarded damages in excess of those demanded in his pleadings?

Rule: A claimant may be awarded damages in excess of those demanded in his pleadings if he is entitled to those damages under the evidence.

American Nurses' Association v. Illinois (1986)

Facts: The American Nurses Association brought a class action suit against the state of Illinois, charging sex discrimination in employment violating both Title VII of the Civil Rights Act of 1964 and the Equal Protection Clause of the Fourteenth Amendment. The state claimed that the Association's complaint was vague and unclear.

Issue: Will a cause of action fail if the plaintiff did not set forth the allegations in his complaint with clarity?

Rule: A cause of action does not fail if a plaintiff does not set forth the allegations of his complaint with particularity. A defendant should not move to dismiss the complaint but should make a motion for a more definite statement.

Zielinski v. Philadelphia Piers, Inc. (1956)

Facts: Zielinski was injured in an accident by a forklift driven by Johnson. Philadelphia Piers officers were present at a deposition where Johnson said he worked for Philadelphia Piers. Philadelphia Piers did not respond then, but later denied that it employed Johnson.

Issue: May a defendant knowingly allow a plaintiff to rely on erroneous facts in the complaint?

Rule: A defendant who knowingly makes false statements upon which a plaintiff relies will be estopped from denying such statements at trial.

Oliver v. Swiss Club Tell (1963)

Facts: Oliver alleged in his complaint that Swiss Club Tell was an unincorporated association. Swiss Club Tell denied the allegation, claiming it lacked information on that point and that it believed it was not an unincorporated association.

Issue: May a party deny an allegation based on lack of information or belief?

Rule: A party cannot deny an allegation based on lack of information and belief when such information is within the actual knowledge of the party.

Ingraham v. United States (1987)

Facts: Ingraham and the Bonds alleged in two separate actions that they were negligently injured as a result of medical malpractice by the Air Force's employees. In both cases, the plaintiffs were awarded damages. After entry of judgment, the Air Force moved to limit recovery under the Medical Liability and Insurance Improvement Act of Texas.

Issue: Can a defendant wait until judgment is entered to plead a defense?

Rule: An affirmative defense must be timely pleaded or it is considered waived.

Moore v. Moore (1978)

Facts: Reuben and Cindy Moore were involved in a custody dispute over their daughter. Cindy did not originally seek custody, child support, separate maintenance, or counsel fees. Nevertheless, the court granted her these reliefs. The court allowed Cindy to amend her pleadings after trial to include the reliefs it had initially granted her.

Issue: When may a court permit post-trial amendments to the pleadings?

Rule: A court may permit post-trial amendments to pleadings when issues not raised in the pleadings are tried by express or implied consent of the parties.

Beeck v. Aquaslide 'N' Dive Corp. (1977)

Facts: Beeck was injured while using a water slide. Aquaslide 'N' Dive Corp. initially admitted it was the slide's manufacturer, but later moved to amend its answer to deny manufacturing the slide. The motion was granted.

Issue: When may a court grant a motion to amend an answer?

Rule: A court may grant a motion to amend an answer unless the opposing party can show he would be prejudiced if the motion is granted.

Worthington v. Wilson (1992)

Facts: Worthington was arrested on February 25, 1989 by two police officers, and was injured during the arrest. Exactly two years later, Worthington filed a complaint against the police department and "three unknown named police officers" for deprivation of his constitutional rights stemming from the actions of the officers during the arrest. On June 17, 1991, Worthington filed an amended complaint naming the actual officers involved in the arrest. The officers moved for dismissal, claiming that the two-year statute of limitations had run before the amended complaint was filed.

Issue 1: May an amended complaint that changes the name of the defendant relate back to the time of filing of the original complaint, for the purposes of the statute of limitations?

Rule 1: Relation-back is governed by FRCP 15(c), which allows an amended complaint that changes the name of a defendant to relate back to the filing of the original complaint if it arises out of the same conduct as the original complaint, and the named party is made aware of the action within 120 days of the filing of the original complaint.

Issue 2: Is relation back permitted when lack of knowledge as to the proper defendant, and not mistake, causes a failure of the original complaint?

Rule 2: An amended complaint which fails due to an initial lack of knowledge concerning the proper defendant does not involve a "mistake," and is therefore not entitled to relation-back under FRCP 15(c).

Schiavone v. Fortune (S.Ct. 1986)

Facts: Schiavone filed a libel action within the statutory period but failed to correctly name Fortune in his complaint. Schiavone amended his complaint within the 120-day period allowed for service pursuant to FRCP 4(j). However, by that time the statute of limitations had expired on the action.

Issue: Can an amended complaint filed after the statute of limitations has expired but within the time allowed for service of process relate back to the original complaint?

Rule: (Blackmun, J.) In order for an amendment adding a party to relate back to the original complaint, the party to be added must have received notice of the action before the statute of limitations has run.

Surowitz v. Hilton Hotels Corp. (S.Ct. 1966)

Facts: Surowitz brought a shareholder derivative action against the officers and directors of Hilton Hotels Corp. for allegedly defrauding the corporation of several million dollars. In an oral examination, Surowitz revealed that although she had verified her complaint, as required by FRCP 23(b), she did not understand it at all, and had relied mainly on information given to her by her son-in-law in proceeding with the suit.

Issue: Does a party who verifies a complaint in a derivative suit have to possess full understanding of the complaint to satisfy the requirements of FRCP 23.1?

Rule: (Black, J.) A party who verifies a complaint in a derivative suit pursuant to FRCP 23.1 may do so based on the advice of a competent person, and not necessarily based on the party's personal knowledge.

Concurrence: (Harlan, J.) Verification need not come from the actual party, but may also come from party's counsel.

Business Guides, Inc. v. Chromatic Communications Enterprises, Inc. (S.Ct. 1991)

Facts: Business Guides published various trade directories. The directories contained "seeds," which were deliberate errors planted to provide evidence of copyright infringement if they turn up in competitors' directories. Business Guides sought a temporary restraining order against Chromatic Communications, alleging that its directory contained ten seeds. A one-hour investigation, by a law clerk revealed that nine of the ten were actually legitimate listings. Chromatic Communications sought Rule 11 sanctions against Business Guides and their attorneys, Finley, Kumble. Because Finley, Kumble was in bankruptcy, the motion was only pursued against Chromatic Communications, which was held liable for $13,866.

Issue 1: What is the standard of care imposed by Rule 11?

Rule 1: (O'Connor, J.) Any party who signs a pleading, motion or other paper has an affirmative duty to conduct a reasonable inquiry into the facts and the law before filing. The applicable standard is reasonableness under the circumstances.

Issue 2: To whom does Rule 11 apply?

Rule 2: Rule 11 applies to those whose signatures are present on court papers, whether an attorney or a party, and whether or not their signatures were required.

Dissent: (Kennedy, J.) The purpose of Rule 11 is to control the practice of attorneys or those who act as their own attorneys. It is an abuse of discretion to sanction a represented litigant who acts in good faith but errs as to the facts.

Boddie v. Connecticut (S.Ct. 1971)

Facts: The Boddies, indigents and welfare recipients, sought a divorce in state court. A state statute required a filing fee when bringing an action for divorce. The Boddies were barred from bringing the action because of their inability to pay. They filed an appeal with the federal district court seeking to enjoin state officials from enforcing the filing fee, claiming the required payment of filing fees as a condition precedent to obtaining a divorce was unconstitutional as applied to the indigents.

Issue: Can a state deny an indigent access to its courts in a divorce action, due to an inability to pay a mandatory filing fee?

Rule: (Harlan, J.) Where the parties are forced to settle their claim through the judicial process, due process prohibits a state from denying individuals access to its courts solely because of their inability to pay a filing fee.

United States v. Kras (S.Ct. 1973)

Facts: Kras filed for bankruptcy. Federal law required the payment of a filing fee before relief may be granted. Kras could not pay, and so was denied relief. He then challenged the constitutionality of the filing fee on due process grounds. The district court held the fee provision unconstitutional as applied to Kras and the United States appealed.

Issue: Is the payment of a filing fee as a condition precedent to a discharge in bankruptcy a violation of a party's constitutional rights?

Rule: (Blackmun, J.) Since there is no constitutional right to obtain a discharge of one's debts in bankruptcy, a fee requirement is not unconstitutional as to indigents.

Concurrence: (Burger, C.J.) Bankruptcy court is but one mode of orderly adjustment. The states have provided their own remedies as well. Where the court requiring a fee is not an exclusive remedy, the fee does not offend due process.

Dissent 1: (Stewart, J.) Since the creditors only hold rights over the debtor due to the existence of substantial debtor law, the courts should allow equal access to provide remedies for the debtors. Since the creditor-debtor relationship, like the husband-wife relationship in *Boddie v. Connecticut*, is the creation of law, a state may not, consistent with due process, pre-empt the right to dissolve this relationship without affording all citizens access to the means prescribed for doing so.

Dissent 2: (Marshall, J.) When a person asserts a claim or right, the only forum where one may adjudicate such a right is in court. To exclude someone from that court solely because of an inability to pay violates due process.

Duke of Somerset v. Cookson (1735)

Facts: The Duke of Somerset brought a bill in equity to compel the undamaged return of his unique altar-piece. Cookson, a goldsmith, demurred to the bill because the Duke had a remedy at law either by an action of trover for money damages or detinue for the return of the altar-piece if it could be found.

Issue: When can an action in equity be maintained if the plaintiff has a remedy at law?

Rule: A party may bring an action in equity if there are no adequate remedies at law. Here, money damages (trover) would not be sufficient to compensate a party for the loss of a unique object, and detinue does not ensure the undamaged return of the object.

Heroux v. Katt (1949)

Facts: Heroux brought an action at law in trespass and ejectment when he discovered that Katt's building wrongfully occupied 451 square feet of the premises that Heroux had leased from another.

Issue: May a party bring an action at law if the usual remedy is in equity?

Rule: Although a party may not bring an action in equity if there is an adequate remedy at law, he may choose to bring an action at law if a valid and more effective equitable remedy exists.

Boomer v. Atlantic Cement Co., Inc. (1970)

Facts: Boomer and other landowners sued the Atlantic Cement Company for damages and for an injunction against further operation of its cement plant because of alleged injury to property from dirt, smoke, and vibrations emanating from the plant.

Issue: When must an equity court grant an injunction?

Rule: Although the general rule is that a nuisance that results in substantial continuing damage to neighbors must be enjoined, an injunction may be denied if the economic consequences of the injunction are much worse than the injury caused by the nuisance.

Note: Balancing the equities, the court denied the injunction unless Atlantic failed to pay permanent damages.

Lumley v. Wagner (1852)

Facts: Lumley sued to enforce a contract whereby Wagner agreed to sing at Lumley's theater for three months and to refrain from singing at any other location.

Issue: May an equity court restrain a party from committing an act that she has bound herself not to do?

Rule: Although an equity court will not compel a party to specifically perform a personal services agreement, it may restrain a party from committing an act that she has bound herself not to do.

Aetna Life Insurance Co. v. Haworth (S.Ct. 1937)

Facts: Haworth stopped paying the premiums on his five insurance policies because he claimed he was permanently disabled. The insurance company sought a declaration of rights because it feared that evidence needed to disprove Haworth's disability would not be available if Haworth instituted suit in the future.

Issue: When is a declaratory judgment action justiciable, rather than hypothetical?

Rule: (Hughes, C. J.) A declaratory judgment action is a justiciable case or controversy if it involves a concrete dispute between adverse parties that admits itself of specific relief.

American Machine & Metals, Inc. v. De Bothezat Impeller Co. (1948)

Facts: American Machine & Metals, Inc. (American) conveyed to De Bothezat Impeller Co. (De Bothezat) certain patent rights and equipment to be used for the production of fans. De Bothezat desired to exercise its unilateral right to terminate the arrangement and sought a declaration of rights because American contended that De Bothezat would be prohibited from selling any type of ventilating equipment if De Bothezat terminated the contract and also led the plaintiff to believe that they would sue.

Issue: When may a declaratory judgment be granted to prevent the accrual of avoidable damages?

Rule: Where there is an actual controversy over contingent rights, a declaratory judgment may be granted to prevent the accrual of avoidable damages.

Serrano v. Priest (1977)

Facts: Serrano and others challenged the procedure California implemented to finance public education. Serrano prevailed, and the court awarded reasonable attorney's fees. Because Serrano in this case was not obligated to pay fees, the defendants contended that the award was improper.

Issue: When does a trial court have the equitable power to grant reasonable attorney's fees?

Rule: If, as a result of the efforts of plaintiffs' attorneys, rights created or protected by the state constitution are protected to the benefit of a large number of people, plaintiffs' attorneys are entitled to reasonable attorney's fees from the defendants under the Private Attorney General Equitable Doctrine (even where plaintiffs are under no obligation to pay their attorneys).

Zaldivar v. City of Los Angeles (1986)

Facts: Zaldivar sued Los Angeles to block a recall election, claiming violation of the Federal Voting Rights Act. The lower court dismissed the case and imposed FRCP 11 sanctions on Zaldivar and his attorneys.

Issue: When may sanctions be applied under FRCP 11?

Rule: For sanctions to be imposed, the action must not only be brought for improper purpose, but it must also be brought without a well-grounded basis in fact and existing law.

Stromillo v. Merrill Lynch, Pierce, Fenner & Smith, Inc. (1971)

Facts: Stromillo alleged that her stockbroker used her account for his own benefit. Merrill Lynch made a motion to require Stromillo to state her claim more definitely.

Issue: When will a court grant a motion for a more definite statement?

Rule: A motion for a more definite statement will be granted only if a pleading is so vague or ambiguous that a party cannot reasonably be required to frame a responsive pleading.

Rannard v. Lockheed Aircraft Corp. (1945)

Facts: The Rannards alleged that they were the victims of medical malpractice by Lockheed's employee in the course of his employment. After trial, the court sustained Lockheed's motion for judgment on the pleadings, arguing, in part, that the complaint failed to state the fact which caused the injury.

Issue: Will a motion for a judgment on the pleadings be granted if the complaint merely alleges a negligent action by the defendant?

Rule: A motion for judgment on the pleadings can be granted if an essential allegation is lacking.

Lubliner v. Ruge (1944)

Facts: Lubliner alleged that he was injured in an automobile accident as a result of Ruge's negligence. The trial judge refused to allow Lubliner to show that Ruge was intoxicated at the time of the accident because it was not alleged in Lubliner's complaint.

Issue: Must a party who plans to submit proof that his adversary contributed to the alleged negligence include such facts in his pleadings?

Rule: When a party contemplates submitting affirmative proof of contributory negligence, such proof must be pleaded by him.

Albany Welfare Rights Organization Day Care Center., Inc. v. Schreck (1972)

Facts: Albany Welfare Rights brought action against officers of the Albany County Department of Social Services for violation of its constitutional rights under both the First and Fourteenth Amendments. After trial the court dismissed the complaint on the ground that it failed to allege facts sufficient to constitute a claim upon which relief can be granted.

Issue: Can a claim be dismissed if it alleges discrimination but presents no facts to support its allegation?

Rule: Conclusory allegations of politically motivated discrimination are insufficient as a matter of law to state a claim upon which relief can be granted.

Penton v. Canning (1941)

Facts: Penton sued Canning on the grounds of malicious prosecution. Canning demurred on the grounds that the complaint did not state facts sufficient to constitute a cause of action, but his objection was overruled.

Issue: When will a demurrer be denied?

Rule: Where the complaint sufficiently alleges all of the relevant elements of the action alleged, a demurrer must be denied. However, this complaint did not sufficiently allege that the original "malicious prosecution" was without probable cause.

Riggs, Ferris & Greer v. Lillibridge (1963)

Facts: The New York law firm of Riggs, Ferris & Greer sued Lillibridge for services rendered, originally valued at $35,000. Riggs, Ferris & Greer made a written offer to settle for $25,000 but Lillibridge refused. At the pretrial conference Riggs, Ferris & Greer amended its pleadings to demand $50,000. The jury returned a verdict for Riggs, Ferris & Greer in the amount of $56,000.

Issue: Can a jury in a federal court, relying solely on federal law, award a damage amount in excess of that claimed in the amended ad damnum clause?

Rule: A jury can award a damage amount in excess of that claimed. But, when a default judgment is entered against a party, recovery is limited to that prayed for in the demand for judgment.

David v. Crompton & Knowles Corp. (1973)

Facts: David was injured by an allegedly defective machine manufactured by Crompton & Knowles. In its answer Crompton averred that it was without sufficient knowledge to admit or deny the allegation. Thereafter Crompton sought to amend its answer to deny that it manufactured the said machine.

Issue: When may a defendant, who avers that it is without sufficient knowledge and information to admit or deny plaintiffs allegations, be estopped from amending its response to deny those allegations?

Rule: Where a defendant avers that it is without sufficient knowledge and information to admit or deny plaintiffs allegations, and defendant is actually in possession of such information, it may not amend its pleadings. Thereafter, plaintiff's allegations will be deemed admitted.

Sinclair Refining Co. v. Howell (1953)

Facts: Howell's son was electrocuted to death due to a Sinclair Refining Co. employee's negligence. Howell was awarded $30,000. However, the court required Howell to amend his complaint to assert that his son was not subject to the workmen compensation laws of Alabama.

Issue: When may a defendant be deemed to have admitted plaintiff's averments as true?

Rule: A defendant may be deemed to have admitted plaintiff's averments if the averments are in a pleading to which a responsive pleading is required, unless the averment relates to the amount of damages.

Fuentes v. Tucker (1947)

Facts: The plaintiff's sons were killed by an automobile operated by the defendant. The defendant admitted liability in his answer, yet the court permitted the plaintiff to show that the defendant was intoxicated, and to show the distance the boys were thrown by the impact.

Issue: May a court receive evidence that is material only to an issue to which the party has already admitted?

Rule: Once a party admits an issue in the answer, it is error to receive evidence that is material to that matter.

Black, Sivalls & Bryson v. Shondell (1949)

Facts: Shondell bought five of Black, Sivalls & Bryson's oil storage tanks, which were allegedly defective. The court ruled in favor of Shondell. Black appealed, alleging for the first time that Shondell's complaint did not state a cause of action.

Issue: May a defendant waive all defenses and objections that he does not present either by motion or in his answer?

Rule: Only the defense of failure to state a claim upon which relief can be granted may be made by a later pleading, if one is permitted, or by motion for judgment on the pleadings, or at the trial on the merits. All other defenses are deemed to be waived if not made either in an initial motion or in the answer.

Friedman v. Transamerica Corp. (1946)

Facts: Friedman brought a class action against Transamerica for irregularities in stock transactions. Friedman then successfully amended its pleadings three times. The present suit regards Friedman's petition to amend the complaint a fourth time.

Issue: Does FRCP 15(a), which provides that leave to amend "shall be freely given," create an absolute right?

Rule: FRCP 15(a) provides that leave to amend "shall be freely given when justice so requires." The word "freely" was used with deliberate intention to obviate technical restrictions on amendment. But this does not mean that leave to amend is to be granted without limit; otherwise, the right to amend would be absolute and would not rest in the discretion of the court.

Note: Most courts use an informal "three strikes" rule, allowing a party to freely amend a complaint three times, but only to do it afterwards where absolutely necessary.

Manning v. Loew (1943)

Facts: The plaintiff sued the defendant for breach of contract, alleging that the defendant had promised to make her a movie star. The plaintiff alleged that consideration for the implied contract consisted of her devotion and companionship to the defendant. At trial, the plaintiff's testimony was at variance with her pleading. The court then directed a verdict for the defendant.

Issue: Can a court issue a directed verdict because a pleading varied from the trial testimony?

Rule: A court may direct a verdict for a defendant when a plaintiff's pleading and testimony vary.

Mangum v. Surles (1972)

Facts: The plaintiff alleged that the defendant by fraud obtained her signature to the challenged deed. The plaintiff did not state with particularity the circumstances constituting the alleged fraud.

Issue: Can a court admit evidence where the opposing party does not object on the ground that it is outside the issue raised by the pleadings?

Rule: Where no objection is made to evidence on the ground that it is outside the issues raised by the pleadings, the issue raised by the evidence is nevertheless before the court for determination. The pleadings are regarded as amended to conform to the proof even though the defaulting pleader made no formal motion to amend.

Humphries v. Going (1973)

Facts: In July 1968, the Humphries were injured in an automobile accident by a car driven by Going. Original complaints were filed in October, 1969. In May 1970, Humphries amended their pleadings to show that the vehicle was owned by Colonial Flooring and that Going was driving it with Colonial Flooring's consent and in furtherance of Colonial Flooring's business. In 1971 the statute of limitation ran out on the action in question. In March 1973, Humphries amended their motion to show that Going was treated for alcoholism prior to the accident and that Colonial Flooring had full knowledge of the treatment.

Issue: Does an amendment to a complaint made after the statute of limitations has run relate back to the date of the original complaint?

Rule: An amendment to a complaint relates back to the date of the original complaint providing the amendment does not create a new cause of action and the defendant is neither prejudiced nor deprived of notice or any other right in the action.

Azada v. Carson (1966)

Facts: Three days before the statute of limitations ran, Azada filed a complaint for injuries sustained in a car accident. Carson was not served until after the statute of limitations had run. Carson then tried to file a counterclaim on the same accident.

Issue: May a counterclaim be filed after the statute of limitations has run, in response to an original claim that was timely filed?

Rule: A counterclaim filed after the statute of limitations has run will be considered timely if the counterclaim was filed in response to a timely complaint.

Stoner v. Terranella (1967)

Facts: Stoner brought an action against Terranella and Glenos seeking damages for decedent's death in a car accident in June 1964. Terranella and Glenos filed answers but only Glenos filed counterclaims. In July 1965 the statute of limitations expired. In September 1965 Terranella also filed an amended answer and counterclaim.

Issue: Will a counterclaim not relate back to the date of the filing of the original suit if the party had ample opportunity to file the counterclaim before the statute of limitations expired?

Rule: FRCP 13(f) states that when a pleader fails to set up a counterclaim through oversight, inadvertence, excusable neglect, or when justice requires, he can set up the counterclaim by amendment by leave of court.

Sierocinski v. E.I. Du Pont De Nemours & Co. (1939)

Facts: Sierocinski filed suit against E.I. Du Pont De Nemours & Company (Du Pont), but the complaint was ordered amended when the court granted Du Pont's motion for a more definite statement. Sierocinski's second complaint alleged negligence on Du Pont's part in the manufacturing and distributing of dynamite caps. Du Pont filed a motion to strike Sierocinski's amended pleading as failing to set forth specific acts of negligence. The court granted Du Pont's motion and Sierocinski appealed.

Issue: How specific does FRCP 8(a)(2) require a complaint to be in order to avoid dismissal?

Rule: A complaint may not be dismissed for lack of specificity when, on its face, the complaint, if proved, would entitle the complainant to relief.

Coleman v. Frierson (1985)

Facts: Coleman, a special investigator, sued the Village of Robinson and various officials under 42 U.S.C. § 1983, alleging he had been dismissed to cover up corruption Coleman had been investigating. The Village denied the allegations, but was so delinquent during discovery that the judge decided, as a sanction, that the Village had defaulted on the issue of liability. The jury then found for Coleman and the Village appealed.

Issue: What effect is given a default judgment?

Rule: A default judgment is given the same effect as a judgment on the merits, and may not be retried.

Williams v. Robinson (1940)

Facts: Robinson sued Williams, accusing him of committing adultery with Robinson's wife. Williams then sued Robinson for libel and slander. Robinson moved to dismiss Williams' complaint, arguing that Williams failed to assert his claim in the original case.

Issue: Does the failure to raise a claim by way of a counterclaim in answer to a defendant's cross-complaint bar subsequent litigation of the claim?

Rule: The FRCP require a defendant to state any counterclaim he has against a plaintiff, if it arises out of the same transaction or occurrence that is the subject matter of the plaintiffs claim, and failure to assert the claim bars raising it in an independent suit.

Blair v. Durham (1943)

Facts: Durham sued Blair for personal injuries when a board fell from a scaffold on her head. Durham subsequently amended her complaint to allege negligent construction of the scaffolding. Blair moved to dismiss the amended complaint, alleging it stated a new cause of action and was barred by the Tennessee statute of limitations. The court denied the motion.

Issue: For statute of limitation purposes, when does an amended pleading relate back to the date of the original pleading's filing?

Rule: If the claim alleged in an amended pleading arose out of the same conduct, transaction, or occurrence set forth or attempted to be set forth in the original pleadings, the amendment does not set up a new cause of action; it relates back to the date of the original pleading.

Anonymous (1304)

Facts: The defendants claimed that they could not be held accountable for cutting and carrying away the plaintiff's trees because they did not use force or arms.

Issue: May a party recover for trespass even if the act is not accomplished with force and arms?

Rule: Force and arms is not a necessary element of trespass.

Williams v. Holland (1833)

Facts: When Holland's "gig" collided with Williams' cart, causing immediate injury to his children, Williams brought an action on the case for negligence. Traditionally, an action for damages caused by a collision is brought under a writ or trespass.

Issue: May an action on the case be maintained if an action in trespass due to immediate injury is appropriate?

Rule: Where injury is occasioned by the carelessness of the defendant, the plaintiff is at liberty to bring an action on the case for negligence even if an action in trespass due to immediate injury is appropriate.

Swift v. Moseley (1838)

Facts: Eliphalet Swift had leased his property to Jirah Swift for one year. Without Eliphalet's permission, Jirah sold Eliphalet's sheep to Moseley for well under the market price. Eliphalet sued Moseley under a writ of trover prior to the termination of the lease. To maintain an action on trover, the plaintiff must have had either custody of the item taken, or a property interest in it.

Issue: Does a lessor retain an interest in the leased property, to allow an action of trover for misuse of the property?

Rule: If leased property is destroyed or put to a different use from that for which it was leased, the lessor has a right to immediate possession and may maintain an action of trover.

Watkins' Case (1425)

Facts: W.B. brought a writ of trespass on the case on assumpsit when Watkins did not build the mill by the agreed-upon date. Watkins asserted that there was no cause of action because W.B.'s attorney failed to allege either consideration paid for Watkins' promise or a misfeasance.

Issue: May an action for trespass on the case on assumpsit be maintained without allegations of consideration paid or misfeasance?

Rule: A separate opinion was rendered by each justice. But Chief Justice Babbington, in his opening majority opinion, held that the plaintiff must allege each element of the claim in order to be able to recover.

Concurrence 1: (Martin, J.) Defective performance by the defendant is required for an action in trespass on the case on assumpsit, while nonfeasance gives rise to an action on the covenant.

Concurrence 2: (Babbington, CJ.) A party is required to allege the provisions of the agreement to receive damages for injuries caused by misfeasance.

Concurrence 3: (Cokayne, J.) Nonfeasance that results in injury will give rise to an action for trespass on the case on assumpsit.

Courtney v. Glanvil (1615)

Facts: Glanvil sold Courtney a jewel valued at twenty pounds for a price of 360 pounds. An action was brought and settled in a court of law. Dissatisfied with the result, Courtney sued in a chancery (equity) court to get the prior judgment overturned on equitable grounds.

Issue: May a court of equity relieve a party from a judgment at law?

Rule: A court of equity cannot modify or reverse a judgment at law even to avoid injustice.

Carmen v. Fox Film Corp. (1920)

Facts: Carmen entered into a contract with Keeney Corp. without informing it that she had already signed a contract with Fox Film Corp. while still a minor. Carmen repudiated her contract with Fox and then sued for an injunction when Fox began to interfere with her contractual relations with Keeney.

Issue: Under what grounds will a court of equity refuse to grant relief?

Rule: Equity will refuse its aid in any manner to a party seeking its active interposition if that party has been guilty of unlawful or inequitable conduct with respect to the subject matter of the litigation.

Avery v. Spicer (1916)

Facts: Avery sued for damages when Ingalls cut down trees for Spicer on property that Avery allegedly owned. Avery proved he had legal title to the land but did not show possession, a necessary element of trespass.

Issue: Must a party establish all essential facts of his claim?

Rule: If a party bases his right to recovery on his capability to establish certain essential facts, he is required to establish those facts.

Manhattan Egg Co. v. Seaboard Terminal & Refrigeration Co. (1929)

Facts: Seaboard Terminal & Refrigeration Co. alleged that the 220 cases of eggs that Manhattan Egg Co. sold to it were stolen and then sold back to Manhattan. When Manhattan refused to return the eggs to Seaboard, Seaboard declined to pay for them. Manhattan sued for the contract price and Seaboard counterclaimed in quasi-contract for the value of the stolen eggs.

Issue: May an action in quasi-contract be set up as a counterclaim to an action on an independent contract?

Rule: In an action on contract, any other cause of action on contract, including quasi-contract, existing at the commencement of the action may be set up as a counterclaim. Provisions dealing with counterclaims should receive a liberal construction in order to avoid multiplicity of actions.

Raab v. Bowery Savings Bank (1974)

Facts: Raab entered monthly payments into an escrow account to be held by the mortgagee bank, out of which taxes were to be paid on her house. Raab brought an action for interest on the amount of money in the escrow that exceeded the amount expended.

Issue: May a party be compensated in equity if there is no legal basis for the suit?

Rule: A party must demonstrate a cause of action or a basis for liability in order to be granted relief in equity.

Apex Smelting Co. v. Burns (1949)

Facts: Burns contracted to provide security for Apex's plant. When one of the guards that Burns hired set fire to Apex's plant, Apex sued Burns for negligent hiring. After receiving an unfavorable judgment, Apex appealed on a breach of contract theory.

Issue: May an appellate court consider theories of liability not tried below?

Rule: A reviewing court will not consider new theories of recovery not originally called to the attention of the trial court unless a great injustice will result.

Wasik v. Borg (1970)

Facts: Wasik sued Borg to recover for personal injuries sustained in an automobile accident. Borg joined Ford, the automobile manufacturer, as a third-party defendant, alleging that the accident was based on a defect in the design or manufacture of the automobile. The jury found for Wasik against Ford, even though Wasik had never brought a claim against Ford.

Issue: Can a third-party defendant be held liable to a plaintiff who never brought a claim against it?

Rule: Under the FRCP 15(b), a third-party defendant may be held liable to a plaintiff if it had the opportunity to fully litigate the issue of its liability.

Robbins v. Jordan (1950)

Facts: Robbins sued Jordan for medical malpractice. At trial Robbins moved to amend its pleadings to state that Jordan was a specialist in obstetrics and gynecology. The court disallowed the request and directed a verdict for Jordan.

Issue: Should an amendment to pleadings be permitted at trial when the amendment alters the legal theory of the case, but does not state a new cause of action?

Rule: Pleadings can be amended freely when presentation of the merits of the action will be served and the objecting party fails to show that admission of such evidence would prejudice his position.

Burlington Transp. Co. v. Josephson (1946)

Facts: Josephson sued Burlington to recover for false arrest. Josephson's pleadings only specified general damages, but at trial he also sought recovery for special damages.

Issue: Can a court award special damages to a party whose pleadings only requested general damages?

Rule: Special damages may only be awarded when the defendant was apprised of the nature of the claim against him by allegations of specific facts set forth by the plaintiff.

Decker v. Massey-Ferguson, Ltd. (1982)

Facts: Decker instituted a shareholder derivative action against Massey-Ferguson. The initial complaint, 69 pages long, contained several charges that were not actionable, and many other complaints that were not, as required by FRCP 9(b) regarding claims of fraud, stated with specificity. Many other charges were false on their face. One other claim charged Massey's foreign subsidiaries with bribing officials.

Issue: What must a complaint contain to get past the pleadings stage?

Rule: The charges leveled against the defendant must not be patently false. If the charges deal with fraud, FRCP 9(b) requires that they be stated with particularity. Only the charge of bribery satisfies these claims.

Leggett v. Montgomery Ward & Co. (1949)

Facts: Leggett sued to recover for malicious prosecution. In his complaint, he acknowledged that he had waived his rights at the preliminary hearing on the charge of embezzlement. Montgomery Ward claimed that Leggett's waiver proved that probable cause, which operates as a defense to malicious prosecution, existed.

Issue: Should a claim be dismissed where the plaintiff's pleadings allege facts that constitute a valid defense without avoiding such defenses?

Rule: A complaint alleging both facts which constitute a cause of action and a valid defense may be summarily dismissed.

Heimbaugh v. City & County of San Francisco (1984)

Facts: Heimbaugh claimed that the city's regulations regarding Softball and baseball playing violated his First, Fourth and Fourteenth Amendment Rights. The city moved to dismiss the motion and to impose FRCP 11 sanctions against Heimbaugh.

Issue: Under what standards should a lawsuit be dismissed?

Rule: A suit should be dismissed if, construing all the evidence in favor of the plaintiff, he has no possibility of recovery.

Drewett v. Aetna Casualty & Surety Co. (1975)

Facts: Drewett sued Aetna to recover under flood insurance policies issued pursuant to the Flood Recovery Act of 1968. Drewett further demanded penalties and attorney's fees under the state insurance law. Under FRCP 12(f), Aetna moved to strike Drewett's demands for penalties and attorney's fees.

Issue: May a court grant a motion to strike specific allegations in a complaint?

Rule: FRCP 12(f) provides that the motion to strike be directed toward an insufficient defense or toward a redundant, immaterial, impertinent, or scandalous matter. A motion to strike may not be directed to a specific allegation.

Gunder v. New York Times Co. (1941)

Facts: Gunder asserted a libel action against the New York Times. After New York Times answered the complaint, Gunder moved to strike all of New York Times' affirmative defenses as being insufficient. Gunder's complaint itself did not allege enough facts to state a cause of action.

Issue: May a defendant who has filed an insufficient answer, move to dismiss a complaint that itself fails to state a cause of action?

Rule: A defendant may challenge the validity of a complaint after the plaintiff has made a motion to strike the defendant's affirmative answers.

Molasky v. Garfinkle (1974)

Facts: The Molaskys and other shareholders alleged that Garfinkle and others fraudulently manipulated the stock market, rendering it impossible for the plaintiffs to sell their shares of Ancorp in the open market. They brought a suit under Securities and Exchange Commission Rule 10(b)(5), but could not allege in the pleadings that they were either purchasers or sellers of stock, as required by judicial decisions interpreting the Securities Exchange Act.

Issue: Must a plaintiff allege all the elements of an action in order to maintain a cause of action?

Rule: A complaint that has not set forth facts sufficient to maintain a cause of action must be dismissed.

Gomez v. Toledo (S.Ct. 1980)

Facts: In a suit under 42 U.S.C. § 1983, Gomez alleged that in dismissing him from the Puerto Rican Police Force, the city of Toledo violated the principles of procedural due process. Gomez neglected to allege that the city had acted in bad faith, although the city was perfectly within its rights to dismiss Gomez in good faith.

Issue: Is it necessary for a plaintiff to allege that an official acted in bad faith to state a claim against a public official under 42 U.S.C. § 1983?

Rule: (Marshall, J.) In an action against a public official whose position might entitle him to immunity if he acted in good faith, a plaintiff need not allege bad faith on the part of the official in order to state a claim for relief under 42 U.S.C. § 1983.

St. Mary's Honor Center v. Hicks (S.Ct. 1993)

Facts: Hicks sued St. Mary's, his employer, for violations of Title VII of the Civil Rights Act of 1964. Hicks established a prima facie case of discriminatory intent by the defendant. St. Mary's produced rebuttal evidence justifying its conduct, but the court, was unpersuaded. Hicks argued that the defendant's failure to produce a "legitimate, nondiscriminatory reason" for its conduct entitled Hicks to judgment.

Issue: Does a defendant's failure to persuade the trier of fact that it did not act with discriminatory intent entitle the plaintiff to judgment in a Title VII action?

Rule: (Scalia, J.) A defendant must produce evidence to rebut a plaintiff's prima facie case in a Title VII action, however, this requirement is merely a procedural device, and the plaintiff still bears the burden of proof. A defendant's failure to persuade the trier of fact that it *did not* act with discriminatory intent does not necessarily prove the plaintiffs claim that the defendant *did* act with discriminatory intent, and does not entitle the plaintiff to a judgment in his favor.

Dissent: (Souter, J.) In a Title VII action, a prima facie case is a proven case and produces a presumption in favor of the plaintiff. Unless the defendant successfully rebuts the plaintiffs prima facie case, that presumption remains, and the plaintiff should be entitled to judgment.

Leatherman v. Tarrant County Narcotics Intelligence and Coordination Unit (S.Ct. 1993)

Facts: Plaintiffs sued several municipal bodies for civil rights damages under 42 U.S.C. § 1983 in a Fifth Circuit district court.

Because municipalities are generally immune from respondeat superior liability under § 1983, the Fifth Circuit required plaintiffs suing municipalities under the statute to plead with specificity why the defendant municipalities were not immune from liability.

Issue: May a federal court impose a higher pleading standard than that required by FRCP 8 and FRCP 9?

Rule: (Rehnquist, C.J.) A federal court may not impose a higher pleading standard than that required by Rules 8 and 9 of the FRCP. To permit the Circuits to raise the pleading standards and require greater specificity in pleading would interfere with the primary purpose of "notice pleading" under the FRCP, which is merely to provide the defendant with fair notice of what the plaintiffs claim is and the grounds upon which it rests.

Mitchell v. E-Z Way Towers, Inc. (1959)

Facts: Mitchell alleged that E-Z Way Towers' business practices violated the Fair Labor Standards Act. E-Z Way made a motion for a more definite statement and for dismissal based thereon.

Issue: When will a motion for a more definite statement be granted?

Rule: A motion for a more definite statement cannot be used merely to assist a party in obtaining additional facts in preparation for trial. A motion is sufficient where the defendant has enough information to frame responsive pleadings.

Matarazzo v. Friendly Ice Cream Corp. (1976)

Facts: Matarazzo alleged that Friendly Ice Cream Corp. violated both the Sherman and Clayton Acts in its dealings with its franchises. Matarazzo made a motion to amend his pleadings to allege facts with more specificity and to set forth an alleged supplemental state claim of misleading advertising.

Issue 1: Will an amendment predicated on a new theory be granted in the absence of any new issues?

Rule 1: If predicated upon a new theory, an amendment should be permitted even in the absence of a discussion of any new issues.

Issue 2: Do federal courts have the power to exercise jurisdiction over state claims?

Rule 2: Federal courts have the power to exercise jurisdiction over state claims if the claims are derived from a common nucleus of operative facts.

Helfend v. Southern California Rapid Transit District (1970)

Facts: Helfend brought a tort action against Southern California Rapid Transit (SCRT), and Mitchell, an employee. Helfend pleaded special damages for doctor bills, hospital bills, and medicine costs. At trial, SCRT sought to introduce evidence that a portion of Helfend's medical bill had been paid by Helfend's insurance plan.

Issue: May a party introduce evidence that the plaintiff had received the benefits of medical insurance coverage?

Rule: When an injured party receives some compensation for his injuries from a source wholly independent of the tortfeasor, such payment will not be deducted from the damages that plaintiff would otherwise collect from the tortfeasor.

Pacific Mutual Life Insurance Co. v. Haslip (S.Ct. 1991)

Facts: Haslip sued Pacific Mutual for the fraudulent sale of insurance by one of its agents. The jury found Pacific Mutual guilty and imposed a large punitive damage award. Pacific Mutual appealed, claiming that the punitive damage award violated the Due Process Clause because the award had been left to the discretion of the jury.

Issue: Do punitive damage awards left to the discretion of the jury violate the Due Process Clause?

Rule: (Blackmun, J.) Punitive damage awards do not violate the Due Process Clause when the jury's discretion operates within reasonable constraints, and when the trial court exercises meaningful and adequate review of the jury award amount. Because the nature and purpose of punitive damage awards were explained to the jury in this case, and because the trial court conducted a meaningful review of the award amount, the punitive damage award comports with the Due Process Clause.

Dissent: (O'Connor, J.) A court examining the constitutionality of a punitive damage award procedure should examine: (1) the private interest at stake; (2) the risk that existing procedures will wrongly impair this private interest, and the likelihood that additional safeguards can effect a cure; and (3) the governmental interest in avoiding these additional procedures. The punitive damage awarded in this case violate the Due Process Clause because no meaningful criteria for reaching an award decision was provided to the jury.

Weinberger v. Romero-Barcelo (S.Ct. 1982)

Facts: Romero-Barcelo brought suit to enjoin the United States Navy from conducting weapons training on an island off the coast of Puerto Rico. Romero-Barcelo's complaint alleged violations of the Federal Water Pollution Control Act (FWPCA). The district court refused to enjoin the Naval operations on the island, holding that an injunction was not necessary to ensure prompt compliance. The Court of Appeals for the First Circuit reversed and remanded, holding that, under the Act, the court's equitable discretion had been impliedly withdrawn.

Issue: When does the district court retain discretionary power to grant or deny equitable remedies?

Rule: (White, J.) Absent express statutory withdrawal of discretion, the power to issue injunctions always rests within the discretion of the court.

Dissent: (Stevens, J.) In the FWPCA, Congress has so narrowly proscribed the court's discretion that injunctions should be issued in all but the most narrow category of cases.

Connecticut v. Doehr (S.Ct. 1991)

Facts: DiGiovanni submitted an application to the Connecticut Supreme Court for an attachment on Doehr's home. The relevant prejudgment remedy statute provided that ex parte attachments of real property were allowable upon verification that there was probable cause to sustain the plaintiffs claim. The attachment was granted without giving Doehr prior notification, and Doehr filed a federal suit claiming that the statute was unconstitutional under the Fourteenth Amendment.

Issue: Does a state statute that allows prejudgment attachments of real estate without prior notice or hearing violate the Due Process Clause of the Fourteenth Amendment?

Rule: (White, J.) A prejudgment remedy statute which concerns deprivation of real property must satisfy a three part inquiry: consideration of the private interest affected by the measure, examination of the risk of error and value of providing additional safeguards, and the interest of the party seeking the remedy. Under this test, the relevant statute was found to violate the Due Process Clause.

Lawson Products, Inc. v. Avnet, Inc. (1986)

Facts: Upon filing supporting affidavit with the court, Lawson Products moved for a preliminary injunction against Avnet, Inc., its competitor. The court denied the motion and Lawson appealed.

Issue: What standard of review is applied in reviewing a trial court's denial of a motion for a preliminary injunction?

Rule: When a reviewing court evaluates a preliminary injunction order, factual determinations are reviewed under the clearly erroneous standard and legal conclusions are given de novo review.

United States v. Kubrick (S.Ct. 1979)

Facts: Kubrick sued the United States in 1972, under the Federal Tort Claims Act (28 U.S.C. § 2401(b)), for injuries he allegedly sustained due to negligent treatment by a physician in a Veteran's Administration Hospital. Kubrick discovered his injuries in 1969. The United States argued that Kubrick's claim was time-barred.

Issue: When does a tort claim accrue within the meaning of the Act for statute of limitation purposes?

Rule: (White, J.) A tort claim accrues within the meaning of the Act when a party knows both the existence and cause of his injury, or should have known, using a due diligence standard.

Dissent: (Stevens, J.) The Court assumes that Kubrick did not use due diligence. That should be an issue for the jury, not the Supreme Court to decide.

Evans v. Jeff D. (S.Ct. 1986)

Facts: Jeff D. and other children suffering mental and emotional handicaps sued the Governor and several state officials of Idaho on both federal and state constitutional grounds. The Idaho Legal Aid Society represented the children and instructed its employee, attorney Johnston, to reject any settlement offer conditioned on a waiver of fees or costs. Nevertheless, Johnston accepted a new settlement offer that included a provision for a waiver of any claim to fees. Subsequently, Johnston filed a motion, based on the Civil Rights Attorney's Fee Awards Act (CRAFAA) of 1976, with the district court, requesting that the court reject settlement portions dealing with waiver of attorney's fees. The court denied the motion.

Issue: Where attorney's fees are guaranteed by law, may a client waive his own attorney's fees?

Rule: (Stevens, J.) The law guaranteeing attorney's fees was not intended to stand in the way of settlements that include a waiver of that right.

Dissent: (Brennan, J.) CRAFAA was intended to insure that civil rights violations, were prosecuted. By allowing clients to waive their attorney's rights, the Court makes it more difficult for victims of civil rights violations to obtain attorneys to represent them.

Logan v. Southern Cal. Rapid Transit District (1982)

Facts: Following an altercation with a passenger, Logan was fired from his job as a bus driver. He admitted in his pleadings that he was provided with a hearing, but claimed that his due process rights were violated. Apparently, he was not allowed to testify at the hearing or call an important witness. However, he did not allege these facts in his complaint. The defendants demurred on the ground that Logan failed to state a cause of action.

Issue: What facts must be alleged in a complaint in order to state a cause of action?

Rule: To successfully state a cause of action, a complaint must allege ultimate facts, not evidentiary facts or conclusions of law. Here, the defendants' demurrers were sustained because Logan claimed his due process rights were violated, but failed to allege any ultimate facts as to how his due process rights were violated.

Note: This is a California case. Courts that follow the Federal Rules have largely abandoned the evidentiary fact/ultimate fact/conclusion-of-law distinction in favor of more general allegations.

Campbell v. Laurel (1990)

Facts: Campbell alleged that Laurel, her probation officer, informed her that her status as a lawful, complying probationer depended on her willingness to have sex with him. Her complaint alleged violations of a state civil rights act, intentional infliction of emotional distress, gross negligence and violation of 44 U.S.C. § 1983. 42 U.S.C. § 1983 provides a cause of action where conduct committed by a person acting under state law deprives a person of rights, privileges, or immunities secured by the Constitution or laws of the United States. Laurel made a FRCP 12(b)(6) motion to dismiss for failure to state a claim.

Issue: What facts must be alleged in a complaint in order to state a cause of action?

Rule: To be sufficient, pleadings must allege enough information to outline the elements of a claim or permit the inference that these elements exist. Conclusory allegations that require courts to conjure up unpleaded facts to support the allegations are not sufficient. The demurrer here was properly sustained because the facts alleged by Campbell only support claims under state law (i.e., tort). She failed to allege facts to support a § 1983 action, such as the acts were a policy or custom of the agency, negligence in training, etc.

Rannels v. S.E. Nichols, Inc. (1979)

Facts: Rannels stopped payment on a check due to a dispute over defective merchandise she purchased from Nichols. Nichols filed a criminal complaint alleging violation of a bad check statute, although it knew why she had stopped payment. Rannels brought the present suit for wrongful prosecution and alleged those facts in her complaint. The district court dismissed the action on grounds that the complaint failed to aver lack of probable cause (an element necessary for a wrongful prosecution claim).

Issue: Under the federal rules, must a complaint allege facts necessary to support every element of a cause of action?

Rule: The federal rules only require that a complaint contain a short, plain statement of the claim to give the defendant fair notice of what the plaintiff's claim is and the grounds on which it rests. Malice, intent, knowledge, and other conditions of mind need not be specifically averred.

DiLeo v. Ernst & Young (1990)

Facts: DiLeo was an investor in Continental Illinois Bank (Continental), which lost four billion dollars. Ernst & Young (E & Y) was Continental's accountant. DiLeo brought an action against E & Y for securities fraud. The central allegation of the complaint was that before investors bought their stock, E & Y "became aware that a substantial amount of the receivables reported in Continental's financial statement were likely to be uncollectible." They became uncollectible.

Issue: What must a complaint allege in an action for fraud?

Rule: Although states of mind may be pleaded generally, circumstances constituting fraud must be stated with particularity. Here, the plaintiff did not provide any facts to indicate that the change in the stated condition of the firm was even due to negligence, let alone fraud.

Fisher v. Flynn (1979)

Facts: Fisher brought a Title VII sex discrimination suit against Bridgewater State College for her dismissal as an assistant professor. Her only allegation of specific conduct was that "some part" of the reason for her dismissal was that she refused the romantic advances of her department chairman.

Issue: What must a complaint allege in a civil rights action?

Rule: Complaints based on civil rights violations must do more than state simple conclusions; they must at least outline the facts constituting the alleged violation. Fisher did not allege a sufficient nexus between her refusal of the romantic overtures and her termination because she did not allege that the department chairman had the authority to terminate her employment.

Layman v. Southwestern Bell Tel. Co. (1977)

Facts: Southwestern Bell (Bell) had a subcontractor dig up part of Layman's property. Layman brought a trespass action. Bell's answer contained only a general denial. At trial, Bell sought to introduce evidence that it had an easement across the property (an affirmative defense).

Issue: May a party introduce evidence supporting an affirmative defense when it has only pled a general denial in its answer?

Rule: A defendant is obligated to plead affirmative defenses in its answer. If a defendant only pleads a general denial, it may not offer evidence establishing affirmative defenses.

Barnes v. Callaghan & Co. (1977)

Facts: Barnes was fired from her job at Callaghan. She brought suit against Callaghan, alleging sexual discrimination. Barnes amended her complaint to state a claim for slander. The statute of limitations for slander had run by the time the complaint was amended, but had not yet run when the original complaint was filed. Barnes' original complaint did not allege malice or publication, which are elements of a well-pleaded slander action. FRCP 15(c) provided that an amended claim relates back to the date of the original pleading if it arose out of the conduct, transaction, or occurrence set forth in the original pleading.

Issue: What are the requirements for an amended claim to relate back to the original complaint?

Rule: An amended complaint relates back to the original pleadings if the original pleadings contained timely, specific allegations of the conduct or transaction on which the amended claim is based such that the defendant has adequate notice of the action. Because Barnes' original complaint only alleged facts that stated Title VII and breech of contract claims, the slander claim was regarded as a new cause of action (which was consequently time-barred).

CHAPTER 5

JOINDER

I.   ABILITY TO SUE

A.   Justiciability

1. The Supreme Court and lower federal courts will only hear justiciable cases, i.e., cases appropriate for federal adjudication on the merits.

2. Sources of Justiciability Standards
The conditions necessary for justiciability are derived either from interpretations of the Article III, § 2 requirement that there be a "case or controversy," or from general Supreme Court policies developed apart from the Constitution.

3. Requirements for Justiciability
A suit is justiciable when certain conditions are present.
Mnemonic: **SCRIMPS**

   a.   **S**tanding
   A plaintiff must have standing to invoke the adjudicatory power of the federal courts. Standing is created when the plaintiff has a personal stake in the suit's outcome. The "personal stake" requirement is met where:

   i.   There is distinct and palpable (not speculative) injury to the plaintiff;

   ii. A fairly traceable causal connection exists between the claimed injury and the challenged conduct; and

   iii. There is a substantial likelihood that the relief requested will prevent or redress the claimed injury.

   iv. Taxpayer Standing
   A taxpayer will have standing to challenge a Congressional expenditure only if it meets the dual-nexus test established in *Flast v. Cohen*.

(1) The expenditure must be an exercise of power under the Taxing and Spending Clause.

(2) The expenditure must violate a specific constitutional provision which limits the taxing and spending power, such as the prohibition against an established religion. In reviewing a suit that requests more than one type of relief, the Supreme Court will impose a separate standing test for each.

b. Case or Controversy
The issues must arise out of an actual and current case or controversy between adverse litigants. Adjudication of hypothetical or removed disputes would result in advisory opinions – something federal courts may not issue.

c. Ripeness
The case must be ripe for review, i.e., the issues must be fully crystallized and the controversy concrete. Ripeness is established when litigants claim actual interference with their rights. Hypothetical threats to those rights do not invoke federal adjudicatory power.

d. Mootness (*DeFunis v. Odegaard*)
A federal case must involve controversies that are active and ongoing at the time of adjudication. A case becomes moot, and thus ineligible for judgment on the merits, once the controversy between the parties ceases to be definite and concrete and when a court's decision would no longer affect the litigants' rights.

e. Political Questions
A suit is nonjusticiable as a political question if:

i. The issues involve resolution of questions committed by the Constitution's text to a coordinate governmental branch;

ii. There is a lack of judicially discoverable and manageable standards for resolving the case, or if a decision would require a policy determination clearly outside judicial discretion; and

iii. Judicial intervention would produce an embarrassing diversity of pronouncements on the issue by various governmental departments.

f. Self-restraint/Discretion

There must not be a risk that federal adjudication would breach principles of judicial self-restraint and discretion. For example, federal courts and the Supreme Court avoid suits that would entail interfering with:

i. State courts' ability to resolve federal question cases;

ii. Pending state court proceedings; or

iii. Execution of state court judgments.

iv. Judicial self-restraint recognizes the importance of preserving the balance between state and federal interests. Such restraint also prevents the unwarranted federal constitutional decisions that may result when federal courts interpret state statutes.

4. The Problem of "Jus Tertii"

The Supreme Court and lower federal courts will not recognize the standing of a plaintiff who represents the constitutional rights of third parties ("jus tertii"), i.e., those not parties to the case. This rule is not constitutionally based; it is founded on policies of judicial self-restraint.

a. The Court hesitates to permit assertions of "jus tertii" (third-party rights) because:

i. Nonparties may not want to assert their own rights;

ii. Nonparty rights may be unaffected by the litigation's out-come; and

iii. Third parties are often the best proponents of their own interests.

b. Federal courts may recognize "jus tertii" standing when:

i. The nonparties' rights are inextricably bound up with the activity the litigant wishes to pursue;

ii. The plaintiff is no less effective a proponent of third party rights than the third parties themselves; and

iii. There is a genuine obstacle to the nonparties' representing their own interests.

B. Real Party in Interest (FRCP 17(a))

1. Defined

Every action shall be prosecuted in the name of the real party in interest (RPI). The RPI is the individual or individuals who will be directly affected by the action at hand.

2. Insurers

An insurer that has fully paid a claim to an insured individual would be the RPI in any action to recover damages, since the insured has already been compensated. Had the claim been only partially paid, however, both the insured and the insurer could be real parties in interest.

C. Capacity to Sue and Be Sued (FRCP 17(b))

1. Defined

States sometimes condition some groups' ability to enforce rights and obligations. For instance, minors and mental incompetents often cannot sue or be sued, except in specific cases.

2. Individuals

The ability of an individual to enforce rights or duties against others is determined by the state in which the person is domiciled.

3. Corporations
A corporation's capacity to sue or be sued is determined by the law of the state under which the corporation is incorporated.

4. Unincorporated Associations
Even if state law does not grant unincorporated associations the capacity to sue or be sued, FRCP 17 grants such capacity to these groups where federal or constitutional rights or obligations are at stake.

II. JOINDER OF CLAIMS

A. Generally (FRCP 18)
A party may join several causes of action as long as they arise out of the same transaction or occurrence, or series of transactions or occurrences. This transactional test applies whether the second claim is brought by a plaintiff against a defendant, by a defendant against a plaintiff (counterclaim), or by one party against a co-party (cross-claim).

B. Counterclaims (FRCP 13)
Defendant asserts a claim against a plaintiff. If the defendant's claim is not transactionally related to the claim asserted by the plaintiff, the judge has the discretion not to unduly complicate the case by refusing the joinder.

C. Compulsory Counterclaims (FRCP 13(a))
Some jurisdictions require all transactionally related counterclaims to be brought by the defendant. A compulsory counterclaim that has not been asserted cannot be raised in a subsequent lawsuit in federal court and compulsory counterclaim jurisdictions.

D. Cross-Claims (FRCP 13(g))
Parties to a lawsuit (either plaintiffs or defendants) can assert cross-claims against their co-parties (co-plaintiffs or codefendants, respectively) if the claims arise out of the same transaction as the case at hand.

III.   JOINDER OF PARTIES

A.   Permissive Joinder (FRCP 20)
Outside parties to an action may consent to be joined by leave of the court. The joined parties must have claims that are transactionally related to the original action.

B.   Necessary Parties (FRCP 19(a))

1. Generally
Necessary parties to an action must be joined if possible, but their nonjoinder will not result in dismissal. A court will deem a party to be necessary if:

   a.   The party's absence will preclude complete relief to present parties;

   b.   The party's absence will preclude complete relief to that party in a subsequent suit; or

   c.   The party's absence may subject a present party to multiple liabilities.

2. Involuntary Necessary Party
A necessary party who does not consent to joinder may be made a defendant or an involuntary third-party plaintiff upon order of the court. However, if the court does not have proper jurisdiction over the party, or if venue is improper, the court may continue the action without this "necessary" party.

C.   Indispensable Parties (FRCP 19(b))

1. Generally
Indispensable parties are those whose presence at trial is so necessary that their joinder will be compelled, even at the cost of dismissing the action, if that party cannot be joined.

2. Factors
A court may deem a necessary party to be indispensable by weighing how that party's absence will affect the following factors:

a. Prejudice to parties present as well as the necessary party;

b. Judicial options that may alleviate that prejudice;

c. Adequacy of the judgment without the party; and

d. Alternative remedies for the plaintiff in case of dismissal.

D. Consolidation (FRCP 42)

1. Consolidating Cases
Where several transactionally related actions are before the same court, the judge may order all of those actions to be consolidated in one suit.

2. Policy
Combined discovery, shared costs, and general reduction in delay.

3. Separation
Alternatively, where consolidation actually hinders speedy adjudication of the suits, the judge may also order separation.

4. Multidistrict Litigation (28 U.S.C. § 1407)
Transactionally related claims occurring in separate federal courts may be consolidated for concurrent discovery and other pretrial procedures upon a proper determination by a judicial panel on multidistrict litigation. This measure has been used frequently with asbestos liability and other mass tort litigation.

E. Impleader (FRCP 22)

1. Generally
Impleader is a device by which the defendant joins a third party to a suit under the theory that if the defendant is liable to the plaintiff, then this third party is also at least partially responsible.

2. Policy

    a.   Judicial efficiency

    b.   Prevent multiple liability, or windfall decisions
       Prevents a plaintiff from first suing the defendant and
       then the third party, recovering twice from both.

3. Jurisdiction
The impleaded party must have independent subject matter jurisdiction regarding the plaintiff, and cannot destroy diversity jurisdiction.

F.   Intervention (FRCP 24)

1. Generally
Intervention allows a third party to join an action, even if neither the plaintiffs nor the defendants request that party's presence. The intervenor may present both new claims and defenses to charges.

2. Permissive Intervention (FRCP 24(b))
Courts have the discretion to allow a petitioner to intervene if either:

    a.   A federal statute confers such a right to intervene; or

    b.   The petitioner's claim or defense is transactionally related to the main action.

3. Intervention as of Right
The court must allow a petitioner to intervene if either:

    a.   A federal statute confers such an absolute right; or

    b.   The petitioner presents:

        i.   A transactionally related claim or defense;

        ii. Without adjudication, the petitioner's rights would be impaired or impeded; and

iii. Existing parties would not adequately represent the petitioner's interests.

c. Courts will generally use the same analysis in determining whether a petitioner may intervene as of right as it does when determining whether a party is indispensable under FRCP 19.

G. Interpleader

1. Generally

Interpleader allows one party to join various adverse claimants who each have separate claims to single piece of property or fund, where that property cannot be split amongst the adverse claimants to the satisfaction of all the claims. This procedure is used most often by insurance companies who must pay out a limited fund to several parties.

2. Rule Interpleader (FRCP 22)

As long as general jurisdictional requirements are met, and none of the interpleaded parties ruin the requirement of complete diversity, FRCP 22 allows the debtor to join all the parties. Diversity in this context means that none of the claimants may be from the same state as the debtor.

3. Statutory Interpleader (28 U.S.C. § 1335)

Since most interpleaders will not satisfy the traditional elements of diversity jurisdiction, Congress enacted a second interpleader statute. This statute differs from rule interpleader in several respects.

a. The amount in controversy need be only $500, as opposed to the $75,000 normally required for diversity jurisdiction.

b. Minimum, not complete diversity is required. So long as any two claimants are diverse regarding one another, diversity is satisfied.

c. The property being disputed must be deposited with the court throughout the proceedings.

CASE CLIPS

Harris v. Avery (1869)

Facts: Harris called Avery a thief and confined him to a county jail. Avery's petition alleged two causes of action: false imprisonment and slander. Harris demurred, stating that the two issues were improperly joined.

Issue: Can two causes of action be joined in a single petition?

Rule: A petition may unite several causes of action where they arise out of the same transaction.

United States v. Heyward-Robinson (1970)

Facts: Heyward-Robinson entered into subcontracts with D'Agostino for construction of a naval base and for another, nonfederal project. D'Agostino sued Heyward-Robinson for nonpayment for the naval job to which Heyward-Robinson asserted a counterclaim alleging overpayment for both jobs. D'Agostino interposed a reply counterclaim for monies due on the nonfederal job. Since no diversity of citizenship existed, subject matter jurisdiction existed only with respect to claims relating to the federal job.

Issue: When is a federal court barred from asserting jurisdiction over a permissive counterclaim?

Rule: A federal court cannot assert ancillary jurisdiction over permissive counterclaims which do not rest on independent federal jurisdiction.

Great Lakes Rubber Corp. v. Herbert Cooper Co. (1961)

Facts: Great Lakes Rubber Corporation's federal complaint against Herbert Cooper Company was dismissed for lack of diversity jurisdiction. However, since jurisdiction of Herbert Cooper's counterclaim arose under federal law, it was retained. Great Lakes Rubber then tried to reassert its claims against Herbert Cooper as a counterclaim to Herbert Cooper's claims. Great Lakes asserted that its claims must be heard in federal court, despite the lack of subject matter jurisdiction because, under federal laws, the claims were compulsory.

Issue: When may a compulsory counterclaim be heard in federal court despite a lack of independent subject matter jurisdiction?

Rule: If a compulsory counterclaim bears a "logical relationship" to the opposing party's claim, and arise out of same transaction, federal courts may hear the claim despite the lack of any independent subject matter jurisdiction.

Lasa Per L'Industria del Marmo Societa Per Azioni v. Alexander (1969)

Facts: Lasa Per L'Industria del Marmo Societa Per Azioni sued Alexander, Southern Builders and Contract Casualty for breach of a construction contract. Both Alexander and Southern Builders filed counterclaims, and Alexander filed cross-claims against both Southern Builders and Contract Casualty.

Issue: When may a party assert a cross-claim against its co-party?

Rule: FRCP 13 and 14 (governing cross-claims and third-party claims) are intended to "dispose of the entire subject matter arising from one set of facts in one action," thus allowing several claims to be tried at the same time.

Ellis Canning Co. v. International Harvester Co. (1953)

Facts: The Ellis Canning Company alleged that the International Harvester Company negligently started a fire on its tractor while servicing it. Ellis Canning had been paid in full for the damage by its insurance company, but under an agreement with the insurance company, brought suit against International Harvester to recover the insurance company's loss.

Issue: Is an insured, after having been paid for his loss, legally entitled to maintain an action in his own name for the benefit of the insurer?

Rule: Where the insured has been fully paid to damages sustained, it is the insurance company that is the real party in interest and therefore must maintain its own action for reimbursement.

Ryder v. Jefferson Hotel (1922)

Facts: The Ryders, husband and wife, were forced to leave the Jefferson Hotel due to an employee's rudeness and insults. The Ryders suffered injury individually, yet the suit was brought in a single action.

Issue: Can several plaintiffs, each alleging individual personal torts arising out of the same occurrence, maintain a single action?

Rule: Two plaintiffs alleging separate tortious conduct, even arising out of a common occurrence, must try their actions separately. To maintain a joint action, the alleged tortious conduct must produce common damage to all the plaintiffs.

Tanbro Fabrics Corp. v. Beaunit Mills, Inc. (1957)

Facts: Three lawsuits arose out of a single business dispute concerning the sale of fabrics between Beaunit, Tanbro, and another party, Amity. Beaunit sued Tanbro first, seeking to recover the price of cloth it had sold to Tanbro. Tanbro counter-claimed, alleging that Beaunit's cloth had been defective. Tanbro then sued Amity in a separate action, seeking to recover the cloth it had sent to Amity. Amity counter-claimed for its contract price. Tanbro then tried to sue both Beaunit and Amity on a theory of alternative liability. Beaunit and Amity moved separately to dismiss Tanbro's last suit on the ground that there were prior actions pending between the parties with respect to the same cause of action.

Issue: What factors are necessary to permit consolidation of several actions?

Rule: To consolidate actions, it is no longer necessary that there be an identity of duty or contract between the parties. It is necessary that the alternative liability arise out of a common transaction or occurrence involving common questions of law and fact.

Bank of California National Association. v. Superior Court (1940)

Facts: Sara Boyd died testate, naming Bank of California as her executor. Her will named several legatees. Bertha Smedley, one of the legatees, brought an action to enforce an alleged contract between her and Boyd by which she was to receive the entire estate. Although the complaint named the Bank of California and all the beneficiaries, only the Bank of California and the residuary legatee had been served with process. No other legatees had been notified, nor did they appear in court.

Issue: When may parties be deemed necessary and indispensable to an action?

Rule: Parties subject to compulsory joinder are those whose interests might be affected by the outcome of the decision, or whose interests are such that the court cannot proceed without them (i.e., complete relief cannot be awarded in their absence).

Provident Tradesmens Bank & Trust Co. v. Patterson (S.Ct. 1968)

Facts: A car owned by Dutcher and driven by Cionci got into an accident with a truck driven by Smith. Cionci, Lynch (a passenger) and Smith, were killed and Harris (another passenger) was injured. Provident, the administrator of Lynch's estate, settled with Cionci's estate for $50,000, but Cionci had no money to pay. Actions against Dutcher by Smith's estate and by Harris had yet to go to trial. Dutcher had an insurance policy with Lumbermens Mutual Casualty Company worth $100,000 that Lynch's estate wanted to use to recover the value of its settlement with Cionci. Lynch's estate could only recover if it was proven that Cionci had Dutcher's permission to drive his car. Lynch's estate sued Cionci and Lumbermens to collect the $50,000 settlement out of Dutcher's policy, but did not join Dutcher as a defendant because that would have destroyed diversity.

Issue: When should a court dismiss a case that lacks an indispensable party?

Rule: (Harlan, J.) If in "equity and good conscience" the court can proceed without an absent party, it must. Four "interests" should be weighed in determining whether the court should proceed. First, the plaintiffs interest in selecting the forum, including the possibility of a satisfactory alternative. Second, the defendant's interest in avoiding multiple litigations. Third, the necessary party's interest in being present when his interests may be affected (even if the case would have no *res judicata* effects on him). Fourth, the courts' interest in complete, consistent, and efficient settlement of controversies. The court should strive to shape relief to accommodate these interests. Furthermore, some interests might have greater or lesser weight if the issue is raised at trial or on appeal.

Jeub v. B/G Foods (1942)

Facts: Jeub brought suit against B/G Foods for injuries sustained by eating contaminated ham. B/G Foods interposed a third-party complaint against Swift Premium, the canner, for judgment against it in the event that Jeub should recover against B/G Foods.

Issue: May a defendant implead a third-party who is liable to the defendant for any amount awarded to the plaintiff?

Rule: The purpose of FRCP 14 is to provide an efficient means of determining all parties' rights in a single proceeding. Thus, if a third party is liable to a defendant for any damages sustained, there is no reason a defendant shouldn't avail himself of the ability to implead such third party.

Hancock Oil Co. v. Independent Distributing Co. (1944)

Facts: Hopkins leased land to Hannock Oil for which he was to receive owner's royalties. Independent Distributing Co. subsequently claimed it owned the land. Hannock brought suit against Hopkins and Independent to determine to whom the royalties were owed.

Issue: When may a debtor interplead several claimants to a debt?

Rule: Common law interpleader has four elements: (1) the same debt must be claimed by both/all parties; (2) all claims must arise from a common source; (3) party seeking relief must have no claim or interest in the subject matter; and (4) the party owing the debt must not have incurred independent liability to any claimant.

New York Life Insurance Co. v. Dunlevy (S.Ct. 1916)

Facts: A judgment creditor of Dunlevy brought a garnishment proceeding in Pennsylvania on money due to Dunlevy from a fund set up by Gould, Dunlevy's father, through New York Life. New York Life admitted its indebtedness, but both Dunlevy and Gould had claims to the fund. New York Life interpleaded Dunlevy.

Dunlevy was given notice in California but never appeared. After the Pennsylvania court awarded the insurance claim to Gould, Dunlevy brought an action in California against New York Life to recover the value of the policy. She claimed that the Pennsylvania court had no jurisdiction over her as she was a resident of California and had no contacts with Pennsylvania.

Issue: Where a party is interpleaded to determine an interest in property, must the court have personal jurisdiction over the interpleaded party?

Rule: (McReynolds, J.) Interpleader actions bring about a final and conclusive adjudication of personal rights; consequently, a court must have personal jurisdiction over the parties.

Pan American Fire & Casualty Co. v. Revere (1960)

Facts: The Pan American Fire & Casualty Company sought to interplead all parties to a multivehicle accident. Several suits had already commenced. It set aside the insurance proceeds, claiming it was a "disinterested stakeholder," while denying any liability.

Issue: Is interpleader available to an insurer in the federal courts even though the insurer claims that the proceeds should go to none of the claimants but should remain with the insurance company itself?

Rule: The common-law rule of interpleader no longer applies. FRCP 22 only requires that the claims be such that plaintiff is, or might be, exposed to multiple liability. It does not matter that the insurer itself has a claim to the money.

State Farm Fire & Casualty Co. v. Tashire (S.Ct. 1967)

Facts: State Farm sought to interplead all prospective claimants involved in a multivehicle accident. The insurance proceeds would not cover the amount of the claims that had already been filed.

Issue: Is a federal interpleader action appropriate before claims have been adjudicated?

Rule: (Fortas, J.) Insurance companies can interplead prospective claimants prior to judgment being rendered; however a plaintiff is not entitled to enjoin prospective claimants from bringing suit outside the jurisdiction of the interpleader action.

Brune v. McDonald (1938)

Facts: Brune was a passenger in McDonald's car when an accident occurred. Brune had originally alleged that McDonald was drinking, but later amended the complaint, deleting the averment about the alcohol. McDonald's insurance policy with Pacific Indemnity would not apply to an accident that occurred during a social event (such as when liquor is a factor). Pacific Indemnity, McDonald's insurer, attempted to intervene, seeking to halt prosecution of Brune's action until it determined whether McDonald had breached the terms of the insurance agreement by using alcohol while driving.

Issue: Can a party attempt to intervene when its rights are not directly tied to the litigation?

Rule: A third party may intervene when its rights will be directly and immediately affected by the present litigation. Such a case exists here.

Smuck v. Hobson (1969)

Facts: In a prior class-action case between parents of minority children and the Board of Education, the court held that minority children had been denied the right to equal educational opportunities. When the Board chose not to appeal, the superintendent and several nonminority parents filed motions to intervene.

Issue: Must parties attempting to intervene in a case have real and present interests, the protection of which can only be realized through intervention?

Rule: Federal courts will grant a petition for intervention when denying the petition to intervene would prohibit the petitioners' ability to protect their interests, and when the petitioners are not effectively represented by parties in the litigation.

Atlantis Development Corp. v. United States (1967)

Facts: Anderson "discovered" coral reefs in 1962, staked a claim to the reefs and then sold his interest to the Atlantis Development Corporation. Meanwhile, the United States brought an action for trespass against a second group of corporations who had begun to develop the reefs themselves. Atlantis sought to intervene in the action, alleging it had title to the reefs.

Issue: Ta what extent must a party have a direct interest that will be prejudiced by an action in order to intervene?

Rule: Where a present action may impair or impede a party's ability to protect its own interests, intervention is permitted even if the consequences of the action would not be binding on the potential intervenor.

Ex-Cell-O Corp. v. City of Chicago (1940)

Facts: A manufacturer of machines for the production of paper milk bottles and a manufacturer of paper milk bottles brought an action challenging a legislative act banning paper milk bottles.

Issue: Does a party that will indirectly suffer inevitable financial pecuniary damage as a result of a legislative act have standing to challenge the act?

Rule: In order to challenge a legislative act a party must be able to show not only that the statute is invalid, but that he has sustained, or is in immediate danger of sustaining, some direct injury as the result of its enforcement.

United States v. Students Challenging Regulatory Agency Procedures (SCRAP) (S.Ct. 1974)

Facts: SCRAP, an unincorporated association of law students, brought an action challenging a surcharge on railroad freight rates approved by the Interstate Commerce Commission. SCRAP alleged that the increase in rates made it less economical to ship refuse to recycling plants and that, as a result, more refuse was discarded in Washington parks, thus diminishing SCRAP members' use and enjoyment of these parks.

Issue 1: Is injury to a plaintiff's aesthetic and environmental well-being sufficient "injury in fact" for purposes of establishing standing?

Rule 1: (Stewart, J.) An injury to a plaintiffs aesthetic and environmental well-being is sufficient "injury in fact" to confer standing, as "injury in fact" is not confined to a showing of "economic harm."

Issue 2: Can the fact that many people share the same injury be sufficient reason to disqualify an injured party from seeking review of a governmental agency's action?

Rule 2: The fact that many people share the same injury is not sufficient reason to disqualify an injured plaintiff from seeking review of an agency's action. (Such a rule would mean that the most injurious government actions could not be questioned.)

Duke Power Co. v. Carolina Environmental Study Group, Inc. (S.Ct. 1977)

Facts: Forty individuals who lived within close proximity to a planned private nuclear facility brought an action challenging the Price-Anderson Act, which set an upper liability limit of $560 million for damages caused by nuclear accidents.

Issue 1: Do individuals who live within close proximity to a planned nuclear facility have standing to challenge a federal act that places an upper liability amount on claims resulting from a nuclear accident?

Rule 1: (Burger, CJ.) Individuals have standing to challenge a federal act when they can show that they have a "personal stake" in the controversy and that there is a "fairly traceable" causal connection between the claimed injury and the challenged conduct (i.e., passage of the act). But for the federal act, the private company would not be able to build the facility; therefore, a causal connection existed.

Issue 2: Do the federal courts have subject matter jurisdiction over this controversy?

Rule 2: The individuals' claims appear to occur under the Fifth Amendment of the Constitution, thus making this case one of a federal question, despite the fact that the individuals claim that their suit was brought under 28 U.S.C. § 1337 (granting jurisdiction over issues related to restraint of trade).

Dissent: (Rehnquist, J.) The Fifth Amendment claim only becomes relevant if the Duke Power Company actually invokes the Price-Anderson Act as a defense to the individual's tort action (which is governed by North Carolina state law). No federal claim appears on the basis of the plaintiffs' "well-pleaded complaint."

Orlando v. Laird (1971)

Facts: Draftees in the United States Army brought separate actions against the Secretary of Defense, the Secretary of the Army, and their commanding officers, seeking to enjoin them from carrying out deployment orders sending plaintiffs to Vietnam.

Issue: May courts decide whether Congress constitutionally ratified the executive's military activity?

Rule: Judicial scrutiny of Congress' duty to authorize or ratify the executive's declaration of war is not foreclosed by the political question doctrine; the constitutional propriety of the means by which Congress has chosen to ratify and approve military operations is, however, a political question (i.e., courts can pass on the substance of Congress' ratification, not the form Congress chooses to use in ratifying).

Matter of State Industrial Commission (1918)

Facts: Members of a state commission, debating among themselves as to whether they had the authority to require that insurance companies and self-insurers pay into a state fund, requested that courts determine the commission's authority.

Issue: May a state court, if requested, grant an advisory opinion regarding a question of law?

Rule: The courts will only decide an issue if it is incidental to a pending case or controversy. Courts do not grant advisory opinions.

De Funis v. Odegaard (S.Ct. 1974)

Facts: De Funis sued the University of Washington Law School claiming that the school's affirmative action policies injured him. He obtained a preliminary injunction and was able to attend law school throughout the ensuing trial and subsequent appeals. When the case eventually reached the United States Supreme Court, plaintiff had already registered for the final semester of his last year. The school conceded that De Funis would not now be prevented an opportunity to complete his degree.

Issue: May the Supreme Court decide an issue of great public interest although the outcome will not effect the original parties?

Rule: (Per Curiam) Federal courts are without power to decide questions that cannot affect the rights of litigants. Great public interest in an issue will not save a case from mootness.

United States v. Aetna Casualty & Surety Co. (S.Ct. 1949)

Facts: Aetna partially paid out a claim to one of its insured, even though that insured may have been able to recover damages by suing the United States in a tort action. Aetna then sued the United States in its own name based on its partial payment to the insured. The insured could have brought the suit as well.

Issue: May an insurance company bring suit against the United States upon a claim to which it has partially paid the insured, even though the insured could have brought the suit himself?

Rule: (Vinson, CJ.) An insurance company may bring such a suit in its own name even though the United States may have to defend several actions based on the same tort.

Tyler v. Dowell, Inc. (1960)

Facts: Tyler contracted with Phillips, who contracted with Dowell, Inc., to repair an oil well. Dowell's operations resulted in a fire for which Tyler sought to recover damages. Dowell successfully joined Tyler's insurance company, which Dowell contended had become the real party in interest when it entered into a loan agreement with Tyler.

Issue: Does an insurer become a real party in interest when it advances its insured a loan which is to be repaid from the litigation proceeds?

Rule: Courts have generally viewed agreements whereby an insured receives a loan that is to be repaid with litigation proceeds as payment of the loss. Thus, the insurance company becomes the subrogee of the insured and the real party in interest.

Oskoian v. Canuel (1959)

Facts: Canuel and two others, members of the then defunct Independent Union tried to sue the International Union, alleging malicious and unlawful interference with an employment contract. Canuel served process on Oskoian and two others, representatives of a local chapter of the International Union. Oskoian and the others claimed that they lacked the capacity to be sued as representatives of the national union. FRCP 17(b) allows an unincorporated association (like International) to be sued in its common name if the association had no capacity to be sued under state law. Canuel did not comport with the applicable Rhode Island law because the officers required to be served by that law were not subject to Rhode Island's jurisdiction. The court also inferred that Rhode Island law would allow the suit if all of the members of International could be sued in a class action under FRCP 23(a)(l).

Issue: Must the named parties in a class action have individual capacities to be sued as representatives of an association?

Rule: Since a class action affects all members of the class equally, where state law contemplates that capacity to be sued will be satisfied by a suit on all members of the association, the named parties need not have individual capacities to be sued as representatives of the association.

Mulcahy v. Duggan (1923)

Facts: Mulcahy sued Duggan, alleging Duggan had physically attacked him. Duggan set up a counterclaim for libel, alleging that the fight between them resulted from the libelous remarks published by Mulcahy.

Issue: Can a defendant assert a counterclaim based on an action that allegedly led to claims asserted in the present suit?

Rule: As here, a counterclaim must arise out of the transaction or occurrence that is the foundation of the plaintiff's original complaint.

Rosenthal v. Fowler (1952)

Facts: Rosenthal alleged that his landlord overcharged him rent and did not provide basic services in his apartment. Fowler interposed two counterclaims: that the basic services were Rosenthal's responsibility, and that Rosenthal injured Fowler by inducing an appraiser to reduce his estimate of the property's worth. Rosenthal moved to dismiss the counterclaims for lack of subject matter jurisdiction.

Issue: May a counterclaim be maintained despite a lack of independent subject matter jurisdiction?

Rule: Any counterclaim bearing a logical relationship to the main claim in the lawsuit may be maintained despite a lack of independent subject matter jurisdiction.

Chamberlain v. White and Goodwin (1622)

Facts: Chamberlain sued White and Goodwin for slander. White and Goodwin appealed, alleging impermissible joinder of parties.

Issue: May a plaintiff maintain a slander action against multiple defendants?

Rule: A plaintiff cannot maintain a slander action against multiple defendants because "the speaking of one is not the speaking of the other." Thus, they should have been "severally charged," since the complaint alleges distinct causes of action against each defendant.

Akely v. Kinnicutt (1924)

Facts: 193 plaintiffs sued the defendants, claiming fraud in each individual stock purchase, based upon a fraudulent prospectus.

Issue: When may separate and distinct causes of action be joined in one complaint?

Rule: All parties may be joined in one action where, as here, any common question of law or fact would arise were they to be tried separately.

Shields v. Barrow (1854)

Facts: Barrow sold property to Shields that was to be paid for in installments. The unpaid balance was endorsed by six guarantors, four claiming Louisiana citizenship and two claiming Mississippi citizenship. When Shields defaulted, a compromise agreement was entered into between all parties that Barrow sought to rescind only as against the two Mississippians. Shields argued that the other guarantors were indispensable parties.

Issue: When is a partied deemed indispensable such that a court may not decide the case without their being present?

Rule: Parties are considered indispensable when they have an interest in the controversy of such a nature that a decree would either (1) substantially affect their interest, or (2) leave the controversy in such a state that its termination would be inconsistent with equity and good conscience. Absent such indispensable parties, the court cannot proceed.

Keene v. Chambers (1936)

Facts: The plaintiffs owned a life estate in a half interest in land in Chicago. Chicago Title & Trust, an Illinois corporation, had rights to the other half. The plaintiffs sued the defendants, New York residents, in New York for nonpayment of rent. The defendants unsuccessfully attempted to join Chicago Title & Trust. New York had no jurisdiction over Chicago Title and Trust. Illinois had jurisdiction over Chicago Title & Trust, but not over the New York defendants.

Issue: May the court join a party over whom it does not have jurisdiction whose rights may possibly be affected?

Rule: It is illogical to command that a party be joined where the party cannot be served, and where there is no jurisdiction over the party.

Schutten v. Shell Oil (1970)

Facts: Schutten sought to evict Shell Oil from his land in a federal diversity action. Shell Oil contended that it leased the land from the Board of Commissioners of the Orleans Levee District, and that the Board is an indispensable party since it also claimed title to the land. However, joining the lessor would destroy diversity jurisdiction.

Issue: Is an adverse claimant to property an indispensable party to an eviction proceeding?

Rule: A party claiming an adverse property interest is an indispensable party to an eviction proceeding even though such a classification might destroy diversity jurisdiction and force dismissal of the case.

United States v. De Haven (1953)

Facts: De Haven contracted with Vander Broek for roofing repairs and signed a promissory note for the sum due. The note was assigned to the United States. De Haven defaulted, alleging breach of contract, and attempted to implead Vander Broek when it was sued by the United States for collection on the note.

Issue: Is a party to a contract for whom a note had originally been signed a necessary party such that the party should be impleaded under FRCP 14 on a suit for collection of the promissory note by a third party?

Rule: A court will deny impleader under FRCP 14 when trial of the third-party suit requires determination of facts and issues unrelated to the primary suit.

Indianapolis Colts v. Mayor of Baltimore (1984)

Facts: After learning that the Maryland Senate had enacted a law granting Baltimore the power to acquire the Indianapolis Colts through eminent domain, the Colt's owner moved the Colts to Indiana under the cover of darkness, and executed a lease that the Colts and Indiana had been negotiating for about a month. Baltimore brought a condemnation suit against the Colts, who claimed that its obligations under its lease with Indiana conflicted with Baltimore's eminent domain claim.

Issue: Is the lessee of property subject to an eminent domain action a party who may be subject to an interpleader?

Rule: An interpleader is a suit over a fund to which several parties have claims. A leaseholder does not have a direct interest in the property over which eminent domain is being asserted.

Haas v. Jefferson National Bank (1971)

Facts: Haas brought a federal diversity action seeking to enforce an alleged contract made with Glueck in 1963 to sell Haas 169^1/2 shares of the Jefferson National Bank's stock. The trial court ordered Haas to join Glueck as an indispensable party, and then dismissed the case because Glueck's joinder destroyed diversity.

Issue: Should a case be dismissed if joining a party under FRCP 19(a) would destroy diversity?

Rule: A case should be dismissed where judgment rendered in the absence of a party who could not be joined might be prejudicial to either the party absent or to those parties already present.

Babcock & Wilcox Co. v. Parsons Corp. (1970)

Facts: Babcock & Wilcox lent machinery to Parsons which became damaged. Babcock & Wilcox recovered for the damage. In the subsequent diversity suit between Parsons and its insurer, Babcock & Wilcox intervened. Were Babcock & Wilcox to successively intervene, diversity would be destroyed.

Issue: Must a permissive intervention be supported by independent jurisdiction grounds?

Rule: Permissive intervention must be supported by independent subject matter jurisdiction. In dicta, the court stated that compulsory intervention does not require independent subject matter jurisdiction.

Lambert v. Southern Counties Gas Co. (1959)

Facts: The Lamberts rented their bulldozer to several ranch owners. The bulldozer was destroyed when it hit Southern Counties Gas Company's gas pipeline and exploded. The Lamberts sued the ranch owners and the gas company. The gas company sought to dismiss the claims against it due to a state law that made the owner of a motor vehicle responsible when the vehicle was negligently driven by someone with the owner's permission. One of the Lamberts' allegations stipulated that the driver of the tractor had been negligent. The Lamberts responded that their tractor is not a vehicle under the state law, that the driver may or may not have been negligent, and if not, the gas company is negligent.

Issue: Can a defendant use an allegation of a codefendant's negligence to defeat allegations of its own negligence?

Rule: A plaintiff may plead alternate and inconsistent causes of action in separate counts. A count sufficient within itself may not ordinarily be defeated by importing, from another count, an allegation to which the sufficient count makes no reference.

Pan American World Airways, Inc. v. United States District Court (1975)

Facts: In a suit involving an airline crash against Pan Am, the district court had ordered that all potential plaintiffs be notified of the impending litigation.

Issue: Can a court take it upon itself to notify all potential claimants of pending litigation?

Rule: Absent statutory authority or compulsory joinder considerations, a court may not take it upon itself to notify potential plaintiffs of pending litigation.

Associated Dry Goods Corp. v. Towers Financial Corp. (1990)

Facts: Associated brought a diversity action against Towers, seeking a declaratory judgment that Towers had breached a sublease agreement. Towers claimed that the parties could not obtain complete relief unless the head-lessor was joined. Associated could not join the head-lessor as a plaintiff without destroying diversity. Towers could have joined the head-lessor as a codefendant in a compulsory counterclaim over which the court would have had ancillary jurisdiction, but Towers refused to do so. Instead, Towers moved to have the case dismissed for Associated's failure to join an indispensable party.

Issue: May a court dismiss an action for a plaintiffs failure to join an indispensable party, when the plaintiff cannot join the party without destroying diversity jurisdiction and the defendant can join the party without destroying the court's jurisdiction?

Rule: A court may not, in equity and good conscience, dismiss a case for a plaintiff's failure to join an indispensable party, when the plaintiff cannot join the party without destroying diversity and the defendant can join the party without destroying the court's jurisdiction. The FRCP 19(b) notion of equity and good conscience assumes that the parties before the court are obliged to pursue any avenues available for eliminating the threat of prejudice.

American Motorcycle Association v. Superior Court (1978)

Facts: Gregos, a teenager, was injured in a cross-country motorcycle race. He sued the American Motorcycle Association for damages. The Association denied the allegations and cross-claimed Gregos' parents as responsible for Gregos' negligence and damages as evidenced by their signing a parental consent form prior to Gregos entering the race.

Issue: May a defendant assert a cross-claim against a third party who the plaintiff has not brought into the action.

Rule: A defendant may bring anybody it claims may share liability into the action.

Fairview Park Excavating Co. v. Al Monzo Construction Co. (1977)

Facts: On a job for Robinson Township of Pennsylvania, Monzo, the Pennsylvania-based general contractor, hired Fairview Park or Ohio as a subcontractor. Fairview brought a federal diversity action against Robinson Township, Monzo and Monzo's Maryland insurer for nonpayment. Monzo cross-claimed against Robinson. Fairview's claim against Robinson was dismissed because state law limited a township's liability to contractors, not subcontractors. The lower court then dismissed Monzo's cross-claim against Robinson for lack of independent subject matter jurisdiction.

Issue: Must a cross-claim have independent subject matter jurisdiction if the original claim against the cross-claimed party has been dismissed?

Rule: Cross-claims brought against a party who was properly brought within the court's jurisdiction may be maintained even if the original complaint against the party has been dismissed.

Bustop v. Superior Court (1977)

Facts: A minority student sued to end racial segregation in her school district. The school district began to develop a plan for integration that included busing. Bustop, a nonprofit corporation of 65,000 parents of white children, petitioned to intervene.

Issue: When may a party intervene in a proceeding?

Rule: A party that has social, educational or economic interests in a matter may intervene in a proceeding where those interests are not already adequately represented.

Valley Forge Christian College v. Americans United for Separation of Church and State, Inc. (S.Ct. 1982)

Facts: The Department of Health, Education and Welfare gave land to Valley Forge Christian College. Americans United for Separation of Church and State sued Valley Forge, claiming the gift violated the First Amendment.

Issue: Does every group have standing to challenge the constitutionality of government action?

Rule: (Rehnquist, J.) Without a claim of actual or personal injury as a consequence of the action, a litigant has no standing. The injury must be more than that shared by the general populace as taxpayers.

Dissent: (Brennan, J.) The Constitution does not bar the suit of a party who has suffered injury merely because others are similarly aggrieved.

Virginia Electric & Power Co. v. Westinghouse Electric Corp. (1973)

Facts: Virginia Electric brought a federal diversity action on behalf of itself and its insurer to recover damages resulting from the failure of a plant constructed by Westinghouse. Were the insurer to be joined diversity would be destroyed.

Issue: May an insured bring a claim on behalf of its insurer without bringing the insurer into the action?

Rule: Since the insured is representing the insurer in all respects and has a stake in the issues before the court, there is no reason to join the insurer as a real party in interest.

Plant v. Blazer Financial Services (1979)

Facts: Plant executed a note in favor of Blazer. Plant brought suit under the federal Truth in Lending Act for failure to make required disclosures. The defendant brought a counterclaim on the underlying debt. There was no independent jurisdictional basis for the federal court to adjudicate the counterclaim (i.e., federal question or diversity jurisdiction), such that the court could only hear the counterclaim if it was compulsory.

Issue: When is a counterclaim compulsory?

Rule: A counterclaim is compulsory when there is a logical relationship between the claim and the counterclaim that indicates that they arose from the same aggregate of operative facts. Because both actions in this suit arose from a single loan transaction and depend on overlapping evidence, the court held that the action on the underlying debt was a compulsory counterclaim to the truth-in-lending action.

Watergate Landmark Condo Unit Owners Association v. Wiss, Janey, Elstner Assoc. (1987)

Facts: The plaintiffs employed Legum & Norman to manage their condominiums. Legum and Norman hired the defendant, an engineering firm, to draw plans to repair crumbling balconies. Based on the defendant's plans, the plaintiff employed Brisk Waterproofing to repair the balconies. The plaintiff sued Legum & Norman (the managers) and the defendant engineers because they were not satisfied with the repairs. The complaint conceded that Brisk's work was performed properly. Legum & Norman filed a third party complaint against Brisk Waterproofing.

Issue: When is a third party complaint proper?

Rule: A third party claim is only appropriate if the third party plaintiff is claiming that the third party defendant is derivatively liable to him (i.e., the third party defendant must reimburse the original defendant for all or part of anything he must pay the original plaintiff). It is not appropriate in suits such as this, where the defendant makes a third party claim in order to state, "It was him, not me."

Amco Constr. Co. v. Mississippi State Bldg Comm'n (1979)

Facts: Mississippi State Building Commission (Commission) hired Amco to construct a park. Amco posted a performance and payment bond, using Houston General as surety. Amco also hired subcontractors. Amco subsequently abandoned the project. A subcontractor sued Houston General in federal diversity jurisdiction for payment on the bond. Houston General filed third party claims against Amco and Commission for indemnification. Amco then file& a cross-claim against Commission, claiming that Commission furnished defective plans and specifications. There was no diversity between Amco and Commission.

Issue: When is it proper for a federal court to extend ancillary jurisdiction to a cross-claim that has no independent basis of jurisdiction?

Rule: A claim is ancillary if it arises out of the same aggregate of operative facts as an original claim over which the court has jurisdiction. The claim arises out of the same facts if the same facts serve as the basis of both claims or the facts upon which the original claim rests activates additional previously dormant legal rights in a defendant. In the instant case, the original suit was for performance on a bond, whereas the cross-claim was for breach of contract. The claims arose from different transactions, required substantially distinct fact-finding efforts, and the cross-claim did not depend on the original claim for its existence. Therefore, supplemental jurisdiction did not extend to the cross-claim.

Helzberg's Diamond Shops v. Valley West Des Moines Shopping Center (1977)

Facts: Helzberg entered into a lease agreement with Valley West that provided that Valley West would not lease space to more than two additional jewelry stores. Valley West leased space to a third jewelry store, Lord's. Helzberg sued Valley West, seeking injunctive relief. Lord could not be joined as a party to the action because it was not subject to personal jurisdiction. Valley West moved to dismiss, for failure to join an indispensable party.

Issue: When should a suit be dismissed for failure to join an indispensable party?

Rule: A suit should be dismissed for failure to join an indispensable party if a judgment rendered in the party's absence would be prejudicial to that party or another defendant. A party is not indispensable to an action to determine rights under a contract simply because that party's rights or obligations under an entirely separate contract will be affected by the result.

Natural Resources Defense Council v. United States Nuclear Regulatory Comm'n (1978)

Facts: The Natural Resources Defense Council sought an injunction to prevent the U.S. Nuclear Regulatory Commission and the New Mexico Environmental Improvement Agency from issuing licenses to uranium mills without first preparing environmental impact statements. Kerr-McGee, a potential license recipient, moved to intervene in the suit, pursuant to FRCP 24. The trial court denied the motion on the ground that the movant's interests were well represented by other parties. FRCP 24(a)(2) provided that one can intervene in an action if he has an *interest* relating to the subject of the action and is so situated that the disposition of the action may *impair* his ability to protect that interest, unless the interest is *adequately represented* by existing parties.

Issue: When does a party have a sufficient interest in an action to intervene under FRCP 24(a)(2)?

Rule: A party has a sufficient interest in an action when there is a genuine threat to a substantial degree. A general interest in the public welfare is not a sufficient interest. Any significant legal effect in the applicant's interest satisfies the impairment requirement. The interest is not adequately protected by existing parties if there is even a small possibility that their interests will diverge. The court consequently granted Kerr-McGee's motion.

CHAPTER 6

CLASS ACTIONS

I. GENERALLY

A. Defined
    Class actions are lawsuits brought (or defended) by several representative members on behalf of all group members, pursuant to FRCP 23.

B. Jurisdiction
    The class representative must satisfy the requirements of subject matter jurisdiction, personal jurisdiction, and venue.

II. PREREQUISITES (FRCP 23(A))

A. Policy
    Before certifying a class, the judge must determine that certain prerequisites have been met. The prerequisites for a class action mandate the principle that one cannot automatically file a class action unless there is a definable class with specific interests at issue in the controversy.

B. Elements
    FRCP 23(a) requires that four conditions be satisfied before there is any possibility of a class action:
    Mnemonic: **CAN'T**

    1. **C**ommonality
    The class must present common questions of law and fact.

    2. **A**dequacy
    The representatives must fairly and adequately represent the interests of the class.

    3. **N**umerosity
    The size of the class must be very large so that joinder is not possible (i.e., people are from different jurisdictions or cannot afford to join).

4. <u>T</u>ypicality
The representatives must present claims and defenses typical of those of the class.

III. NAMED REPRESENTATIVE

A. Policy
After certifying the class, the court will seek out an individual who will represent that class. Every class of litigants is represented by what is known as a named plaintiff. This is generally the individual who initially files the class action.

B. Elements

1. Satisfy Requirements
Named representatives must satisfy the four requirements pursuant to FRCP 23.

2. Common Injury
Named representatives filing a class action must show a common injury.

3. Common Claims
Named representatives must be suing on similar legal grounds.

C. Headless Class Actions
In cases of class action defendants, or where the original class action plaintiff withdraws from the litigation or is disqualified, there may be a situation where a valid class action exists without a named representative. These are so-called headless class actions. A court then has several options:

1. Voluntary Replacement
The court may allow the attorneys for a disqualified named representative to locate a new individual, who fulfills all of the qualifications for named representative, to voluntarily pick up where the disqualified representative left off.

2. Assigned Representative
For class action defendants, and some class action plaintiffs, a court may simply assign a named representative to prevent dismissal of an action.

3. Retained Representative
The court may decide to maintain the original named representative despite a technical disqualification, such as mootness (as regarding the individual named plaintiff). But the court must be sure that the named individual will proceed in the best interests of the class.

IV.   CERTIFICATION

A.   Policy
Having certified the class and located a named representative, a judge must then decide what type of class action will proceed. FRCP 23(b) sets out three types of class actions. These classifications are not mutually exclusive, and a single class action may be certified under more than one classification. Furthermore, some issues may be certified under one classification, while other issues in the same class action may be certified under others.

B.   Types of Class Action

1. Legal Class Action (FRCP 23(b)(1))
The most common type of class action occurs if either of two criteria are present:

a.   Inconsistent Results
Often there is a danger that, if litigated separately, severe injustice could accrue to one or more of the class members. Examples are where substantive rights are at issue that might determine future conduct (e.g., patent infringement); or

b.   Dispositive Adjudication
Occasionally, one litigation could effectively litigate a claim of a party not present. For instance in mass tort litigation, were suits to be brought individually a

defendant may go bankrupt paying out large claims (or simply by defending individual suits) to the first few plaintiffs, before others, who may be even more seriously injured, get a chance to even litigate. This class action would allow all injured parties to at least get partial adjudication.

2. Injunctive Relief (FRCP 23(b)(2))
   Class actions will be certified under FRCP 23(b)(2) where the court has properly certified the class and has determined that injunctive or declaratory relief may be necessary.

3. Predominating Issues of Law or Fact (FRCP 23(b)(3))
   That individual class members are not identical with regard to the claims against the common defendant (or defenses against a common plaintiff) will not preclude certification if some issues of law or fact, common to all class members, predominate. A court will look at the following factors:
   Mnemonic: **COIL**

   a. **C**oncentration
      Desirability of concentrating litigation in one forum, where the class members may be from many different jurisdictions, and subject to different laws.

   b. **O**versight
      Difficulties in managing a class action with many different claims and parties who may have different interests.

   c. **I**ndividual Control
      Interest of individuals in controlling their own suits, as opposed to being thrown into a class-driven suit, where their individual concerns may not be as adequately addressed.

   d. **L**itigation
      Extent of litigation already started by other class members that may be impeded by the onset of a class action.

C.   Conditional Certification (FRCP 23(c)(l))
A certification order may be made conditional, or altered or amended to reflect a change in circumstances (i.e., a court determines a certain subclass should be decertified, or the class should be expanded, or the case requires injunctive relief, etc.)

V.   NOTICE

A.   Policy
It is not normally possible to individually notify all the class members because they are too numerous, or because not all the members can be positively identified. FRCP 23(c)(2) and 23(c)(3) require different notice depending on the type of class action certified.

B.   Requirements for FRCP 23(b)(3) Class Actions (FRCP 23(c)(2))

1. Best Notice Practicable
The court must notify FRCP 23(b)(3) class members in the best practicable way. The Supreme Court has held that this means that every class member must receive individual notice.

2. Opt-Out Provisions
Notice to FRCP 23(b)(3) members must include notification that individuals may be able to "opt out" of the class. If they opt out, an adverse judgment will not be binding on them, but neither will they receive any benefit of a favorable judgment. If they neglect to opt out (even if they do not actively opt in) any judgment will be binding, whether they participate actively or not.

C.   Requirements for FRCP 23(b)(l) and 23(b)(2) Class Actions (FRCP 23(c)(3))

1. Judicial Discretion
Courts have wide discretion in notifying class members under FRCP 23(b)(l) and 23(b)(2). This may include individual notice, or notice by publication. Some courts have gone so far as to require the named representative to take out

large newspaper, magazine and television advertising to contact as many potential class members as possible.

2. No Opt-Out

Individual class members may not opt out of FRCP 23(b)(1) and 23(b)(2) class actions. That is why notice requirements are not as stringent. However, this means that a class member may become bound by a suit to which the member neither had notice nor input.

D.   Costs of Notice

Often, the named representative must bear the cost of notice. However, if the individual defendant (or plaintiff) can afford to notify the class members less expensively, a court may require that defendant to notify all class members, with a reimbursement by the named representative if the costs are substantial.

VI.   JUDGMENTS

A.   Preclusive Effect

Class actions have the same preclusive effect in all class members as any other suit may have. (See Chapter 11.) A judgment in a class action is binding on all members of the class unless there is an opportunity to opt out of the class and the class member takes advantage of that opportunity.

B.   Attorney's Fees

The court's award of attorney's fees is separate from the plaintiff's award. This is unusual because in most cases attorney's fees are paid by the plaintiff out of whatever award is granted (if any).

C.   Settlements (FRCP 23(e))

Class actions may be settled by agreement between the named representative and the individual defendant (or plaintiff), as long as:

1. Notice is provided to members of the class, and

2. The settlement is approved by the court.

CASE CLIPS

Hansberry v. Lee (S.Ct. 1940)

Facts: Hansberry, a black man, purchased land that may have been subject to a racially restrictive covenant. Lee, an owner of land subject to the same covenant, sought to enforce the restriction. According to the covenant, the restriction would only be valid if signed by 95 percent of the landowners. In a prior case, to which neither Hansberry nor any other minorities were a party, a state judge had held that 95 percent of the landowners had signed.

Issue: Can an individual be bound by a prior action in which he was not a party based on the fact that both he and the party in the previous suit are members of the same class?

Rule: (Stone, J.) Due process requires that members of a class not present as parties to an action be bound by the judgment only if they were adequately represented by the parties present. Such members are also bound if they participate in the litigation, if they have joint interests, or if a legal relationship exists between the parties present and those absent such as to entitle the former to stand in judgment for the latter. None of these criteria was present in this case.

Wetzel v. Liberty Mutual Insurance Co. (1975)

Facts: Wetzel brought a Title VII class action in federal district court claiming that her employer had practiced discriminatory hiring and promotion policies. Having found that the class could be maintained under either FRCP 23(b)(2) (for injunctive relief) or FRCP 23(b)(3) (requiring notice of the suit be sent to all class members so they may opt out of the suit if they so desire), the court maintained the class under FRCP 23(b)(2) and refused to require that notice be sent to the nationwide class. The court later decided that injunctive relief would be inappropriate.

Issue 1: Where a court originally certifies a class action under FRCP 23(b)(2) but later determines that there is no need for injunctive relief, must the court recertify the suit under another classification if possible?

Rule 1: Where a class action is particularly fit for FRCP 23(b)(2) treatment because of common class characteristics (in this case, sex), the basic nature of the action is not altered because the need for injunctive relief has been subsequently eliminated.

Issue 2: If the requirements of both FRCP 23(b)(2) and FRCP 23(b)(3) are met, should the court certify the class under FRCP 23(b)(3) to provide the procedural protection of "notice" and "opting out"?

Rule 2: An action maintainable under both FRCP 23(b)(2) and FRCP 23(b)(3) should be treated under FRCP 23(b)(2). Not only will such an action benefit from its superior res judicata effect, but the procedural complications of FRCP 23(b)(3) that serve no useful purpose under FRCP 23(b)(2) will also be eliminated.

Issue 3: Does due process require a party who brings a FRCP 23(b)(2) action to give notice to all class members prior to any determination of liability?

Rule 3: The very nature of a FRCP 23(b)(2) class is that there are no conflicting interests among members of the class. As long as representation is adequate, there is no unfairness in giving res judicata effect to a judgment against all members of the class even if they have not received notice.

Phillips Petroleum Co. v. Shutts (S.Ct. 1985)

Facts: Shutts brought a class action suit in Kansas state court on behalf of royalty owners possessing rights to leases with Phillips Petroleum. The members of the class resided throughout the world. Almost all of the leases and class members had no connection with Kansas.

Issue: Can a class action suit be brought in state court though most members of the suit do not have any "minimum contacts" with the forum state?

Rule: (Rehnquist, J.) A forum state may exercise jurisdiction over the claim of an absent class-action plaintiff who lacks "minimum contacts" with the forum. However, the court must provide minimal due process protections, including reasonable notice, opportunity to be heard as well as participate in the litigation, an "opt out" provision, and adequate representation.

Cooper v. Federal Reserve Bank of Richmond (S.Ct. 1984)

Facts: Cooper and others, who had been class members in a previous discrimination suit, sought to bring individual claims of racial discrimination after the court decided that defendant had engaged in neither a general pattern nor a practice of discrimination.

Issue: Does a class action judgment preclude a class member from maintaining a subsequent civil action on the same issue?

Rule: (Stevens, J.) A judgment in a class action bars class members from bringing another action against the defendant regarding the same issues alleged at similar times.

In Re "Agent Orange" Product Liability Litigation (1988)

Facts: Vietnam War veterans initiated a class action suit to recover damages suffered by the veterans' exposure in Vietnam to herbicides produced by the defendant.

Issue 1: When may a class be certified under FRCP 23(b)(3)?

Rule 1: A class may be certified under FRCP 23(b)(3) where questions of law and facts common to the class predominate over questions affecting individuals, the class action is the best method for resolution of the suit as discovery and proof in such areas of law would be too expensive and complicated for individual attorneys, the plaintiffs are a very large class, common defenses are applicable to the plaintiff class as a whole, and certification may encourage settlement.

Issue 2: When may a class be certified under FRCP 23(b)(l)(A)?

Rule 2: FRCP 23(b)(l)(A) applies where there exists a risk of inconsistent results from trying each case separately. But FRCP 23(b)(l)(A) will no apply where the risk of inconsistent results in individual actions is merely the possibility that defendants will prevail in some cases and not in others.

Issue 3: When may a class be certified under FRCP 23(b)(l)(B)?

Rule 3: Certification under FRCP 23(b)(l)(B) is allowed for punitive damages where individual adjudication would impede the ability of other class members to protect their interests.

Issue 4: To bring a class action, what characteristics must the class members have in common?

Rule 4: FRCP 23(a) requires that the class be so numerous that joinder of all members is impracticable, that there be questions of law or fact common to the class, that the claims of the representative parties be typical of the claims of the class, and that the representative parties adequately protect the interests of the class.

Issue 5: When is a definition of a class too subjective to be applicable in a class action?

Rule 5: Subjectiveness does not affect the applicability of the class trial's findings to members of the class.

Issue 6: How should notice be given in a class action suit under FRCP 23(b)(3) where not all of the class members' locations are known?

Rule 6: FRCP 23(c)(2) provides that notice for class actions maintained under FRCP 23(b)(3) be the most efficient under the circumstances, including individual notice to all who can be identified through reasonable effort.

Note: The total settlement was originally $180 million, although due to interest it accrued, the fund became worth $240 million. The court appointed two special masters to determine how the fund should be distributed. $170 million went to a "Death & Permanent Disability Fund." The maximum award any single veteran received from the fund was $12,790 if the veteran had been completely disabled, to be paid out over ten years. Families of deceased veterans received a lump sum of about $3,400. $52 million went towards a "Class Assistance Foundation" to fund programs designed to benefit the entire class, but would be rendered virtually meaningless were it to distributed in tiny amounts to each class member. $5 million went to trust funds to compensate class members who were citizens of Australia and New Zealand. Attorneys for the plaintiffs received over $13 million to pay for their services and any expenses incurred.

United States Parole Commission v. Geraghty (S.Ct. 1980)

Facts: Geraghty had been convicted of a federal offense and imprisoned. Geraghty was later denied parole based on guidelines established by the United States Parole Board. Geraghty then brought a class action claiming that the guidelines established by the Board violated the Parole Commission and Reorganization Act. Class certification was denied. Plaintiff appealed but was released from prison before any brief could be filed.

Issue: Will an action brought on behalf of a class become moot upon expiration of the named plaintiffs substantive claim?

Rule: (Blackmun, J.) Actions brought on behalf of a class do not become moot upon expiration of the named plaintiffs substantive claim because class action claims capable of repetition yet evading review may be litigated by a plaintiff even after losing his personal stake; because a plaintiffs substantive claims are moot due to an occurrence other than a judgment on the merits does not mean that the claims of the class are also moot. A new named party should be found, or if none, the suit may continue with the inadequate named party if it is determined he is sufficiently motivated to adequately represent the class.

Lindy Brothers Builders, Inc., of Philadelphia v. American Radiator & Standard Sanitary Corp. (1973)

Facts: The plaintiffs – builders and owners in a class action – reached a settlement agreement establishing a single fund to satisfy the claims of represented and unrepresented claimants. Kohn and Berger, attorneys for the builders, petitioned for attorney's fees. The court awarded attorney's fees without holding an evidentiary hearing.

Issue 1: Does a court have authority to award attorney fees to plaintiffs who settled an action rather than pursuing it to successful judgment?

Rule 1: A court may use its equitable powers to compensate individuals whose actions in commencing, pursuing, or settling litigation benefit a class of persons not participating in the litigation.

Issue 2: What standards should a court follow in exercising its discretion to award attorney's fees in class action suits?

Rule 2: Awarding attorney's fees in class actions serves to compensate the attorney for the reasonable value of services rendered that benefitted the unrepresented claimant. Before such an award is granted a court must inquire into the quantity of hours spent by the attorneys, the value of services rendered to the class, and the extent to which the unrepresented claimants benefitted from these services as compared with the rest of the class. An evidentiary hearing should be held to provide a basis for resolving disputed factual matters.

Gonzales v. Cassidy (1973)

Facts: Gonzales sought to represent a class in an action that had already been litigated in a prior lawsuit involving the same class, the same defendant, and the same issues. The previous class representative, Gaytan, did not appeal an order which granted relief for himself but not for the class.

Issue: Will the failure of a class representative to appeal an order denying relief to everyone in the class except for the class representative preclude any res judicata effect?

Rule: A class action judgment will bind only those members of the class whose interests have been adequately represented by parties to the litigation. A class representative who obtained relief only for himself and failed to prosecute an appeal on behalf of the other class members inadequately represented the class.

General Telephone Co. v. Falcon (S.Ct. 1982)

Facts: Falcon, a Mexican-American, brought a class action suit against his employer, General Telephone Co., claiming illegal discrimination in its promotion policies. Falcon then sought to maintain a discrimination class action based on General Telephone's hiring policies.

Issue: Can a plaintiff maintain a class action on behalf of a class to which he is not a member, but which is factually related to issues relating to his class action suit?

Rule: (Stevens, J.) The type of injury claimed by the plaintiff must be the same as that type of injury claimed by the class purported to be represented. That all the class members share a common bond (such as race) is not necessarily enough. Nor is it enough that all class members claim discrimination. The type of discrimination must have affected the named plaintiff as well as the class members.

In Re Northern District of California, Dalkon Shield IUD Products Liability Litigation (1982)

Facts: Injured purchasers of Dalkon Shield's IUD devices, as well as the manufacturer appealed a district court order conditionally certifying the more than 166 pending suits in the court's district, and thousands of cases throughout the country as both a nationwide class action on the issue of punitive damages and a statewide class action on the issue of liability. Only one plaintiff and no defendants supported the class action measure. The court asserted jurisdiction pursuant to the federal interpleader statute of minimum diversity, holding that since the aggregate claims exceed the net worth of the company, the company itself is a limited fund subject to interpleader.

Issue: May a court compel class certification over the objections of both the plaintiffs and the defendants?

Rule: A court should not certify a statewide class if individual issues outnumber common issues, if the court cannot adequately fulfill the typical plaintiff requirement because of differing state standards, and if a class action is not superior to individual actions.

Eisen v. Carlisle & Jacquelin (S.Ct. 1974)

Facts: Eisen filed an antitrust and securities class action. The trial court determined that of the six million members in the class, only 7000 members would be notified personally of the lawsuit. Notice to the other class members would be accomplished by publication. The cost of notice would be distributed between both plaintiffs and defendants after a hearing on the merits.

Issue 1: Is publication sufficient notice for known members of a large class on grounds that personal notice would be too costly?

Rule 1: (Powell, J.) Due process requires that notice be made in the best method possible under the circumstances, including individual notice to all known members.

Issue 2: Can a court hold a preliminary hearing on the merits in order to determine who should pay for notice?

Rule 2: A preliminary hearing on the merits of a class action may prejudice the defendant. The plaintiff must therefore bear the cost of notice to the class except where a fiduciary duty preexisted between plaintiff and defendant.

Oppenheimer Fund, Inc. v. Sanders (S.Ct. 1978)

Facts: Representatives of the Oppenheimer Fund, in a class action suit brought under FRCP 23(b)(3), requested that Sanders help compile a list of the names and addresses of the members of the plaintiff class so that individual notice required by FRCP 23(c)(2) could be sent.

Issue 1: Can a court require a defendant to send notice to all plaintiffs in a class action?

Rule 1: (Powell, J.) Generally, the representative plaintiff should finance his own law suit. But a court can shift the responsibility of performing tasks necessary for sending notice to a defendant if the defendant could perform the tasks with less difficulty or at a lesser expense than the plaintiff.

Issue 2: Can a court require a defendant to pay for the cost of sending notice to all plaintiffs in a class action?

Rule 2: If an expense necessary for sending notice to the plaintiff class is substantial, it must be borne by the plaintiff. Only if the expense involved is minimal may such an expense be shifted to the defendant.

Grunin v. International House of Pancakes (1975)

Facts: A class action suit against International House of Pancakes (IHOP) by several franchisees had been settled. All class members received notice and an opportunity to be heard on the settlement before the court approved. Then Grunin, a franchisee, sued IHOP, claiming notice had been inadequate. Grunin had been present at the settlement hearing.

Issue: Upon what standards may a class member appeal the settlement of a class action?

Rule: Unless the class did not receive notice reasonably calculated to apprise interested parties of the settlement, or the court abused its discretion in approving the settlement, a class action settlement will not be overturned.

Vasquez v. Superior Court (1971)

Facts: Vasquez and others had purchased meat from the Bay Area Meat Company. Collection on these contracts was assigned to three finance companies. The purchasers brought a class action against the Company and the finance companies, even though no single plaintiff had a claim against each finance company.

Issue: May a class action be maintained even though no class member has a claim against all defendants?

Rule: A class action may be maintained if there is a definable class and a well-defined community of interest in the questions of law and fact involved.

Henson v. East Lincoln Township (1987)

Facts: Henson brought a class action against both a local welfare department and local welfare departments in various other counties to compel the departments to comply with eligibility and notice-and-hearing procedures.

Issue: Can a defendant class be certified under FRCP 23(b)(2)?

Rule: A defendant class cannot be maintained in an action under FRCP 23(b)(2) as such an action presents practical as well as due process problems. The factors a court should consider include the strong incentive that local welfare departments have in voluntarily bringing themselves into compliance with proper procedures, the fact that there is no provision in FRCP 23(b)(2) for "opting out" or "notice," and that many class action plaintiffs would have no claim against most of the class action defendants.

Saylor v. Lindsley (1972)

Facts: Saylor, a class representative in a shareholder derivative action, appealed the settlement made by his attorney. Plaintiff had neither known of any settlement negotiation nor approved of the settlement offer. Plaintiffs attorney had engaged in little discovery before accepting settlement.

Issue: May an attorney representing a plaintiff in a class action derivative suit settle the case without approval of the plaintiff-representative?

Rule: An attorney must keep his client informed of settlement negotiations, advise the client before signing a stipulation of settlement on his behalf, and inform the court of any objections made by the client so that it can devise procedures to allow the plaintiff to conduct further inquiry. Furthermore, settlement in a class action shareholder derivative suit by the plaintiffs attorney should not be approved over plaintiffs opposition when doubt exists as to whether there has been a truly adversary discovery prior to the stipulation of settlement.

Mosley v. General Motors Corp. (1974)

Facts: Mosley and nine others jointly filed suit alleging that General Motors and their union discriminated against them on the basis of race and/or sex. FRCP 20(a) provided that all persons may join in one action as plaintiffs if they assert any right to relief arising out of the same transaction(s) and if any questions of law or fact are common to all. The district court severed the action, having found that there were a variety of issues having little relationship to each other beyond a common defendant.

Issue: Does a Title VII action brought by several plaintiffs who allege discrimination by a common employer satisfy the FRCP 20(a) joinder requirements?

Rule: Parties may join as plaintiffs in a suit brought on the basis of a company-wide policy of discrimination because it arises out of the same series of transactions and depends on similar questions of law and fact, even if the actual effects of the policy (i.e., damages) vary throughout the class.

CHAPTER 7

PRETRIAL

I. DISCOVERY
Discovery is the obtaining of information, prior to trial, from opponents and witnesses regarding matters that are relevant to the cause of action.

A. Policies

1. Goals

   a. Preserve evidence when a witness will not be available for trial.

   b. Narrow the issues that will be introduced at trial. '

   c. Control the course of the trial and prevent trial delays and surprises.

   d. Promote just and informed settlements.

2. Concerns

   a. Control costs of discovery

   b. Prevent use of discovery as a method of one party imposing unreasonable costs on another.

   c. Prevent discovery as a method of harassing the other party.

   d. Prevent parties from gaining evidence through the hard work of others.

B. Scope of Discovery

1. Relevancy
The information must be reasonably calculated to lead to the discovery of admissible evidence.

   a. Discovery may not be used as a "fishing expedition."

b. Discovery may not be used to determine an adversary's legal analysis or strategy.

c. Nonparties may not be deposed more than 100 miles from where they live. FRCP 45(d)(2).

d. Depositions may not be used against a party without notice of the deposition. FRCP 32(a).

2. Discovery Scope and Limits (FRCP 26(b))

   a. Court Discretion (FRCP 26(b)(l))

   b. Court may limit discovery if:

      i. It is unreasonably duplicative and cumulative;

      ii. The information is more easily obtainable elsewhere; or

      iii. The discovery request is unduly burdensome.

   c. Insurance Agreements (FRCP 26(b)(2))

   d. Insurance agreements are always discoverable.

   e. Materials Used in Trial Preparation (FRCP 26(b)(3))

   f. Only discoverable if there is a substantial need and the party cannot, without undue hardship, obtain the information or equivalent by other means.

   g. Experts (FRCP 26(b)(4))

      i. Experts Who Will Testify at Trial (FRCP 26(b)(4)(A))
      Through interrogatories, a party may discover the name, subject matter, summary of facts and opinions, and grounds for each opinion.

      For further discovery, a court order is needed and the discovering party is responsible for costs. FRCP 26(b)(4)(C).

    ii. Experts Retained By Counsel But Will Not Testify
No discovery unless it is impracticable to get the information by other means. There is no discovery of experts consulted but not retained. FRCP 26(b)(4)(B).

    iii. Fees
The discovering party must pay experts a reasonable fee. FRCP 26(b)(4)(A)(ii).

3. Protective Orders (FRCP 26(c))
The court may prevent or restrict discovery to protect a party from annoyance. The court can also tailor discovery to prevent prejudice.

  a. Purpose
To protect the privacy of parties and to limit abuses of the discovery process.

  b. Good Cause
The party requesting protection must show good cause.

  c. Discretion
Courts have broad discretion in protecting a party from annoyance, embarrassment, oppression or undue burden or expense.

  d. General uses

    i. Trade Secrets

    ii. Privileged Information

4. Sequence and Timing of Discovery (FRCP 26(d))
A court may order discovery in a certain order at its discretion.

5. Supplementation of Responses (FRCP 26(e))
Normally not required, with the following exceptions:

  a. Questions Addressing:

    i. The identity and location of persons; or

      ii. The identity of experts expected to be called at trial, subject matter of testimony and substance of testimony.

  b. New Information

      i. Party knows information given is incorrect; or

      ii. Information given, though true at the time, is no longer true.

6. Verifications and Sanctions (FRCP 26(g))

  a. Documentation must be signed by an attorney or an unrepresented party.

  b. There must be a good faith belief after reasonable inquiry that information:

      i. Is consistent with the rules and warranted by existing law or a good faith extension, modification or reversal of the law;

      ii. Is not interposed for an improper purpose such as harassment or delay; and

      iii. Is not unduly burdensome or costly given the stakes.

7. Privilege
Unless the privilege is waived, privileged matters are not discoverable. Examples include information involving:

  a. The lawyer-client relationship.

  b. The doctor-patient relationship.

  c. Husband-wife (i.e., marital confidences).
Some jurisdictions limit the knowledge protected to that gained after the wedding, some jurisdictions protect only information gained before divorce, some protect only information between those two points, and some jurisdictions may not have it at all.

     d. Self-incrimination.

     e. Priest-penitent.

8. The Work-Product Doctrine (FRCP 26(b)(3) and 26(b)(4)) Information obtained by an attorney while preparing for litigation is not discoverable.

     a. Examples include:

        i. Mental impressions

        ii. Conclusions

        iii. Opinions

        iv. Legal theories

     b. Purpose
To promote full investigation of a case.

     c. Exceptions

        i. Any party can obtain his or her own statement.

        ii. The doctrine cannot be used to hide evidence or to severely prejudice a party.

C.   Mechanics of Discovery

1. Requests to Perpetuate Testimony (FRCP 27)

     a. Before Action (FRCP 27(a))
A court order allows parties to depose for the purpose of perpetuating testimony, in preparation for a yet unfiled suit. The potential adverse parties must be named, and the subject matter of the deposition must be disclosed.

     b. Pending Appeal (FRCP 27(b))
Such court orders are infrequent, and good cause must first be shown.

2. Authorization (FRCP 28)
All depositions must take place before a person authorized by the government to take depositions.

3. Oral Depositions (FRCP 30)

    a.   Once an action has been filed, no court order is required.

    b.   A deposition is initiated through the use of a subpoena.

    c.   Purposes

        i.   See how a witness will behave in court under pressure.

        ii.   Freeze testimony so witness will not recant.

    d.   Timing (FRCP 30(a))
       A deposition may be taken within 30 days of service of summons and complaint upon a defendant or service made under FRCP 4(e), unless:

        i.   Defendant seeks own discovery; or

        ii.   Witness will abscond the jurisdiction.

    e.   Corporation as Party (FRCP 30(b)(6))
       The corporation will supply appropriate experts, so that the expert is considered a party whose deposition may be used in the witness' absence.

    f.   Motion to Limit (FRCP 30(d))
       Depositions will be limited or terminated if they were conducted in bad faith or in a manner calculated to harass the deponent or party.

    g.   No Show (FRCP 30(g))

        i.   Nonparty
           If a nonparty does not show and was not subpoenaed, the deposing party bears the costs.

     ii. Party
         If a party does not show, a motion may be made to compel compliance and no subpoena is necessary.

  h. Request for Documents (FRCP 30(b)(5))
     The deposing party may attach a request for documents , pursuant to FRCP 34 to the notice of deposition. If the deponent is a nonparty the request must take the form of a subpoena duces tecum.

4. Written Depositions (FRCP 31)

  a. No court order is needed.

  b. Questions and answers are in written form only.

  c. Cheaper method but less useful since there is little flexibility, and the answers will be written by nit-picky literal-minded lawyers.

5. Interrogatories (FRCP 33)

  a. Parties Only (FRCP 33(a))
     Written questions under oath with 30 days to answer.

  b. Documents (FRCP 33(c))
     Businesses may provide documents as an answer, but only if the burden is the same for the deponent or the deposing parties to find the answer within the documents.

  c. Goals

     i. Allocate costs based on the knowledge the parties have and their available resources.

     ii. The deposing party must do the research.

     iii. Do not let the deponent do the deposing party's math and statistical analysis.

d. Concerns

    i. Answers are not generally candid.

    ii. Lawyers, and not the party, generally draft the answers.

6. Requests for Evidence (FRCP 34)
Parties may request production of documents or the right to inspect another party's land or premises if the request is reasonable.

a. Enforceability (FRCP 34(c))
A separate action may be brought to enforce this order.

b. Class Actions
This order may even be enforced against class action plaintiffs, even if they are not the named representatives.

7. Physical and Mental Examinations (FRCP 35)

a. Only enforceable against parties.

b. Court will try to protect the person's privacy as much as possible.

    i. The health of the party must be in controversy.

    ii. The scope of the examination must be specifically stated.

    iii. Court order is required and will only be granted if good cause is shown.

c. Failure to comply will bring sanctions, but generally not contempt.

d. The party examined may generally not see the report unless the party waives all doctor/patient privileges, so both sides will get each other's medical reports.

8. Requests for Admissions (FRCP 36)

   a. A party may request another to admit a matter presently at issue.

   b. The failure to admit or deny an issue is an admission.

   c. If a party denies an issue that has already been proven, forcing the other party to reprove it at trial, sanctions may be imposed.

   d. FRCP 37(c).

   e. An admission may be retracted at the court's discretion.

9. Nonparty Documents (FRCP 45(b))
Are only accessible if a court issues a subpoena duces tecum.

D.   Sanctions for Noncompliance (FRCP 37)

1. Motions To Compel Discovery
The refusing party must pay reasonable expenses incurred in obtaining a court order if refusal was without sufficient justification.

2. Failure to Comply with Court Order

   a. Opposing party can be held in contempt of court.

   b. Failure to respond to requests could be deemed admission of the facts.

   c. Opposing party can be fined or imprisoned.

   d. An action or defense can be dismissed.

II.   PRETRIAL CONFERENCE

A.   Purposes
A pretrial conference is used for trial preparation to:

1. Clarify issues.

2. Amend pleadings.

3. Identify witnesses and documents.

4. Discuss settlement or extrajudicial procedures (i.e., alternate dispute resolutions, special proceedings).

B.   Scheduling
In most cases, a judge is required to issue a scheduling order within 120 days after the complaint is filed.

C.   Limits
A pretrial conference may not be used to:

1. Serve as a substitute for trial.

2. Steal opponent's trial preparation.

III.   PRETRIAL ORDER

A.   Purposes
A pretrial order serves to:

1. Document the issues agreed upon at the pretrial conference.

2. Control the parties' courses of action.

B.   Effects
Failure to comply with the pretrial order can result in:

1. Striking of pleadings or defenses.

2. Exclusion of evidence at trial.

3. Dismissal of action.

4. Mistrial.

5. Attorney's fees.

CASE CLIPS

Kelly v. Nationwide Mutual Insurance Co. (1963)

Facts: Kelly sued for damages. Kelly answered all of Nationwide's interrogatories, but Nationwide moved to require more complete answers.

Issue: What information may be discovered through the use of interrogatories?

Rule: Interrogatories may discover information that is not privileged, that would be admissible as evidence in the action, and that is relevant to an issue in the action, as distinguished from merely being relevant to an issue in the pleading.

Lindberger v. General Motors Corp. (1972)

Facts: Lindberger alleged General Motors' negligence in manufacturing a front end loader sold to Lindberger's employer. General Motors refused to answer interrogatories about changes made after production of the loader.

Issue: Can a party avoid answering interrogatories by claiming that the information sought is inadmissible at trial under FRCP 26(b)?

Rule: Even if the information sought would be inadmissible at trial, a party cannot avoid answering interrogatories under FRCP 26(b) when the information asked for is relevant to the subject matter of the litigation.

Marrese v. American Academy of Orthopaedic Surgeons (1985)

Facts: The American Academy of Orthopaedic Surgeons (Academy) refused to admit two surgeons who had applied for membership. The surgeons alleged violations of antitrust laws by the Academy. The Academy then refused to produce confidential membership applications requested during discovery.

Issue: Can a motion under FRCP 26(c) to limit discovery bar a party from access to all confidential information?

Rule: A motion under FRCP 26(c) does not bar discovery of confidential information that is essential to developing a case.

Membership files are discoverable in appropriate circumstances subject to adequate safeguards.

Seattle Times Co. v. Rhinehart (S.Ct. 1984)

Facts: Rhinehart, the leader of a religious group called the Aquarian Foundation, brought a state action in Washington against the Seattle Times, alleging defamation of character and invasion of privacy. The trial court ordered Rhinehart to provide information requested in discovery and issued a protective order prohibiting the Seattle Times from using the information except for at trial.

Issue 1: Under Washington's Civil Rule 26(c), may a trial court prohibit parties from publicly revealing confidential information?

Rule 1: (Powell, J.) Rule 26(c) confers broad discretion on a trial court to decide when a protective order is appropriate and what degree of protection is required.

Issue 2: Does a protective order prohibiting publication of materials violate First Amendment rights of free speech?

Rule 2: If a protective order, limited to pretrial civil discovery, is granted on a showing of good cause, the First Amendment is not violated when the protective order does not restrict dissemination of the protected information if gained from other sources.

Note: Washington's Civil Code is modeled on the Federal Rules of Civil Procedure.

Less v. Taber Instrument Corp. (1971)

Facts: Less subpoenaed Teledyne, a nonparty corporation, in order to depose its director, Henry E. Singleton. Although the corporation was properly served, Singleton was not.

Issue: Does FRCP 30(a) require a nonparty director of a nonparty foreign corporation to be personally served?

Rule: FRCP 30(a) does not distinguish between parties and nonparties. When a nonparty corporation is properly served, its nonparty directors, though not personally served, may be deposed.

Hart v. Wolff (1971)

Facts: In a defamation suit against him, Wolff moved pursuant to FRCP 34 to have Hart produce certain corporate documents. Hart contended that the records were not in his possession, custody, or control since he was no longer an officer of the corporation, but merely an employee.

Issue: Under FRCP 34, when are documents in a person's possession, custody, or control?

Rule: A prima facie showing that the party served has some control over the documents sought must be made. Even if the party does not have absolute control, a showing that the party refused to use any influence it might have in producing the documents is sufficient.

Schlagenhauf v. Holder (S.Ct. 1964)

Facts: Holder and other bus passengers involved in a collision between a Greyhound bus and a tractor trailer sued Schlagenhauf (the bus driver), Greyhound (the bus line), Contract Carriers (the tractor owner), McCorkhill (the truck driver), and National Lead (the trailer owner). Contract Carriers and National Lead claimed the accident was due to Schlagenhauf's negligence and requested, pursuant to FRCP 35(a), that Schlagenhauf submit to four physical and mental examinations.

Issue: Under what circumstances may a court order a party to submit to mental and physical exams pursuant to FRCP 35?

Rule: (Goldberg, J.) FRCP 35 requires an affirmative showing that each condition to which an examination is sought is really and genuinely in controversy and that good cause exists for ordering each particular exam. FRCP 35 applies to all parties to the action, even if they are not party to the specific claim.

Concurrence: (Black, J.) Where allegations of a party put another party's health "in controversy," an examination may be made pursuant to FRCP 35.

Dissent: (Douglas, J.) Ordering defendants to submit to physical examination must be very limited. In an examination there is no judge present to ensure that a doctor's probing is limited only to what is relevant to the case. The right to keep one's person inviolate should not be affected simply because one has been sued.

Richmond v. Brooks (1955)

Facts: Richmond, a California resident, sued her ex-husband, a New Yorker named Brooks in New York. Richmond, who did not personally attend the trial, offered her deposition as evidence. The court dismissed the action for failure of proof.

Issue: When may a nonresident party's deposition be admitted as evidence?

Rule: If the requirements of FRCP 32(a)(3)(B) are met (i.e., the party is unavailable), that party may submit to the court a deposition in lieu of personal appearance at the trial.

Hickman v. Taylor (S.Ct. 1947)

Facts: Taylor, the owner of a tugboat that sank, had obtained statements from survivors. Hickman, representing the deceased, requested copies of the statements but Taylor refused.

Issue: What written statements, private memoranda, and personal recollections may a party secure from an opponent?

Rule: (Murphy, J.) A party may secure written statements, private memoranda, and personal recollections from an opponent only if the party shows necessity or undue prejudice.

Concurrence: (Jackson, J.) Discovery should not be allowed to enable counsel to perform its functions on wits borrowed from its adversary. To rule otherwise would be to force attorneys to tell their opponent everything they have learned via their own hard work.

Upjohn Co. v. United States (S.Ct. 1981)

Facts: Upjohn lawyers conducted an internal investigation to determine whether illegal bribes had been made to foreign governments by the company's subsidiaries. The lawyers made notes and memos about the investigation. The government sought discovery of the notes and memos to aid in its prosecution of Upjohn for those same alleged offenses.

Issue: What documents produced by attorneys are protected by the work-product rule?

Rule: (Rehnquist, J.) An attorney's notes and memos are protected by the work-product rule and, therefore, are not subject to discovery, when they reveal the attorney's mental processes in evaluating attorney-client communications.

Perry v. W.S. Darley & Co. (1971)

Facts: Perry was struck by W.S. Darley's fire truck and sued for damages. W.S. Darley demanded the names of Perry's expert witnesses who examined the truck after the accident.

Issue: Must a party disclose the names of expert witnesses who will not testify at trial?

Rule: A party does not have to disclose the names of expert witnesses who will not testify unless there is a showing of exceptional circumstances or the experts were witnesses or parties with respect to the subject matter of the suit.

Cine Forty-Second Street Theatre Corp. v. Allied Artists Pictures Corp. (1979)

Facts: The Cine Forty-Second Street Theatre Corporation (Cine) sued Allied Artists Pictures Corporation (Allied) under antitrust laws. Allied served Cine with detailed interrogatories. Cine then failed to obey two court orders requiring more specific answers to Allied's requests for discovery.

Issue: When is failure to obey an order compelling discovery sufficient to justify the harshest disciplinary measures available under FRCP 37?

Rule: Since the basic purpose of FRCP 37 is strict adherence to the responsibilities counsel owe to the court and to opposing counsel, gross negligence is sufficient to justify the harshest disciplinary measures under that rule.

G. Heileman Brewing Co. v. Joseph Oat Corp. (1989)

Facts: A federal magistrate ordered Joseph Oat to send a corporate representative with the authority to make a full settlement to a pretrial conference, in the interests of discussing disputed issues and possibly obtaining a settlement. Joseph Oat sent two attorneys to the meeting, but failed to send a corporate representative. The court determined this omission to be a violation of the court order, and imposed a sanction pursuant to FRCP 16(f). Joseph Oat appealed the sanction, contending that the silence of FRCP 16(a)(5) as to a court's authority to compel such an appearance prohibited the court from making such an order.

Issue: May a federal court order litigants already represented by counsel to appear before it in person at a pretrial conference for the purpose of discussing settlement of the case?

Rule: The absence of specific language in FRCP 16 authorizing a court to compel a represented defendant to appear at a pretrial conference does not signify that the power to do so is prohibited. FRCP 16 is intended to allow courts to actively manage and prepare cases for trial, and should therefore not be construed as a device to limit the authority of the district judge in the conduct of pretrial conferences.

Payne v. S.S. Nabob (1962)

Facts: In a pretrial memorandum, duly noted in the judge's pretrial report, Payne stated that he was relying on the condition of a winch to prove his cause of action. It also included a list of witnesses. At trial, S.S. Nabob's objection was sustained when Payne asserted that other elements (aside from the winch) would be used to prove his cause of action. In addition, two witnesses not listed in the memorandum were not allowed to testify.

Issue: Is a judge's pretrial memorandum invalid because it is not titled as an "order"?

Rule: A pretrial memorandum is not merely preparatory to the conference. Its contents must be accorded weight similar to an "order."

Smith Contracting Corp. v. Trojan Construction Co. (1951)

Facts: Trojan Construction Company leased equipment to Smith Contracting Corporation that was returned in a damaged condition not resulting from normal wear and tear. At trial, Smith Contracting attempted to introduce evidence not mentioned in the pretrial order.

Issue: Can a party amend its answer at trial to include a counterclaim even if such evidence is not included in the pretrial order?

Rule: Rigid adherence to pretrial orders should be relaxed if one party will not be prejudiced and if disallowing an amended answer results in injustice to the party seeking the amendment.

Dodson v. Persell (1980)

Facts: Dodson sued Persell for personal injuries sustained in a car accident. Persell, claiming "work-product" immunity, refused to disclose surveillance photos Persell took in anticipation of the suit to be brought by Dodson.

Issue: Do surveillance materials fall under work-product immunity?

Rule: Surveillance materials are discoverable if they will be used as evidence at trial. Work product is that work done by an attorney in the process of representing his client and is usually not subject to discovery.

O'Donnell v. Breuninger (1949)

Facts: O'Donnell's wife abandoned him for Breuninger. O'Donnell sued Breuninger for alienation of affection and loss of consortium. O'Donnell refused to disclose information obtained from his attorney about his wife, claiming spousal immunity.

Issue: Must a party answer all questions requested of him during discovery?

Rule: Discovery is limited to questions that are relevant to the subject matter of the litigation. Privileged matters are not discoverable.

Oppenheimer Fund, Inc. v. Sanders (S.Ct. 1978)

Facts: Representatives of the Oppenheimer Fund, in a class action suit brought under FRCP 23(b)(3), requested that Sanders help compile a list of the names and addresses of the members of the plaintiff class so that individual notice required by FRCP 23(c)(2) could be sent.

Issue 1: Can a court require a defendant to send notice to all plaintiffs in a class action?

Rule 1: (Powell, J.) Generally, the representative plaintiff should finance his own lawsuit. But a court can shift the responsibility of performing tasks necessary for sending notice to a defendant if the defendant could perform the tasks with less difficulty or at a lesser expense than the plaintiff.

Issue 2: Can a court require a defendant to pay for the cost of sending notice to all plaintiffs in a class action?

Rule 2: If an expense necessary for sending notice to the plaintiff class is substantial, it must be borne by the plaintiff. Only if the expense involved is minimal may such an expense be shifted to the defendant.

Leumi Financial Corp. v. Hartford Accident & Indemnity Co. (1969)

Facts: Leumi Financial Corporation (Leumi) sued on a bond issued by Hartford Accident Indemnity Company (Hartford) to recover losses from the dishonest, fraudulent, or criminal acts of Leumi's employee. In interrogatories, Leumi asked Hartford to define dishonest and fraudulent.

Issue: When are interrogatories requiring opinions or conclusions proper?

Rule: "Opinion-seeking interrogatories" are proper if the responses would benefit the administration of justice (e.g., narrow the issues) and such benefit outweighs the potential prejudice the answering party's case will bear.

O'Brien v. International Brotherhood of Electrical Workers (1977)

Facts: In a disciplinary action, the International Brotherhood of Electrical Workers (IBEW) fined O'Brien for distributing anti-union information. O'Brien sued, claiming his right of free speech had been violated. IBEW refused to explain why O'Brien was fined.

Issue: When does the basis for an internal disciplinary hearing constitute a legal opinion, which is not subject to discovery?

Rule: An interrogatory that seeks a party's application of law to the central facts of the case (i.e., the party's legal theory) is proper, but an interrogatory extending to issues of pure law (i.e., legal issues or conclusions unrelated to the facts of the case) are not proper.

Payne v. Howard (1977)

Facts: Payne sued Dr. Howard for medical malpractice. Howard refused to produce certain requested documents relating to his dental practice, claiming the information was irrelevant and privileged.

Issue: What documents, inadmissible in trial due to privilege or irrelevance, are nevertheless discoverable?

Rule: Information is discoverable if it appears reasonably calculated to lead to the discovery of admissible evidence. Consequently, pleadings from prior suits are not discoverable because they do not typically lead to admissible evidence; tax returns are discoverable if access to them is essential to discovering relevant information that is not obtainable by other means; and, although patients must consent to disclosure of their records, the names and addresses of patients who underwent the same procedure as the plaintiff are discoverable.

Gray v. Board of Higher Education, City of New York (1982)

Facts: Gray, a black college instructor at the City University of New York (CUNY), was denied promotion and tenure. Gray sought discovery of the votes and discussions of CUNY's committee members.

Issue: When is academic information privileged information?

Rule: When an academic committee fails both to articulate reasons and provide evidence supporting denial of reappointment or tenure, discovery of the committee's deliberations is permissible because it is necessary to prove discriminatory intent.

Brown v. Superior Court In & For Maricopa Cy. (1983)

Facts: Brown's printing company burned down. Continental, Brown's insurance company, paid for the loss, but refused to pay for valuable papers inside the building as well as the loss of certain earnings. Brown and Continental arbitrated the claim, but then Brown refused to accept the arbitral award. Brown then sued Continental, claiming "bad faith." Brown sought, through discovery, Continental's entire claims file on Brown's business. Continental refused, claiming that portions of the file contained legal theories and opinions, which are undiscoverable under FRCP 26(b)(3).

Issue: When are legal theories and opinions discoverable despite FRCP 26(b)(3)?

Rule: When legal theories and opinions are a central issue to a party's claim, they are discoverable.

Langdon v. Champion (1988)

Facts: The Langdons, in their personal injury suit against Champion, requested production of Champion's insurance company adjustors' reports and files that had been created prior to commencement of the suit.

Issue 1: When are papers created prior to litigation exempt from discovery due to the attorney-client privilege?

Rule 1: Although a majority of states exempt statements by the insured to the insurer on the basis of attorney-client privilege, the Alaska court joined the growing minority of states in abolishing that rule. First, the insurance company does not always act as the insured's attorney; it may use the information gained to deny the insured's claim, or to even bring a claim against the insured. Second, there is a general policy in favor of liberal discovery rules.

Issue 2: When are papers created prior to litigation exempt from discovery due to the work-product doctrine?

Rule 2: The Alaska court rejected a minority position holding that all insurance reports are completed "in anticipation of litigation." Instead, it retained the majority view that litigation is not "anticipated" until an attorney has become involved.

McDougall v. Dunn (1972)

Facts: McDougall was injured in a car driven by Dunn. Dunn refused to produce statements made by Dunn, McDougall, and another passenger to Dunn's insurance company.

Issue: Are statements made to a party's insurer before a lawsuit has commenced privileged from discovery?

Rule: Statements not specifically made in anticipation of litigation are discoverable, especially if the party seeking discovery will be prejudiced were the statements not disclosed.

Ager v. Jane C. Stormont Hospital & Training School for Nurses (1980)

Facts: Emily Ager was born a quadriplegic. Her father sued the Jane C. Stormont Hospital & Training School for Nurses. Through interrogatories, the school tried to discover the names of Ager's experts.

Issue: Can a party routinely discover the names of experts?

Rule: The identity of an expert who is not expected to be called as a witness is not discoverable, unless there is a showing of exceptional circumstances.

McSparran v. Hanigan (1963)

Facts: The plaintiff brought an action for wrongful death against McShain. Under FRCP 36, McShain requested that the plaintiff admit that McShain owned the property where the decedent worked. The plaintiff made the admission one week before trial. The state's workmen's compensation law immunized employers from wrongful death suits. McShain read the plaintiffs admission at trial, claiming this admission made him an employer protected by law.

Issue: Is an admission, made via FRCP 36, binding at trial?

Rule: A FRCP 36 admission is binding on a party as the truth.

Drum v. Town of Tonawanda (1952)

Facts: The Town of Tonawanda refused to answer Drum's interrogatories, claiming Drum had access to the information he sought from previous depositions.

Issue: Must interrogatories be answered if the answers sought are contained in previously-taken depositions?

Rule: Since there are restrictions on the use of depositions and interrogatories help narrow the issues, a party must answer interrogatories even if the information sought is already contained in prior depositions.

Hertz v. Graham (1961)

Facts: As a result of a collision between Hertz's and Graham's race horses, Hertz's horse died. Hertz sued Graham for negligence. Graham objected to the introduction at trial of depositions taken from out-of-state witnesses.

Issue: Can depositions of unavailable witnesses be read into the record?

Rule: Depositions of unavailable witnesses are admissible evidence if the elements of FRCP 26(d)(3) (now FRCP 32(a)(3)) are met and the testimony is reliable.

National Hockey League v. Metropolitan Hockey Club, Inc. (S.Ct. 1976)

Facts: As a result of Metropolitan failing to obey a court order requiring it to provide the National Hockey League with answers to certain interrogatories, Metropolitan's antitrust suit was dismissed.

Issue: Can a complaint be dismissed on the grounds that a party failed to respond to discovery orders?

Rule: (Per Curiam) FRCP 37 permits a complaint or portions of pleadings to be dismissed if, in bad faith, a party fails to comply with discovery orders.

Securities and Exchange Commission v. Banca Delia Svizzera Italiana (1981)

Facts: The Securities and Exchange Commission (SEC) prosecuted Banca Delia Svizzera Italiana (BSI) for insider trading. The SEC asked BSI for names of BSI's undisclosed principals who traded the stocks. If BSI complied with the SEC's disclosure request, BSI could possibly be exposed to criminal liability in Switzerland.

Issue: Must a foreign entity answer civil interrogatories if disclosure could lead to foreign criminal liability?

Rule: A foreign party must answer interrogatories when, in bad faith, it uses foreign law to shield itself from the reach of the laws of the United States.

Societe Nacionale Industrielle Aerospatiale v. United States District Court of Southern District of Iowa (S.Ct. 1987)

Facts: Societe Nacionale Industrielle Aerospatiale (SNIA), a French company, refused to comply with an American discovery order made pursuant to the FRCP. SNIA asserted that discovery requests must be made pursuant to the Hague Convention, and not be contrary to French law. The discovery request neither comported with the Hague Convention, nor with French law.

Issue: Must discovery against a foreign defendant comply with the Hague Convention?

Rule: (Stevens, J.) The Hague Convention gives an alternate route through which discovery may be maintained. However, the Hague Convention does not preempt traditional discovery procedures, if available.

Marek v. Chesny (S.Ct. 1985)

Facts: While responding to a call, three police officers shot and killed Chesny's son. Chesny rejected a settlement of $100,000 that included attorney's fees. After receiving a jury award of only $60,000, Chesny requested, under 42 U.S.C. § 1983, $171,692.47 in costs, including attorney's fees. The police contested the request under FRCP 68 which shifted the costs of trial, after the settlement offer had been made, to the plaintiff if a rejected settlement offer is greater than the trial award.

Issue 1: Under FRCP 68, must the rejected settlement offer separately list the amount included to cover costs?

Rule 1: (Burger, C.J.) Settlement offers are presumed to cover all costs, so there is no need to list the costs separately.

Issue 2: Under FRCP 68, do "costs" include attorney's fees?

Rule 2: FRCP 68 includes all costs properly awardable under the relevant statute. Although there is a general aversion in American courts to awarding attorney's fees, 42 U.S.C. § 1983 does explicitly include attorney's fees in "costs."

McCargo v. Hedrick (1976)

Facts: McCargo sued Hedrick, Buch and Green in Federal District Court for wrongful revocation of her horse-racing license. Local Rule 2.08 and FRCP 16 were in conflict with respect to the drafting of pretrial orders. The former demanded that the attorneys confer and effectively express themselves in writing, and FRCP 16 left it within the discretion of the trial judge if he determined such a conference to be helpful. Two pretrial orders were filed but were returned to the attorneys with suggestions to prepare a third pretrial order in compliance with Rule 2.08. After the third order was not filed within the time limits of Rule 2.08, the district court dismissed the action with prejudice. McCargo appealed.

Issue: When may a court dismiss a suit for failure to comply with a pretrial order?

Rule: A district court can dismiss a suit for lack of prosecution either upon a defendant's motion under FRCP 41(b) or on its own, but dismissal should be ordered only in extreme circumstances. Factors the judge should take into account when deciding whether to dismiss include the degree of plaintiff's responsibility in noncompliance, the prejudice to the defendant caused by the delay, the willfulness of the plaintiff's noncompliance, and whether sanctions might be better suited than dismissal.

Note: The court also found that the state rule conflicted with the purposes of the FRCP 16 guidelines, and thus under *Erie*, the federal rule applies.

Pacific Indemnity Co. v. Broward County (1972)

Facts: Also known as "The Case of the Forgotten Issue." An issue was raised in a cross-claim but was not raised at trial and was forgotten until after the case had gone to jury.

Issue: When may the course of litigation deviate from a pretrial order?

Rule: The pretrial order controls the course of the litigation and once entered, pursuant to FRCP 16, it may be modified at trial only to prevent manifest injustice.

Wallin v. Fuller (1973)

Facts: In a suit brought by Wallin's wife against Fuller, Mrs. Wallin only claimed Fuller's negligence, and Fuller responded with a defense of contributory negligence. During trial, Mrs. Wallin tried to amend the complaint to include a claim of subsequent negligence, which would negate any defense of contributory negligence. Evidence on subsequent negligence had been introduced without objection.

Issue: When may a claim, not included in the pretrial order, be included during trial?

Rule: Although FRCP 16 allows amendment of a pretrial order only to prevent "manifest injustice," FRCP 15(b) provides that where, as here, issues outside the pleadings are tried by express or implied consent of the parties, they shall be treated as having been included in the pleadings.

Umphres v. Shell Oil Co. (1971)

Facts: Umphres sued Shell Oil Company alleging, among other things, conspiracy. In a deposition, Umphres refused to describe the conspiracy alleged. Shell moved to compel Umphres to answer.

Issue: In depositions, what information may parties gather regarding their opponents claims?

Rule: A party may request information relating to the factual basis for a claim, but may not inquire as to legal theories behind the claim.

Freed v. Erie Lackawanna Railway (1971)

Facts: Freed sued Erie Lackawanna Railway after being struck by one of its trains. In an interrogatory, Erie had contended that the train was not "within yard limits," requiring a lookout to prevent accidents. There was no lookout. At trial, Erie tried to show that the train was within yard limits.

Issue: Is a party bound by assertions made before trial?

Rule: Pretrial assertions are not binding on the party making the assertion, but may be used as evidence of the truth of the matter asserted in trial.

Identiseal Corp. v. Positive Identification Systems, Inc. (1977)

Facts: Identiseal Corporation's suit was dismissed when it failed to comply with a pretrial order compelling further discovery.

Issue: Does the court have the power, through a pretrial order, to compel a plaintiff to conduct discovery rather than permit him to litigate the entire suit at trial?

Rule: Under FRCP 16 (which authorizes pretrial conferences), the court may not compel litigants to complete discovery, but instead it may require litigants to merely "consider the possibility."

Duplan Corp. v. Moulinage et Retorderie de Chavanoz (1974)

Facts: Duplan Corporation sued Moulinage et Retorderie de Chavanoz (Chavanoz) for antitrust violations and sought discovery of Chavanoz's attorney's work-product material from a previously settled and unrelated action between Chavanoz and another party.

Issue: Is an attorney's work-product material from prior litigation discoverable?

Rule: An attorney's work product from a previously terminated case, including mental impressions, conclusions, or legal theories, is not discoverable in subsequent litigation.

Public Citizen v. Liggett Group (1989)

Facts: A smoker's estate sued the Liggett Group, a cigarette manufacturer, for a smoker's wrongful death from lung cancer. During trial, Liggett produced voluminous research and obtained from the court a protective order preventing use of the research for nonlitigious purposes. The smoker lost, and Public Citizen intervened to obtain the research and overturn the court order.

Issue: When may documents be barred from nonlitigatory discovery?

Rule: FRCP 26(c) creates a presumptive right of access to discovery materials unless good cause for confidentiality is shown. Only trade secrets or other specially confidential materials will be barred.

Coca-Cola Bottling Co. v. Coca-Cola Co. (1986)

Facts: In a suit between the manufacturer of Coca-Cola and some of its bottlers, the distributors requested, during discovery, the formula for Coca-Cola. The manufacturer refused to disclose the formula, even under a strict protective court order. The manufacturer acknowledged that it could be sanctioned for its noncompliance. The bottlers moved for summary judgment under FRCP 37(b), on the basis of the manufacturer's noncompliance.

Issue: Under FRCP 37(b), when will noncompliance with a discovery order warrant a default judgment of the case?

Rule: A court should consider six factors: the extent of the party's personal responsibility; the prejudice to the adversary caused by the failure to meet scheduling orders and respond to discovery; a history of dilatoriness; whether the conduct of the party or the attorney was willful or in bad faith; the effectiveness of sanctions other than dismissal, including alternative sanctions; and the meritoriousness of the claim or defense.

Rubenstein v. Kleven (1957)

Facts: Rubenstein, a single woman, sued Kleven, a married man, alleging he breached a contract whereby she agreed to render companionship to Kleven. Kleven pleaded the Fifth Amendment to Rubenstein's discovery questions, leading to the inference that illicit acts had taken place. If such acts had occurred, the contract would be void for public policy.

Issue: May a party use a refusal, based on the Fifth Amendment, to answer discovery questions to raise an inference of illegal activity?

Rule: If a party fails to answer by claiming the Fifth Amendment, the party is estopped from using the incriminating act as an affirmative defense at trial.

Kothe v. Smith (1985)

Facts: Kothe sued Smith for medical malpractice and sought $2,000,000 in damages. The judge recommended that the case be settled for between $20,000 and $30,000 and stated that if the case went to trial and then got settled for anything in that range, he would sanction the dilatory party. Smith offered $5,000 but Kothe claimed she wouldn't settle for less than $50,000. Kothe confidentially told the judge she would settle for $20,000. After the first day of trial they settled for $20,000, but the judge only sanctioned Smith.

Issue: May a judge impose sanctions to pressure parties to settle?

Rule: Although the law favors voluntary settlement, it does not sanction efforts by trial judgment to effect settlements through coercion, especially when placed on one party alone.

Vinson v. Superior Court (1987)

Facts: Vinson brought suit against a community college for sexual harassment and intentional infliction of emotional distress. The college then moved for an order compelling Vinson to undergo a psychological examination to determine the extent of the emotional distress.

Issue 1: Is a mental examination appropriate in a sexual harassment case?

Rule 1: A mental examination is appropriate in a sexual harassment case only if allegations include emotional and mental damages.

Issue 2: Does a party alleging sexual harassment waive the right to sexual privacy?

Rule 2: A party claiming sexual harassment does not waive the right to privacy regarding sexual history and practices.

Issue 3: Can an attorney be present during the psychological examination of a client?

Rule 3: As long as the client's interest is adequately protected, an attorney is not permitted to be present during the psychological examination of the client.

Herbert v. Lando (S.Ct. 1979)

Facts: Herbert, a public figure, sued Lando, a TV producer-editor for defamation. On First Amendment grounds, Lando refused to answer interrogatories about the editorial process.

Issue: Does the First Amendment protect against inquiry into the state of mind of members of the press?

Rule: (White, J.) Inquiry into the state of mind of members of the press does not offend the First Amendment as long as the inquiry is a reasonable and necessary means to produce evidence material to the proof of a critical element of a cause of action.

Rigby v. Beech Aircraft Co. (1977)

Facts: Rigby brought suit for the wrongful death of his wife and injuries he and his children sustained in a plane crash. Rigby alleged defective design in the aircraft's auxiliary fuel system. Rigby's pleadings and interrogatory answers, as well as the pretrial order, made no mention of the main fuel system. Evidence concerning this allegedly defective main system was excluded at trial as irrelevant.

Issue: May a plaintiff introduce factual issues not contested in the pretrial order?

Rule: The pretrial order controls the course of the trial and only evidence relevant to the pleadings contained in the pretrial order is admissible.

Blank v. Sullivan & Cromwell (1976)

Facts: A group of female lawyers were rejected for associate positions at Sullivan & Cromwell. As part of a Title VII action, they sought to discover information regarding the defendant's partner selections. Under FRCP 26, a party is entitled to discovery of information that appears reasonably calculated to lead to the discovery of admissible evidence, as well as material that is relevant and admissible at trial.

Issue: Is a plaintiff alleging employment discrimination entitled to discover information about the firm's selection practices for other positions?

Rule: In a Title VII case in which a plaintiff alleges discriminatory employment practices, general information on the defendant's labor hierarchy is relevant within the meaning of FRCP 26.

Steffan v. Cheney (1990)

Facts: Steffan "resigned" from the U.S. Naval Academy after admitting he was a homosexual and appearing before an administrative board. He was not charged with actual homosexual conduct. Steffan filed a subsequent action challenging the constitutionality of the Naval regulations. He refused to answer deposition questions directed to whether he had engaged in homosexual conduct during his tenure.

Issue: In an action seeking judicial review of an administrative proceeding, what is the scope of discovery?

Rule: Judicial review of an administrative proceeding is confined to the grounds upon which the action was based. Hence, information that was not the basis for the administrative action is irrelevant and therefore not discoverable. Steffan challenged an administrative determination that he was unfit because he had *stated* that he was a homosexual. Therefore, whether he *engaged* in homosexual acts is irrelevant and not discoverable because it was not the basis for the administrative determination.

Bunzel Pulp & Paper Sales v. Golder (1990)

Facts: Bunzel discovered environmental contamination on land formerly owned by Golder. He filed suit to recover the clean-up expenses. Baggett discovered the contamination during routine testing. He later worked with Bunzel and its counsel in anticipation of the resulting litigation. Golder sought to depose Baggett without complying with the requirements of FRCP 26(b)(4), regarding discovery of facts known and opinions held by experts.

Issue 1: May a party's expert be deposed as a fact witness, thereby circumventing FRCP 26(b)(4)?

Rule 2: An expert may be deposed without complying with FRCP 26(b)(4) to the extent the questions are not addressed to "facts known and opinions held that were acquired or developed in anticipation of the litigation." To the extent the witness was an actor or viewer with respect to transactions or occurrences that are part of the subject matter of the lawsuit, he should be treated as an ordinary witness.

Issue 2: Can a party claim privilege in response to a general request for all relevant documents and things within the party's custody?

Rule 2: A party cannot resist discovery with a broad claim of privilege. Claims of privilege must be made on a question-by-question or document-by-document basis.

Coates v. AC & S, Inc. (1990)

Facts: After Mr. Coates expired, tissue samples were taken and sent to experts to determine the cause of death. The defendants sent the samples to experts, who were designated as experts retained in anticipation of litigation, but were not going to testify at trial. The plaintiff wished to depose the experts and obtain written reports and, test results. FRCP 26(b)(4) provided that a party may discover facts known or opinions held by the opposing party's experts upon a showing of exceptional circumstances under which it is impracticable to obtain the facts or opinions by other means.

Issue: When may a party compel discovery of experts consulted by the opposing party?

Rule: If each party is allowed to consult a number of experts who will disagree with each other, and only call those that will provide favorable testimony, the factfinder may be misled into thinking that professional opinion is evenly divided. The factfinder should know the extent of any disagreement among those whom a plaintiff or defendant employs. Because there is no other practicable means to obtain this information, there is an exceptional circumstance permitting discovery under FRCP 26(b)(4). Moreover, tissue samples are analogous to an autopsy, the results of which are discoverable pursuant to FRCP 35(a).

Refac International v. Hitachi, Ltd (1990)

Facts: Refac brought suit against Hitachi and numerous other defendants for patent infringement. During discovery, Refac repeatedly failed to state which of Hitachi's products were infringing and how. Consequently, judgment was entered in favor of all defendants, but the district judge declined to apply Rule 11 sanctions.

Issue: What is the standard for imposing sanctions for failure to comply with discovery requests.

Rule: To warrant imposition of severe sanctions for noncompliance with discovery requests, a court must consider: (1) the public's interest in expeditious resolution of litigation; (2) the court's need to manage its docket; (3) the risk of prejudice to the defendants; (4) the public policy favoring disposition of the case on the merits; and (5) the availability of less drastic sanctions. In this case, the sanctions were proper because Refac's conduct was willful, in bad faith, and totally unjustified.

Issue 2: Do district courts have discretion to decline to apply Rule 11 sanctions?

Rule 2: A district court has discretion to choose the appropriate sanction for a Rule 11 violation. However, a court has no discretion to refuse to declare a Rule 11 violation where one has occurred.

Pressey v. Patterson (1990)

Facts: A Houston police officer frivolously shot a truck driver in the head and fabricated a story to justify the shooting. During discovery, Houston was requested to produce tapes of an interview of the Police Department's internal affairs division. After several months, Houston responded that the tape had been erased through normal reuse. At a later deposition, it was revealed that the tape was actually burned by a police spokesman. Consequently, the judge struck Houston's answer as an abuse-of-discovery sanction and granted a default judgment against it on liability.

Issue: When is it appropriate to strike a defendant's answers as a sanction for discovery misconduct?

Rule: To warrant such a severe sanction as striking a defendant's answers for improper compliance with discovery requests, the defendant must have acted in bad faith or willfully abused the judicial machinery. In this case, the court found that bad faith or willful abuse was not presented because Houston posited reasonable explanations for some and because Houston did not disobey any direct court orders to produce specific evidence of the misconduct. Consequently, the severe sanctions were an abuse of discretion, although lesser sanctions were deemed appropriate.

McKey v. Fairbairn (1965)

Facts: Water leaked into the house McKey rented from Fairbairn, allegedly causing McKey's mother-in-law to slip and fall. The pretrial order set forth an allegation of negligence for failure to repair and eliminate a dangerous condition after receiving notice. During the trial, McKey sought to amend the pretrial order to permit him to introduce local housing regulations that required roofs and walls to be leakproof. Although the landlord was aware of these regulations, the trial court did not permit the plaintiff to change recovery theories.

Issue: May a plaintiff depart from a pretrial order and present a new theory of recovery at trial?

Rule: Where a plaintiff has not presented a particular theory of recovery until trial, refusing to permit the appellant to change her theory is within the judge's discretion.

Dissent: Whether a plaintiff should be permitted to establish a new theory of recovery during trial is determined by balancing the possible prejudice to the defendant against the injustice that would be prevented by permitting the modification. Because the defendants in this case knew of the regulations, their disadvantage would be small in comparison with the injustice the plaintiff would suffer if relevant evidence is precluded.

CHAPTER 8

ADJUDICATION WITHOUT TRIAL

I. **INTRODUCTION**
    Despite the constitutional right to trial by jury, a suit may very well be dismissed before opening arguments. Courts have several means for disposing of a suit before trial. Given the enormous costs of litigation, as well as the increasing delay brought about by overcrowded courts, it is not surprising that the law is more tolerant of pretrial resolution of disputes, especially if voluntary or if the suit is essentially frivolous.

II. **SUMMARY JUDGMENT (FRCP 56)**

A. Purposes
    Summary judgment serves to:

    1. Determine if a dispute exists.

    2. Avoid useless trials.

    3. Achieve a final determination on the merits.

    4. Eliminate certain issues or claims from trial.

B. Standards and Burdens of Proof

    1. Summary judgment may be granted only if there is no genuine issue of fact.

    2. The moving party (the party who wants summary judgment) must be entitled to judgment as a matter of law (i.e., must have a valid legal claim).

    3. The moving party has initial burden of establishing that there is no factual dispute regarding the matter upon which summary judgment is sought.

    4. All doubts will be resolved against the moving party.

    5. A judge will award summary judgment where a reasonable jury could not possibly decide against the moving party,

according to the appropriate standard the jury would be asked to apply (preponderance of the evidence, clear and convincing evidence, or beyond a reasonable doubt).

6. No summary judgments may be entered against criminal defendants.

C. Partial Summary Judgment
A court need not dismiss the entire case. If several issues are present, but one of the issues has no genuine issue of fact, the court may summarily dismiss that claim while allowing the rest to go to trial.

III. DISMISSAL OF ACTIONS (FRCP 41)

A. Voluntary (FRCP 41(a)(1))

1. The plaintiff can voluntarily dismiss an action by filing a notice of dismissal before the defendant has served an answer.

2. The plaintiff can voluntarily dismiss an action after the defendant has answered by a stipulation signed by all parties or by leave of court.

3. The first voluntary dismissal is without prejudice to the plaintiff. This means they are not precluded from bringing the claim again later.

4. After the second voluntary dismissal, the plaintiff will be precluded from bringing another action on the same claim.

B. Involuntary (FRCP 41(b))

1. Upon motion by the defendant, a court can order dismissal of the plaintiff's action for:

   a. Failure to prosecute, or

   b. Failure to comply with the FRCP.

2. An involuntary dismissal usually constitutes a judgment on the merits, except when the court dismisses without prejudice or the grounds for dismissal are:

   a. Improper venue,

   b. Lack of jurisdiction, or

   c. Failure to join an indispensable party under FRCP 19.

IV.   DEFAULT JUDGMENTS (FRCP 55)

A.   Entry of Default

   1. The clerk enters a default judgment if the defendant:

   a. Does not answer the plaintiff's complaint,

   b. Fails to appear at trial, or

   c. Fails to comply with the FRCP.

   2. If money is allegedly due, the clerk can enter a default judgment for that sum.

B.   Default Judgment

   1. A subsequent hearing may still be held to determine:

   a. Damages, or

   b. Whether the default judgment should be vacated because the defendant had a:

   i.   Valid excuse, and

   ii. A meritorious defense to the action.

   2. A motion to set aside a default judgment should be made within one year after entry.

CASE CLIPS

Lundeen v. Cordner (1966)

Facts: Miss Lundeen, on behalf of Maureen and Michael Cordner, sued Metropolitan Life Insurance to recover on a life insurance policy held by Lundeen's ex-husband, Joseph Cordner, which named Maureen and Michael as beneficiaries. Joseph's second wife, France Cordner, intervened on behalf of her and her child. France introduced evidence that Joseph had completed all the necessary paperwork designating France and her child as the new beneficiaries, and then moved for summary judgment on the grounds that Lundeen had not introduced any controverting evidence. Lundeen contended that the evidence would emerge during cross-examination of an insurance agent.

Issue: Is summary judgment permissible when a party claims that cross-examination of a witness will preclude summary judgment?

Rule: Summary judgment is appropriate when all evidence indicates that no issue of material fact exists between the parties, even if the opposing party contends that cross-examination is essential but fails to show how the testimony would be impeached or how additional testimony will be adduced.

Cross v. United States (1964)

Facts: Cross, a foreign language professor, tried to get a tax refund for the expense of attending a European seminar. The Internal Revenue Service unsuccessfully opposed Cross's motion for summary judgment. The IRS claimed there was a dispute as to the nature of the trip – information it could only get from Cross.

Issue: Is summary judgment appropriate even though the opposing party claims it's only counter evidence will come out during cross-examination?

Rule: Summary judgment is inappropriate where the inferences the parties seek to draw deal with motive, intent and subjective feelings and reactions.

Celotex Corp. v. Catrett (S.Ct. 1986)

Facts: Catrett alleged that her husband died as a result of exposure to asbestos manufactured by Celotex. Catrett sued for negligence, breach of warranty, and strict liability. Celotex moved for summary judgment under FRCP 56 on the grounds that Catrett has not offered any evidence to support the allegation that her husband had been exposed to Celotex products. Catrett argued that Celotex had to produce evidence negating the allegation that her husband had been exposed.

Issue: Must a party submit evidence to support a FRCP 56 motion for summary judgment?

Rule: (Rehnquist, J.) If the opposing party's briefs themselves satisfy the standard for summary judgment, the motion will be granted even if the motion was not supported by affidavits.

Concurrence: (White, J.) It is the defendant's task to negate the claimed basis for the suit.

Dissent: (Brennan, J.) The court sets out no identifiable standard for the granting of summary judgment. Where, as here, the party making the motion for summary judgment would also have to carry the burden of persuasion at trial, that party must support its motion with credible evidence.

Anderson v. Liberty Lobby, Inc. (S.Ct. 1986)

Facts: Liberty Lobby sued Anderson for publishing allegedly libelous articles about it. In support of its summary judgment motion, Anderson asserted that Liberty Lobby couldn't prove actual malice (the standard required for libel suits) by "clear and convincing evidence."

Issue: What standard must be applied to determine whether a motion for summary judgment should be granted?

Rule: (White, J.) In determining whether to grant a summary judgment motion, a judge must decide whether a reasonable jury could possibly find in favor of the party opposing summary judgment according to the standard the jury will ultimately use. In making this determination, the judge should resolve all issues of credibility in favor of the party opposing summary judgment.

Dissent 1: (Brennan, J.) By allowing the judge to determine whether a party has satisfied a certain evidentiary burden, the judge becomes a factfmder.

Dissent 2: (Rehnquist, J.) If the application of standards makes no difference where credibility is concerned, where could it possibly make a difference?

Coulas v. Smith (1964)

Facts: Smith sued Bray who then cross-claimed against Coulas to collect on a promissory note. Coulas answered both the cross-claim and complaint but failed to attend the trial. Smith received a judgment on the merits against Bray and against Coulas who, two years later, moved to have the judgment vacated on the grounds that he did not receive the three days' notice as required by FRCP 55.

Issue: What constitutes a default judgment for purposes of FRCP 55?

Rule: Once a party files pleadings or answers in response to any of the claims against him, any judgment is one on the merits, and cannot be a default judgment for the purposes of FRCP 55.

Arnstein v. Porter (1946)

Facts: A court granted Cole Porter summary judgment for alleged copyright infringement of Arnstein's songs. The court held that the factual dispute was so thin as to be farcical.

Issue: How strong must the factual dispute be to prevent a finding of summary judgment?

Rule: When there exists even a slight doubt regarding material facts, summary judgment is improper, and summary judgment is particularly improper when the parties' credibility is in issue.

Di Sabato v. Soffes (1959)

Facts: In a personal injury suit against Soffes, Di Sabato's summary judgment motion was denied even though Soffes failed to controvert the prima facie showing of negligence.

Issue: Can a court grant summary judgment if the defendant fails to introduce rebutting evidence of his own?

Rule: If the plaintiff's pleadings disclose no real defense and if the defendant fails to controvert plaintiff's evidence and pleadings, the court may find that no triable issue exists and grant summary judgment.

Littman v. Bache & Co. (1958)

Facts: Bache & Co. was granted an extension to file its answer. During that time, Bache & Co. moved to have the action transferred to another district court. Littman objected to the transfer, and then on the day prior to settling the transfer issue, Littman filed a notice of voluntary dismissal.

Issue: When may a plaintiff voluntarily dismiss the action?

Rule: So long as the merits of the controversy are not before the court, a plaintiff can file a notice of voluntary dismissal pursuant to FRCP 41(a) at any time.

Republic of the Philippines v. Marcos, et al. (1989)

Facts: The Philippines sought to gain possession of four New York City properties, claiming that the recently deposed President Marcos had purchased the property with illegally acquired monies. The Philippines issued an injunction to prevent Marcos from selling those properties. Adnan Khashoggi, Joseph Bernstein, and Ralph Bernstein claimed they bought the properties before the injunction. Meanwhile, Karl Peterson, acting on behalf of three of the four building owners, sued the Bernsteins for breaches of fiduciary duty committed as managers of the properties from 1983 to 1986. The Bernsteins claimed that Peterson was merely an agent for Khashoggi. The court ordered Khashoggi and Sami Fadel Barakat, another managing owner, to appear in court for depositions. Khashoggi and Fadel refused, so the judge dismissed the case pursuant to FRCP 37, which allows dismissal upon the noncompliance of a party or a party's agent.

Issue: When, for purposes of FRCP 37, is one person considered another's agent?

Rule: Where one party's interests are so closely intertwined with another's so as to consider one the alter ego of the other, noncompliance by one may warrant sanctions, even the severest sanction of dismissal if a willful or conscious disregard for the discovery process exists.

American Airlines v. Ulen (1949)

Facts: Alleging personal injuries in an airline crash, Ulen was granted summary judgment in her suit against American Airlines. American Airlines' answers to interrogatories revealed that the only dispute was the extent of Ulen's damages.

Issue: When is a party entitled to summary judgment?

Rule: A party is entitled to summary judgment when no genuine issues of material fact exist between the parties. The issue of damages may be dealt with separately.

Adickes v. S. H. Kress & Co. (S.Ct. 1970)

Facts: Adickes, a white schoolteacher, and her six black students entered S. H. Kress & Co. (Kress) for lunch. Kress served the schoolchildren, but not Adickes. Adickes then brought suit, claiming that the community's custom of segregated restaurants violated her Fourteenth Amendment Equal Protection Clause guarantees. To win her case, Adickes would have to prove a specific custom. Adickes did not offer any evidence of any custom in her complaint. S. H. Kress then moved for summary judgment.

Issue: When may a court grant a motion for summary judgment?

Rule: (Harlan, J.) A court may only grant a motion for summary judgment when the party requesting summary judgment has shown the absence of a genuine issue of fact.

Peralta v. Heights Medical Center (S.Ct. 1988)

Facts: Heights Medical center sued Peralta, alleging that he had guaranteed the debt of one of his employees. Peralta did not appear or answer, claiming that he was not properly served with process. A default judgment was entered against him and a lien was placed on his real property, which fetched a deflated price at auction. Peralta appealed, claiming that his due process rights were violated. The Texas courts rejected Peralta's appeals because he did not show that he had a meritorious defense (i.e., retrial might produce a different judgment).

Issue: May a state require that an appellant who seeks review for a due process violation must show that he had a meritorious defense to the original claim?

Rule: (White, J.) To require an appellant who has been deprived of property in a manner contrary to due process to show that he had a meritorious defense to the original action violates the Due Process Clause of the Fourteenth Amendment.

Manshack v. Southwestern Electric Power Co. (1990)

Facts: Manshack sued Southwestern Electric (SWEPCO) in Texas federal court for injuries he sustained while working on a high voltage wire. The court ruled that Louisiana law would apply, thereby limiting Manshack's recovery to workman's compensation. Manshack successfully moved for voluntary dismissal so that he could refile in state court where more favorable law might (or might not) apply. SWEPCO appealed, maintaining that the ruling caused them to suffer clear legal prejudice.

Issue: Does granting voluntary dismissal so that a case can be transferred prejudice a defendant?

Rule: Granting voluntary dismissal so that a case can be transferred may prejudice a defendant if it strips the defendant of an absolute defense, but not where, as here, it merely subjects the defendant to a second suit under the same choice-of-law rules.

Visser v. Packer Engineering Assoc.

Facts: Visser had sided with other employees in a recent battle. Packer called Visser into his office and demanded his loyalty. Visser refused and demanded an apology from Packer. Packer immediately fired him. Because this occurred nine months before Visser would have been eligible for full pension benefits, Visser brought an age discrimination suit. The court granted Packer's motion for summary judgment on the ground that there was no evidence that age or pension cost played a factor in the firing of Visser.

Issue: When should summary judgment be granted on the basis of inadequate evidence to support a claim?

Rule: Summary judgment is appropriate if, based on the evidence presented in the summary judgment proceeding, no rational jury could reach a verdict for the party opposing summary judgment.

Dissent: Summary judgment is inappropriate in this case because there are material issues of fact from which a jury could find that there was age discrimination.

CHAPTER 9

TRIALS AND JUDGMENTS

I.   BURDEN OF PROOF

A.   Burden of Production
Each party must produce sufficient evidence to prevent a directed verdict.

    1. The plaintiff bears the initial burden, then the defendant must rebut the plaintiff's evidence.

    2. The defendant submitting affirmative defenses bears the burden of proving that defense, but the plaintiff may then rebut.

B.   Burden of Persuasion

    1. The plaintiff (or the defendant asserting an affirmative defense) must persuade the jury (or judge) of the existence of the facts claimed.

    2. Generally, the burden is met where a party establishes by a preponderance of evidence (i.e., more likely than not) that the events occurred as claimed.

    3. However, stronger burdens may be applied in certain cases.

        a. Clear and Convincing
This stricter standard is most often used where personal reputation is at stake, such as libel and slander cases. This standard also applies to many aspects of family law as well as probate litigation.

        b. Beyond a Reasonable Doubt
This standard is rarely used in civil cases, since it is the highest burden available at law. It is typically used in criminal cases.

C. Presumptions

1. A presumption is a rule of law holding that when a basic fact is found, another fact is presumed to exist, absent rebuttal.

2. Various types of presumptions exist. Some may be used to satisfy burdens of production; others may not. Some may be used to satisfy burdens of persuasion; others may not. Some presumptions may be mere inferences, not enough on their own to satisfy a burden, but capable of being considered with other evidence.

II. JURY TRIAL

A. Demand For Jury Trial (FRCP 38)
Must be served on all parties not later than ten days after service of last pleading.

B. Jury Selection

1. Voir Dire

    a. Each party's counsel questions potential jurors to discover possible bias.

    b. Judge may also pose questions.

2. Juror Dismissal

    a. Provided dismissal does not violate Fourteenth Amendment (i.e., solely motivated by racial consideration, etc.), each side's lawyer has unlimited challenges for cause (i.e., bias) to juror's suitability to hear case.

    b. Each litigant gets three peremptory challenges (i.e., cause need not be shown).

C. Jury's Role
Juries decide factual issues only.

1. Basic facts
The occurrence or nonoccurrence of a fact which does not itself prove one of the necessary elements of the claim or defense.

2. Ultimate fact
Established basic facts that prove a party's claim.

D.   Jury Charge

1. Judge instructs jury as to the doctrine relevant to a party's claim and its application to factual findings.

2. Each party may submit to the judge instructions the party wants read to jury.

3. Judge's failure to submit correct instruction is reversible error if it prejudices verdict.

E.   Unanimity (FRCP 48)
The verdict must be unanimous unless parties stipulate that a stated majority shall deliver the verdict.

F.   Right to Jury Trial

1. Seventh Amendment

   a.   Guarantees jury trial in actions triable at law.

   b.   Nonjury cases

      i.   Actions in equity and cases where a jury is waived are tried before a judge.

      ii.   Trial judge must make specific factual findings and legal conclusions, clearly and distinctly stating both.

2. Mixed Legal and Equitable Claims

   a.   In federal court, where legal issues are incidental to equitable issues, a right to jury trial for legal issues exists (most state courts hold jury trial waived in this situation).

b. In federal court, where legal issues are not incidental to the equitable issue, the legal issue is tried before a jury (preferably prior to the equitable issue), and the equitable issue is tried before a judge.

3. Statutory Actions and Administrative Proceedings

   a. Congress has broad power to create a statutory right to jury trial where none existed in common law.

   b. A right to jury trial does not extend to administrative proceedings.

4. State Law Right to Jury Trial

   a. Diversity cases
   If state law disallows jury trials where federal law would permit them, federal law controls.

   b. Federal issues in state courts
   A party pressing a federal issue in state court is entitled to a jury if federal law mandates a jury trial.

III. DISPOSITION

A. Nonsuit
If after the plaintiff presents its case, it fails to show a right to relief, its case is dismissed. (The test is same as for directed verdicts.)

B. Judgment as a Matter of Law (FRCP 50)
Effective as of December 1, 1991, judgment as a matter of law encompasses the motions previously known as directed verdict and judgment notwithstanding the verdict (JNOV).

1. Directed Verdict

   a. Takes case away from jury.

   b. The defendant may move for a directed verdict at the close of the plaintiff's case-in-chief; either party may move for a directed verdict when all the evidence is in.

   c. Judge views the evidence in the most favorable light to who ever opposes the directed verdict.

   d. The motion will be granted where:

      i. There exists insufficient evidence to go to the jury; or

      ii. The evidence is such that reasonable people could not differ as to the result.

2. Judgment Notwithstanding the Verdict (JNOV)

   a. The judge substitutes his verdict for that of the jury.

   b. A party must move for a directed verdict before a motion for a JNOV is submitted.

   c. The same standard is applied as with the directed verdict.

C. Motion for a New Trial
Courts have broad discretion in ordering new trials; they may be granted based on either questions of law or fact.

1. Grounds

   a. Misconduct of judge or lawyers.

   b. Juror discovered evidence.

   c. Newly discovered evidence.

   d. Insufficient evidence to support judgment or verdict.

   e. Error in law (e.g., evidentiary rulings, erroneous jury charge).

2. Partial New Trial
Where liability is clearly established, courts can order new trials regarding a damage award that is considered inappropriate.

D.   Motion for Relief From Judgment (FRCP 60)

   1. Defined
      A motion granted where a party is prevented from presenting a full case.

   2. Grounds for Reopening a Case

      a.   Mistake or excusable neglect.

      b.   Newly discovered evidence.

      c.   Judgment satisfied or underlying prior judgment is void, reversed, or vacated.

      d.   Fraud or misrepresentation of a litigant.

      e.   Any other reason advancing the interests of justice.

   3. Other Considerations

      a.   The motion will be granted only where a substantial right is prejudiced.

      b.   The court may correct errors made by a clerk entering judgment.

IV.   VERDICTS

A.   General Verdict

   1. The jury finds for a party and grants relief without articulating specific factual findings.

   2. The implication is that all essential issues were found in favor of the prevailing party.

   3. There exists the potential to conceal the jury's misunderstandings of fact, etc.

B.   General Verdict With Interrogatories

    1. Jury is instructed to deliver a general verdict as well as answers to questions regarding essential factual findings and issues.

    2. Purpose

        a.   Ensures that the jury considered essential facts and issues.

        b.   Permits the court to verify the accuracy of verdict by comparing the verdict with the jury's answers to see if they are consistent.

    3. Generally, if the answers to the interrogatory are consistent with each other but inconsistent with the general verdict, the answers control (court may also grant new trial or direct the jury to deliberate further).

    4. If the answers are inconsistent among themselves and some are inconsistent with the verdict, a new trial results.

    5. The court must try to harmonize the general verdict with the jury's answers.

C.   Special Verdicts (FRCP 49(a))

    1. Juries make factual findings only.

    2. Judges apply the law to the juries' factual findings and render a verdict.

D.   Erroneous Verdicts

    1. Failure by a jury to follow instructions may be grounds to set the verdict aside (e.g., a compromise verdict is erroneous).

    2. An internally inconsistent verdict results when jury findings are inconsistent and irreconcilable (e.g., jury holds employer liable under respondent superior, yet finds employee acted with due care).

      3. If an erroneous verdict is correctable, a court abuses its discretion if, upon motion, it fails to direct further jury deliberations.

      4. Errors are waived unless the prejudiced party timely objects; errors that do not prejudice a substantial right are held harmless.

E.   Contempt Orders

      1. The property of the judgment debtor is seized.

      2. Only that amount of property sufficient to cover the judgment may be levied.

      3. Civil contempt of court

          a.   A party returns to court to show the other party's noncompliance with the judgment.

          b.   A noncomplying party held in contempt may be fined, imprisoned, or both until compliance results.

CASE CLIPS

Beacon Theatres, Inc. v. Westover (S.Ct. 1959)

Facts: Fox West Coast Theatres, Inc. sued Beacon Theatres, Inc., asking for a declaratory statement that it was not violating antitrust laws, and an injunction stopping Beacon from threatening Fox with antitrust suits. The declaratory and injunctive claims are both in equity, and do not receive juries. Beacon counterclaimed, alleging violation of antitrust laws and requested a jury trial pursuant to FRCP 38(b).

Issue: Is a right to a jury trial lost because the only issues for which a jury may be requested occur as part of a counterclaim?

Rule: (Black, J.) Under the FRCP, the right to a jury trial is not precluded merely because the case presents both legal and equitable issues. The same court may try both legal and equitable issues in the same action.

Dissent: (Stewart, J.) FRCP 42(b) allows the judge to hear legal and equitable issues in any manner the judge sees fit. The presence of a legal issue should not destroy another party's equitable suit.

Curtis v. Loether (S.Ct. 1974)

Facts: Curtis alleged that Loether refused to rent an apartment to her because she was black. Following a preliminary injunction, the Title VIII suit went to trial to determine damages. Loether's request for a jury trial was denied.

Issue: Is an action for damages an action to enforce "legal rights," thus allowing a Seventh Amendment right to a jury trial, even though the original suit contained an equitable issue that had already been adjudicated?

Rule: (Marshall, J.) Since the Seventh Amendment applies to subsequently created statutory rights, a jury trial must be available if a Title VIII suit involves rights and remedies typically enforced in an action at law.

Tull v. United States (S.Ct. 1987)

Facts: The government sued Tull for dumping waste on wetlands in violation of the Clean Water Act. The suit included requests for an injunction (equity) as well as for damages (law). Tull sought a jury trial.

Issue: Does the Seventh Amendment guarantee a right to a jury trial for both legal and equitable issues?

Rule: (Brennan, J.) The Seventh Amendment requires that a jury trial demand be granted to determine legal issues, but not equitable issues.

Dissent: (Scalia, J.) Once a jury is convened, it should try all the issues before it.

Chauffeurs, Teamsters and Helpers Local 391 v. Terry (S.Ct. 1990)

Facts: Employees sued their union, claiming that the union had breached its duty of fair representation while negotiating collective bargaining agreements. The employees sought relief in the form of back pay and requested a jury trial. The union moved to strike the jury trial request on the ground that no right to a jury trial exists in a duty of fair representation suit.

Issue 1: When does the Seventh Amendment impart a right to a jury trial?

Rule 1: (Marshall, J.) A party has a right to a trial by jury under the Seventh Amendment if the action will resolve the legal (rather than equitable) rights of the parties. A two-prong test determines whether the action resolves the legal rights of the parties. First, the court determines whether the issues involved in the action are legal or equitable by determining whether analogous 18th century rights were vindicated in a court of law or a court of equity. Second, the court determines whether the remedy sought is legal or equitable. The nature of the remedy sought is a weightier factor than is the nature of the issues involved. In this case, the Court found that, although both legal and equitable issues were involved in the action, the remedy sought was a legal one and the parties were therefore entitled to a trial by jury.

Issue 2: Is a damage award an equitable or legal remedy?

Rule 2: (Marshall, J.) Monetary damages are presumed to be a legal remedy. The court may, however, find damages to be equitable in nature if the monetary award is restitutionary or incidental to or intertwined with injunctive relief.

Concurrence: (Brennan, J.) If the remedy sought in an action is a legal remedy, the parties should have a right to a trial by jury. The historical analysis of issues in the first prong of the Seventh Amendment analysis is outmoded, irrelevant and unwieldy.

Dissent: (Kennedy, J.) The Seventh Amendment "preserves" the right to a trial by jury. Therefore, the language of the Constitution requires that the historical test should be the primary factor in deciding whether a right to a jury trial exists.

Hiatt v. Yergin (1972)

Facts: Yergin had contracted to resell stock to Hiatt that Yergin had purchased earlier. Yergin did not deliver. In a breach of contract action, Hiatt sought equitable relief and damages (i.e., a remedy at law). Hiatt claimed the loss of profits to be $50,000 (thus his action at law) and that unless Yergin were compelled to return Hiatt's stock, Hiatt would suffer irreparable harm (thus his action at equity). Hiatt also demanded a jury trial.

Issue: Does a party have a right to a jury trial when that party raises equitable as well as legal issues?

Rule: There is no right to a jury trial when any essential part of a cause of action is exclusively equitable in nature.

Dobson v. Masonite Corp. (1966)

Facts: Dobson orally agreed to clear timber from Masonite's land. Masonite subsequently terminated the agreement and Dobson sued for lost profits.

Issue: Is the meaning of a contract a factual issue for the jury to decide?

Rule: Since interpretation is always a question of fact, a question of contractual meaning must be determined by the trier of fact.

Segal v. American Casualty Co. (1966)

Facts: Segal demanded a jury trial more than two years after the action had been removed to federal court.

Issue: May the right to a jury trial be waived through implication if not asserted within prescribed time limits?

Rule: A right to a jury trial is not absolute and a court, in its discretion, may conclude the right to be waived if not properly asserted.

Thiel v. Southern Pacific Co. (S.Ct. 1946)

Facts: After having leapt from the window of one of Southern Pacific's trains, Thiel sued the railroad for damages. After demanding a jury trial, Thiel unsuccessfully moved to strike out the entire jury panel on the grounds that the court clerk had deliberately excluded from the jury lists all people who worked for a daily wage. After the jury had been chosen, Thiel unsuccessfully sought to challenge the individual jurors on the same grounds. The jury eventually found for the defendant.

Issue: Does the deliberate exclusion of a particular segment of the population from a jury list constitute reversible error?

Rule: (Murphy, J.) The general principles underlying jury selection make unlawful the deliberate exclusion from a jury panel of an entire class of potential jurors and, hence, such exclusion constitutes reversible error.

Dissent: (Frankfurter, J.) Unless the exclusion is based on impermissible criteria such as race, the decision to exclude some from jury service is a question of judicial administration, not constitutional imperatives.

Flowers v. Flowers (1965)

Facts: In this action for divorce, Mrs. Flowers' attempt to have a potential juror dismissed for cause was denied. The challenged juror had stated before her selection that she knew Mrs. Flowers had been unfaithful before.

Issue: Must a potential juror be dismissed if it appears that she is biased as to any of the parties or the subject matter of the action?

Rule: If challenged, a potential juror with a bias toward any litigant or the action's subject matter must be disqualified, as a matter of law, when the bias or prejudice is clearly established.

Edmonson v. Leesville Concrete Co., Inc. (S.Ct. 1991)

Facts: The defendant in a negligence action brought by an African-American used peremptory challenges to strike prospective African-American jurors. The plaintiff claimed that the defendant must provide a race-neutral explanation for the peremptory strikes.

Issue: May a private litigant in a civil case use peremptory challenges to exclude jurors on account of their race?

Rule: (Kennedy, J.) Peremptory challenges exist only because the government permits them. Peremptory challenges are thus attributable to the government, even when exercised by a private attorney. Therefore, use of peremptory challenges to exclude jurors on account of their race violates the jurors' equal protection rights.

Dissent: (O'Connor, J.) The state does not significantly participate in the peremptory challenge process, and the exercise of a peremptory challenge is not a traditional government function. Because racially motivated peremptory challenges are not state actions, they do not violate the Fifth Amendment.

Galloway v. United States (S.Ct. 1943)

Facts: Galloway claimed he went insane while fighting in World War I, and sued for disability payments from the Armed Services. He argued that the court's directed verdict for the United States deprived Galloway of his Seventh Amendment right to a jury trial.

Issue: Does a court's power to issue a directed verdict violate the Seventh Amendment right to a jury trial?

Rule: (Rutledge, J.) When a party's evidence is legally insufficient to sustain a verdict, the court may constitutionally direct a verdict in favor of the other party.

Dissent: (Black, J.) This decision erodes a large portion of the Seventh Amendment, which is the mainstay of American jurisprudence. Judges should not be allowed to make any determinations of fact.

Denman v. Spain (1961)

Facts: Ross' car and Mrs. Eva Denman's car collided, injuring Betty Denman, her daughter. Ross, Mrs. Denman, and a passenger in Ross' car subsequently died. In her personal injury suit, Denman won a jury verdict against Spain, Ross' estate. No proof of Ross' negligence was offered except speculative circumstantial evidence. Spain's motion for a judgment notwithstanding the verdict (JNOV) was granted.

Issue: Can a court overturn a jury verdict based on speculation?

Rule: Verdicts may not be based on "possibilities." Thus, a court can grant a JNOV motion when evidence is legally insufficient to support the jury's verdict.

Rogers v. Missouri Pacific Railroad (S.Ct. 1957)

Facts: In a suit under the Federal Employers' Liability Act (FELA), evidence reasonably supported a verdict for either party. The court submitted the liability issue to the jury, who found for Rogers. Reversing, the appellate court held that, under FELA, the issue could not, as a matter of law, be submitted to the jury.

Issue: If evidence reasonably supports a verdict for either party, must the court submit the issue to the jury?

Rule: (Brennan, J.) If probative facts reasonably support a verdict favorable to either party, the decision is exclusively for the jury to make.

Daniel J. Hartwig Associates, Inc. v. Kanner (1990)

Facts: Hartwig rendered consulting services and expert witness testimony to Kanner, an attorney. Hartwig allegedly lied to Kanner about his education and had problems on the witness stand when questioned about his education. Kanner withheld payment, and Hartwig sued to recover payment for the services. The district judge directed a verdict in favor of Hartwig. Although Kanner did not dispute the amount of the payments owed to Hartwig, he claimed that there was a material issue of fact as to whether the contract was void due to misrepresentation.

Issue: When is it appropriate for a court to grant a directed verdict?

Rule: A court should grant a directed verdict only if there is no credible evidence to sustain a verdict in favor of the party against whom the motion was made. Since the burden of proof for misrepresentation at trial rested on Kanner, his failure to demonstrate any evidence of reliance or damages left the court with no recourse but to find for the plaintiff.

Note: The court in this case followed Wisconsin statutory law for its decision.

Griffin v. City of Cincinnati (1952)

Facts: Griffin was injured while walking on a public sidewalk. The court refused the city's request for a special jury instruction concerning contributory negligence.

Issue: When should a court grant a party's request for a special jury instruction?

Rule: If a special charge is a correct statement of the applicable law, and failure to give the special charge is prejudicial, the court must grant the party's request for the special charge.

Nollenberger v. United Air Lines, Inc. (1963)

Facts: The Nollenbergers sued and defeated United in a wrongful death action. However, the jury's general award was far less than implied by its answer to special interrogatories concerning damages.

Issue: When a general verdict and interrogatory answers are irreconcilable, what options does a court have?

Rule: When answers to special interrogatories are consistent with each other but irreconcilable with the general verdict, FRCP 49(b) permits the court to either resubmit the matter to the jury for further consideration, grant a new trial, or calculate and enter a judgment in accordance with the special interrogatories' answers. The Rule does not, however, permit additional interrogatories to be submitted after the jury has rendered its general verdict.

Roberts v. Ross (1965)

Facts: Based solely on the pleadings, the trial judge found for Ross and directed Ross to file his proposed findings of fact, conclusion of law, and draft of judgment. Roberts filed objections, but the court signed the judgment prepared by Ross without change.

Issue: Can a judge invite counsel for both parties to submit their factual findings and legal conclusions and then order a judgment based on one lawyer's version without making his own factual findings or stating his own legal conclusions?

Rule: Although a court may invite both sides to submit their factual and legal conclusions, according to FRCP 52(a) the trier of fact must state his specific factual findings and conclusions of law sufficiently to indicate the basis of his decision.

Magnani v. Trogi (1966)

Facts: Magnani's complaint stated two causes of action. Magnani prevailed on both. The trial court, however, ordered a new trial because it was impossible to determine how the damages were to be divided between the two causes of action.

Issue: Does a trial court have the power to grant a new trial in order to correct errors made during the course of the trial by the judge?

Rule: Appellate courts will not disturb a trial court's decision to order a new trial unless a clear abuse of discretion can be shown.

Robb v. John C. Hickey, Inc. (1941)

Facts: In this negligence action, the jury returned a verdict in favor of Robb after deciding that both Robb and Hickey, Inc. were negligent, but that Hickey, Inc. was more negligent. Both parties objected, asserting ambiguity and informality.

Issue: Can a court mold an informal and ambiguous verdict to render it formal and reflective of the jury's intent?

Rule: A court can mold an informal verdict to render it both formal and effective, but where the verdict is uncertain or ambiguous, it can not be molded.

Aetna Casualty & Surety Co. v. Yeatts (1941)

Facts: Aetna Casualty sued for a declaratory judgment that its insured, Yeatts, was not covered for liability resulting from criminally-performed abortions. Following a jury verdict for Yeatts, Aetna Casualty unsuccessfully moved for a judgment notwithstanding the verdict and then moved for a new trial.

Issue: Can a judge order a new trial even if the weight of the evidence would not have supported a directed verdict?

Rule: A judge can grant a new trial if he is of the opinion that the verdict is against the clear weight of the evidence, is based upon evidence which is false, or will result in a miscarriage of justice.

Fisch v. Manger (1957)

Facts: Fisch was awarded $3,000 in damages that covered his actual loss but not his pain and suffering. Fisch's motion for a new trial was dismissed after Manger agreed to increase the verdict to $7,500.

Issue: Can a trial judge dismiss a party's new trial motion if it is conditioned upon the opposing party's consent to increase or decrease the verdict (additur or remittitur)?

Rule: A trial court has discretionary power to deny a new trial when denial is conditioned on the other party's consent to either additur or remittitur.

Doutre v. Niec (1965)

Facts: Doutre was awarded $10,000 for personal injuries from an improperly applied bleach and color treatment to Doutre's hair. Niec successfully moved for a new trial limited to liability.

Issue: Can a new trial be granted only on the issue of liability?

Rule: The questions of liability and damages are so closely intertwined that they may not usually be separated. But where liability is clear, a retrial of only the damages issue is proper.

Hulson v. Atchison, Topeka & Santa Fe Railway (1961)

Facts: Hulson was granted an extension for filing a motion for a new trial. Both the motions for a new trial and judgment notwithstanding the verdict were subsequently filed three weeks after judgment was entered, even though FRCPs 50, 59, and 60 stipulated that such motions must be filed within ten days of the judgment's entry.

Issue 1: Does ignorance of the FRCP constitute a valid defense to untimely motions?

Rule 1: An untimely motion may be entertained by the court only if its untimeliness was due to "mistake, inadvertence, surprise, or excusable neglect." Consequently, under FRCP 60, ignorance of the Rules does not furnish grounds for relief.

Issue 2: Does the fact that the motion for an extension is agreed to by the opposing party constitute waiver of the timeliness provisions in the FRCP?

Rule 2: Counsel cannot waive the strict requirements of the Federal Rules.

Hukle v. Kimble (1952)

Facts: The jury determined its award by a method known as a quotient verdict. Each juror wrote an amount on a piece of paper; the estimates were then averaged to reach a final amount.

Issue: Is a quotient verdict a valid method of damage determination?

Rule: Quotient verdicts are invalid, warranting a new trial.

Note: Today, quotient verdicts are generally allowed if the jurors do not agree to be bound by the quotient before the averaging takes place.

Griggs v. Miller (1963)

Facts: To satisfy a $2,000 judgment in favor of Griggs, Brookshire's entire farm was sold for $50,000, much less than its market value.

Issue: Is it error to execute a levy upon real property without first attempting to divide the property and sell only a portion?

Rule: When real property is levied and executed, the property must be divided (if possible) so that only that amount that is necessary to satisfy the judgment is sold.

Reeves v. Crownshield (1937)

Facts: A state statute allowed a court to order a judicial award to be paid in installments. Reeves refused to pay and was held in contempt.

Issue: Is a state statute that allows for imprisonment for failure to obey a court order to pay a debt unconstitutional as violative of due process?

Rule: After evaluating a judgment debtor's family situation, it is not unconstitutional to imprison him for failure to obey a court order to pay a debt out of income. Further, imprisonment results from not obeying a court order, not from nonpayment of a debt.

Matter of Fornabai (1964)

Facts: Fornabai was declared bankrupt and his realty was sold. The amount recovered was insufficient to satisfy two judgment liens and a U.S. tax lien. The government argued that its tax liens had priority over the judgment liens.

Issue: When is a judgment lien so perfected (choate) that the property so attached cannot be reached by competing creditors, including the U.S. government?

Rule: A judgment lien is perfected to the point of being a choate lien when the lienor, the property subject to the lien, and the lien's amount are established.

Dairy Queen, Inc. v. Wood (S.Ct. 1962)

Facts: Dairy Queen moved to strike Wood's demand for a jury trial on the grounds that Dairy Queen's action was either purely equitable or, alternatively, that any legal issues raised (i.e., the plaintiffs claim for a money judgment) were merely incidental to the equitable issues.

Issue: Does a party lose its right to a jury trial if the legal issues are incidental to the equitable issues?

Rule: (Black, J.) A claim for a money judgment is a claim wholly legal in its nature regardless of how the complaint is framed. Therefore, a damages claim is severable from any equitable issues and shall be tried by a jury if a jury is demanded.

Concurrence: (Harlan, J.) The plaintiff is not asking for damages, but an accounting, which is a wholly equitable relief. But for the case to be truly "equitable," it must be of such a complicated nature that they can be satisfactorily unraveled only by a court of equity.

Ross v. Bernhard (S.Ct. 1970)

Facts: Ross and other shareholders sued Bernhard and other directors of the Lehman Corp. alleging that its brokerage firm, Lehman Bros., controlled the corporation illegally. Ross demanded a jury trial on its claims against the corporation.

Issue: Does the Seventh Amendment right to a jury trial extend to stockholder's derivative actions?

Rule: (White, J.) The right to a jury trial attaches to those issues in derivative actions in which the corporation would have been entitled to a jury trial had it been suing in its own right.

Dissent: (Stewart, J.) The FRCP does not and cannot enlarge the scope of the Seventh Amendment. Shareholder derivative actions, a product of the FRCP, should not receive jury consideration.

Di Menna v. Cooper & Evans Co. (1917)

Facts: Di Menna sued to foreclose a mechanics lien, an equitable claim. His complaint also alleged damages, a legal claim. Cooper & Evans Company interposed a counterclaim involving purely legal issues.

Issue 1: Is a plaintiff entitled to a jury trial when seeking both legal and equitable relief arising out of the same transaction?

Rule 1: When a plaintiff seeks both legal and equitable relief arising out of the same wrong, his legal right to a jury trial is waived.

Issue 2: Can a defendant seek a jury trial on his legal counterclaim even if the plaintiff is seeking equitable relief?

Rule 2: A defendant is entitled to a jury trial on all legal issues arising out of his counterclaim. Further, the jury verdict is conclusive as to issues of fact, even for the equitable claims.

McDonough Power Equipment, Inc. v. Greenwood (S.Ct. 1984)

Facts: Greenwood sued when he was injured while using McDonough Power Equipment's equipment. After a jury verdict for McDonough, Greenwood learned that the jury foreman failed to answer a question during voir dire that may have revealed prejudice.

Issue: Is a party entitled to a new trial because a juror failed to answer a question during voir dire?

Rule: (Rehnquist, J.) The party seeking a new trial must show that the juror failed to honestly answer a material question during voir dire and that a correct response would have provided a valid basis to a challenge for cause (the motives for concealing information may vary, but only those reasons that affect a juror's impartiality can truly be said to affect the fairness of a trial).

Concurrence 1: (Blackmun, J.) Regardless of whether a juror's answer is honest or dishonest, it remains within a trial court's option, in determining whether a jury was biased, to order a posttrial hearing at which the challenging party has the opportunity to demonstrate actual bias or, in exceptional circumstances, that the facts are such that bias is to be inferred.

Concurrence 2: (Brennan, J.) To be awarded a new trial, a litigant should be required to demonstrate that the juror incorrectly responded to a material question on voir dire, and that, under the facts and circumstances surrounding the particular case, the juror was biased against the moving litigant.

Santosky v. Kramer (S.Ct. 1981)

Facts: Pursuant to New York State law, Kramer, commissioner of Social Services, commenced a parental neglect proceeding. Based on a fair preponderance of the evidence supporting the allegation against the Santoskys, their parental rights were terminated.

Issue: Can a state sever parental rights in their natural child based solely on a fair preponderance of the evidence?

Rule: (Blackmun, J.) A state can sever parental rights only in the presence of "clear and convincing" evidence supporting a claim of neglect.

Dissent: (Rehnquist, J.) The balancing of the concern for the welfare of the child over the rights of the parents was not necessarily violated by a finding of neglect based on a preponderance of the evidence as opposed to a clear and convincing standard.

Skidmore v. Baltimore & Ohio Railroad Co. (1948)

Facts: Baltimore & Ohio Railroad requested that the jury return a special (rather than general) verdict.

Issue: Must a judge require a jury to return a special verdict at the request of one of the parties?

Rule: A federal judge may, in his discretion, refuse to grant a party's demand for a special verdict.

Baxter v. Tankersly (1967)

Facts: Nine jurors signed the damages verdict (special), but only six of these signed the liability verdict (general). State law required that all jurors agreeing with a less-than-unanimous verdict sign it.

Issue: If a jury is required to return two verdicts, must these verdicts be signed by the same jurors to be valid?

Rule: Where a jury is required to return special and general verdicts and the two verdicts are not signed by the same jurors, the jury's verdict is uncertain and must be set aside as void.

Guinn v. Millard Truck Lines, Inc. (1965)

Facts: Mrs. Guinn and her daughter were injured in an accident between their car and Millard Truck Lines' truck. The Guinns sued for their injuries and Mrs. Guinn's husband (not a passenger) sued for expenses, loss of consortium, etc. The court denied Millard Truck Lines' motion for a directed verdict, and the jury returned a verdict for the Guinn women, but not for Mr. Guinn. Based on the inconsistency, Millard Truck Lines moved for a judgment notwithstanding the verdict.

Issue: Must a court grant a new trial in a case where a jury awards damages to plaintiffs for personal injuries but finds against a plaintiff with a derivative claim?

Rule: The modern approach in cases of inconsistent verdicts is for the court to attempt to reconcile them. If the jury's sole error was in failing to award one plaintiff damages for his derivative claim, the verdicts are not necessarily irreconcilable and therefore a new trial is not mandatory.

Honigsberg v. New York City Transit Authority (1964)

Facts: The New York City Transit Authority moved to have the jury verdict set aside due to evidence that damages may have been determined by averaging or compromise.

Issue: Is a quotient verdict a valid method of damage determination?

Rule: Absent a showing that the jurors agreed beforehand to be bound by the average of the amounts that individual jurors favored, a quotient verdict is valid.

Gasoline Products Co. v. Champlin Refining Co. (S.Ct. 1931)

Facts: After verdicts for Gasoline Products Company on its cause of action and for Champlin Refining Company on its counterclaim, an appellate court ordered a new trial limited to the issue of damages.

Issue: Can an appellate court order a partial new trial?

Rule: (Stone, J.) The Seventh Amendment allows a partial new trial only if the issue to be retried is so distinct and separable from the other issues that injustice will not result.

Devine v. Patterson (1957)

Facts: At trial, Devine introduced evidence that his damages amounted to more than $19,000. Patterson did not dispute or rebut the figure, but the jury awarded Devine only $500 in compensatory damages and $1 in punitive damages.

Issue: Must a court grant a new trial on the issue of damages when the amount awarded is much less than the undisputed amount established at trial?

Rule: Although granting a new trial is generally a matter of the court's discretion, when the verdict is inconsistent on its face a new trial must be held as a matter of law.

Grunenthal v. Long Island Railroad (S.Ct. 1968)

Facts: The trial judge denied Long Island Railroad's (LIRR) motion to set aside a damage award. LIRR claimed the award was excessive. On appeal, a new trial would be granted unless Grunenthal agreed to a remittitur (reduction in the award).

Issue: May an appellate court reverse a trial court's denial of a motion to set aside an award?

Rule: (Brennan, J.) Unless the trial court grossly abused its discretion, the appellate court may not overturn its decision.

Dissent 1: (Harlan, J.) The majority decision is not based on the Constitution, but upon the reasonableness of the appellate court's judgment.

Dissent 2: (Stewart, J.) The Seventh Amendment prohibits judicial review of a district court's order refusing to set aside a verdict.

Burns, Administratrix v. Penn Central Co. (1975)

Facts: Burns sued Penn Central Company for the wrongful death of her husband caused by Penn Central's negligence. Following the jury's inability to reach a verdict, the judge granted Penn Central's request for a directed verdict.

Issue: When may a judge grant a directed verdict?

Rule: A judge may direct a verdict where no significant evidence exists for the party opposing the directed verdict.

Neely v. Martin K. Eby Construction Co. (S.Ct. 1967)

Facts: Neely won a jury verdict in district court over both directed verdict and motions for a judgment notwithstanding the verdict (JNOV) by Martin K. Eby Construction Co. On appeal, the court reversed the denial of Marin's JNOV motion and dismissed the action.

Issue: When must an appellate court grant a new trial rather than dismiss an action if it determines that the prevailing party's evidence was insufficient to sustain a verdict?

Rule: (White, J.) FRCP 50(d) states that the prevailing party has the right to urge an appellate court to order a new trial rather than set aside a verdict. This rule does not mean, however, that the appellate court must order a new trial in such a case. Hence, appellate courts can enter a JNOV, provided the party prevailing at trial first has an opportunity to establish grounds for a new trial.

Dissent 1: (Douglas, J.) Although the court's interpretation of FRCP 50 was correct, in this case the jury's verdict should nevertheless stand.

Dissent 2: (Black, J.) Whenever a jury verdict is overturned, for whatever reason, the losing party must have an opportunity to request a new jury trial.

Tillman v. Baskin (1972)

Facts: At the close of Tillman's case, which had not been before a jury, the trial judge directed a verdict for Baskin.

Issue: In a nonjury trial, may the judge rule in the defendant's favor even before the defendant presents his case?

Rule: In a nonjury trial, a motion for involuntary dismissal is the proper method by which a defendant may obtain a verdict in his favor following the presentation of the plaintiff's case. However, if the plaintiff has established a prima facie case, the judge may not weigh the evidence and find for the defendant before the presentation of the defense.

Atchison, Topeka and Santa Fe Railway v. Barrett (1957)

Facts: Barrett recovered for a chronic head twitching allegedly caused by the railway's negligence. During trial, Barrett twitched repeatedly in front of the jurors, but afterwards, an attorney for the railway noted that Barrett's twitching had mysteriously gone away.

Issue: May a trial use relevant evidence gained after trial to overturn a previously rendered verdict?

Rule: Setting aside the verdict is within the trial court's discretion pursuant to FRCP 60. Also, as here, a trial court also has discretion not to set aside the verdict.

New York Life Insurance Co. v. Nashville Trust Co. (1956)

Facts: Thomas Buntin disappeared from his home, and his beneficiary, the Nashville Trust Co., obtained the proceeds of his life insurance from New York Life Insurance Company. Eleven years later, Buntin turned up in another city, and New York Life sued for return of the proceeds.

Issue: When may the postjudgment discovery of relevant facts be used to overturn a verdict?

Rule: Where the losing party never had an honest opportunity to present facts that had been discovered later, those facts related to fraud in the conduct of the lawsuit, and the money is both present and redeemable, the award may be set aside.

Hicks v. Feiock (S.Ct. 1988)

Facts: Feiock was ordered to pay child support, and when he failed to do so, he was sentenced to 25 days in jail.

Issue: Is a contempt proceeding involving imprisonment civil or criminal?

Rule: (White, J.) Where the defendant may avoid imprisonment by complying with the court order, the punishment is civil.

American Hospital Supply Corp. v. Hospital Products, Ltd. (1986)

Facts: Hospital Products terminated its contract with American Hospital Supply, its distributor. American Hospital sued for breach and received a preliminary injunction preventing Hospital Products from interfering with the contract during trial. Hospital Products challenged the injunction. Two months later, Hospital Products filed for bankruptcy.

Issue: When may a court issue a preliminary injunction?

Rule: A preliminary injunction may only be granted where the harm to the plaintiff absent the injunction, multiplied by the probability that denial would be an error, exceeds the harm to the defendant with the injunction, multiplied by the probability that granting the injunction would be an error.

Colgrove v. Battin (S.Ct. 1973)

Facts: A local rule of the district court in Montana stated that the jury for civil trial shall consist of six persons.

Issue: Does a rule requiring a six member jury violate the Seventh Amendment?

Rule: (Brennan, J.) The Seventh Amendment only applies to cases in which the right to trial by jury was guaranteed at common law, so a six member jury is not violative except in those cases.

Dissent: (Marshall, J.) It cannot be doubted that the Framers envisioned a jury of twelve when they referred to a trial by jury.

Handel v. New York Rapid Transit Corp. (1938)

Facts: Handel uttered the words, "Save me. Help me – why did that conductor close the door on me?" shortly after falling from a train and shortly before his death. A witness' testimony to that effect was declared inadmissible as hearsay evidence.

Issue: What are the standards for allowing a deceased's utterance under the res gestae exception to the hearsay rule?

Rule: The utterance must be a spontaneous expression of the injured person's observation of the occurrence and made within such a small time frame as to preclude fabrication.

American Machine & Metals, Inc. v. De Bothezat Impeller Co. (1948)

Facts: American Machine & Metals, Incorporated (American) conveyed to De Bothezat Impeller Company (De Bothezat) certain patent rights and equipment to be used for the production of fans. De Bothezat desired to exercise its unilateral right to terminate the arrangement and sought a declaration of rights because American contended that De Bothezat would be prohibited from selling any type of ventilating equipment if De Bothezat terminated the contract and also led the plaintiff to believe that they would sue.

Issue: When may a declaratory judgment be granted to prevent the accrual of avoidable damages?

Rule: Where there is an actual controversy over contingent rights, a declaratory judgment may be granted to prevent the accrual of avoidable damages.

International Longshoremen's Local 37 v. Boyd (S.Ct. 1954)

Facts: The International Longshoremen's Local 37 requested the courts to enjoin Boyd as District Director of the Immigration and Naturalization Service from interpreting a statute to apply to alien workers returning from temporary work in Alaska.

Issue: Should a court rule on a hypothetical legal issue that has yet to arise?

Rule: (Frankfurter, J.) Courts will not rule on hypothetical cases. An actual "case or controversy" is required.

Dissent: (Black, J.) Since the court's refusal to act will prevent permanent resident aliens from taking temporary jobs in Alaska, a real harm, not just an imaginary one, has occurred.

Texas Department of Community Affairs v. Burdine (S.Ct. 1981)

Facts: Burdine alleged that in failing to promote her, and in ultimately terminating her, the Texas Department of Community Affairs violated Title VII of the Civil Rights Act of 1964.

Issue: Must an employer carry the burden to show nondiscriminatory reasons for its actions once a plaintiff has established a prima facie case of discriminatory treatment?

Rule: (Powell, J.) Once a plaintiff has proved a prima facie case of both sex and employment discrimination, the burden shifts to the defendant to clearly explain the nondiscriminatory reasons for its actions.

Reid v. San Pedro, Los Angeles & Salt Lake Railroad (1911)

Facts: Reid's cow was killed when it strayed into the path of an oncoming train. The cow could have wandered onto the track either by a hole in the railroad's fence or through an open gate to Reid's pasture.

Issue: What standard of proof is required in a negligence case?

Rule: A plaintiff must prove negligence by a preponderance of the evidence.

Cruzan v. New York Central & Hudson River Railroad (1917)

Facts: Cruzan, a brakeman for the railroad, was struck by a passing passenger train as he was setting a switch on the side of one of the trains. His estate sued the railroad under the Federal Employees' Liability Act (FELA), but was unable to prove, except by mere assertions, the negligence of any railroad employees.

Issue: May a plaintiff prove negligence through inference?

Rule: Negligence must be proven with actual facts, not mere assertions.

Pennsylvania Railroad v. Chamberlain (S.Ct. 1933)

Facts: At trial, the judge directed a verdict for Chamberlain even though the proven facts gave equal support to both the railroad's and Chamberlain's allegations.

Issue: May the judge direct a verdict where the evidence could support either party's allegations?

Rule: (Sutherland, J.) Where evidence could support either party's allegations, judgment must go against the party that had the burden of proof.

O'Connor v. Pennsylvania Railroad (1962)

Facts: O'Connor sued the railroad for slipping on ice on the railroad's property. The railroad claimed the ice had only recently formed, and they did not have sufficient time to remove it. O'Connor asserted the ice had been there from previous snowfalls. The jury found for O'Connor. O'Connor's only evidence on this point was his own testimony, so the judge granted the railroad's request for a judgment notwithstanding the verdict (JNOV).

Issue: When is a JNOV warranted?

Rule: Where the evidence is heavily weighted towards one party, a judge may grant a JNOV for that party.

Chesapeake & Ohio Railway v. Martin (S.Ct. 1931)

Facts: Martin sued the railway in Virginia state court for misdelivery of goods transported to Virginia from Michigan. The railway's witness claimed that eight days was reasonable. Martin did not offer contrary evidence.

Issue: If no contrary evidence is submitted on an issue of fact, may that fact be deemed to have been proven?

Rule: (Sutherland, J.) Where one party strongly establishes a fact and the other party offers no contrary evidence, that question of fact need not be presented to the jury.

Simblest v. Maynard (1970)

Facts: Simblest's car and Maynard's fire truck collided. Simblest sued Maynard. Both Maynard's and Simblest's witnesses testified that the fire truck did blare its siren and turn on its lights. The jury found for Simblest, but the judge granted Maynard's request for a judgment notwithstanding the verdict (JNOV).

Issue: When should a JNOV be granted?

Rule: The evidence must be such that, without weighing the credibility of the witnesses or otherwise considering the weight of the evidence, there can only be one conclusion as to the verdict that reasonable people could have reached.

Jorgensen v. York Ice Machinery Corp. (1947)

Facts: On the last day of trial, the jury foreman's son died. Only the jury and the court clerk knew. In deliberation, the jury agreed beforehand to abide by a majority vote, as opposed to unanimity. Jorgensen won, even though the foreman and four other jurors felt the defendant should win. After the verdict, upon hearing the circumstances, the judge refused to set aside the verdict.

Issue: When should a judge set aside a jury verdict?

Rule: A judge should not grant a new trial except in cases of gross irregularities by the jury.

Columbia Horse & Mule Commission Co. v. American Insurance Co. (1949)

Facts: The parties asked the jury for a special verdict on some relevant issues of fact, but not on others. From the answers given, the judge inferred answers to questions of fact not submitted to the jury.

Issue: May the court infer findings of fact from special verdicts rendered by the jury?

Rule: Unless a party requests that the jury decide, a judge may infer factual findings from a jury's special verdicts.

Mayer v. Petzelt (1963)

Facts: In Mayer's suit against Petzelt, the jury returned a general verdict for Mayer, but returned a special interrogatory in favor of Petzelt on the important question of due care. Because of the special interrogatory, the judge directed a verdict for Petzelt.

Issue: Where a jury's general verdict and special verdicts conflict, which should rule?

Rule: Unless it is absolutely impossible for the two verdicts to be consistent, the general verdict should control.

Arkansas Midland Railway v. Canman (1890)

Facts: The jury returned a verdict for Canman, but the special interrogatories proved that the jury did not agree upon the exact facts leading to the award.

Issue: Where there are several different routes the jury may have taken to get to the decision the jury reaches, must all the jurors agree on one route?

Rule: Jurors may have differing interpretations as long as they agree that the same party should recover.

Rojas v. Richardson (1983)

Facts: During closing arguments, Richardson referred to Rojas as an illegal alien. Rojas did not object at the time, but appealed on those grounds after the jury found for Richardson.

Issue: Must a party object to a prejudicial statement at the time of its utterance in court?

Rule: A new trial may always be granted where there was "plain error." Plain error must be both obvious and substantial. Here, the reference was so prejudicial that it amounted to plain error.

Dimick v. Scheidt (S.Ct. 1935)

Facts: The jury found for Scheidt, but Scheidt claimed that the verdict was contrary to the weight of the evidence and must have been a compromise verdict, based on the amount of the damages. The court then asked Dimick, without first obtaining Scheldt's consent, to increase the damages or go through a new trial. Dimick consented to the damages.

Issue: May a judge award an additur without the consent of both parties?

Rule: (Sutherland, J.) A court's request for an additur without the recovering party's consent is a violation of the constitutional right to the verdict of a jury.

Dissent: (Stone, J.) The Seventh Amendment does not prescribe any particular procedure by which the benefits of a jury trial may be obtained, or forbid any which does not curtail the function of the jury. It does not restrict the court's control of the jury's verdict.

Fairmount Glass Works v. Cub Fork Coal Co. (S.Ct. 1933)

Facts: The first two trials, in which the juries found for Fairmount Glass Works, were each overturned due to errors in law. A third jury found for Cub Fork Coal Company but only awarded one dollar in damages. The judge then refused Cub Fork Coal's request for a new trial. Cub Fork Coal appealed the judge's ruling.

Issue: When may an appellate court overturn a trial court's refusal to grant a new trial?

Rule: (Brandeis, J.) Only where error is plain may an appellate court reverse the trial court's exercise of discretion. The mere refusal to grant a new trial where the jury awarded only nominal damages is not an abuse of discretion.

Dissent: (Stone, J.) A verdict found in contravention of the instructions of the court may be reversed on appeal as contrary to law.

Donovan v. Penn Shipping Co. (S.Ct. 1977)

Facts: In a "slip and fall" case, Donovan obtained a $90,000 verdict. The judge agreed to order a new trial unless Donovan accepted a $25,000 remittitur. Donovan took the $65,000 "under protest" and then sought an appeal of the judge's action.

Issue: May a party appeal from a remittitur that has already been accepted?

Rule: (Per Curiam) Once a remittitur is accepted, it is binding on the parties.

Montgomery Ward & Co. v. Duncan (S.Ct. 1940)

Facts: Duncan sued Montgomery Ward & Company for personal injuries and won. Montgomery Ward moved for a judgment notwithstanding the verdict (JNOV), and failing that, a new trial. The trial court granted the JNOV motion and thus did not consider the motion for a new trial. On Duncan's appeal, the appellate court reversed the JNOV motion, but refused to consider the new trial motion because only a trial court may grant a new trial.

Issue: Where motions for both a JNOV and a new trial are put forth must the trial court consider both motions at once?

Rule: (Roberts, J.) If the trial court only considers one motion, which is reversed on appeal, the trial court may then consider the second motion.

Marsh v. Illinois Central R. (1949)

Facts: In Marsh's personal injury suit against the Illinois Central Railroad, the jury found for March. The railroad then moved for a judgment notwithstanding the verdict (JNOV), or in the alternative, a new trial. The trial court granted a new trial.

Issue: When should a trial court grant JNOV and new trial motions?

Rule: A judge may only direct a verdict where a reasonable jury could not have decided the case as it did (not the case here). However, a judge may grant a new trial where, even though it was possible for a reasonable jury to decide the case as it did, most of the evidence pointed away from the decision that the jury made.

Cone v. West Virginia Pulp & Paper Co. (S.Ct. 1947)

Facts: Cone sued the West Virginia Pulp & Paper Company, claiming it trespassed on Cone's lands and took his timber. The paper company denied that the lands belonged to Cone. Before the case went to the jury, the paper company unsuccessfully moved for a directed verdict. The jury found for Cone. The paper company then unsuccessfully moved for a new trial, but did not make a motion for a judgment notwithstanding the verdict (JNOV). On appeal, the court granted the JNOV motion.

Issue: May a JNOV motion be made on appeal?

Rule: (Black, J.) An appellate court may not grant a JNOV motion unless it was originally made at trial.

In Re Boise Cascade Securities Litigation (1976)

Facts: Boise Cascade tried, unsuccessfully, to acquire two other companies. When the deal fell through, five separate suits were filed against various officers of Boise Cascade alleging violations of various federal and state securities laws. The plaintiffs requested a jury trial, but Boise Cascade objected and moved to strike the jury request on the grounds that the issues involved are too complicated for jury consideration.

Issue: May a court deny a motion for a jury on the grounds that the litigation is too complex?

Rule: Although the Seventh Amendment favors jury trials, the use of juries is not without limits. The Seventh Amendment does not expand the right to jury trial in complex commercial civil actions.

United States v. Cirami (1976)

Facts: The Internal Revenue Service (IRS) brought an action against the Ciramis to recover allegedly unpaid taxes. Then the IRS moved for summary judgment under FRCP 56. The Ciramis did not file an opposing brief, so the trial judge granted the motion and entered judgment against the Ciramis, which again the Ciramis did not oppose. The Ciramis appealed, claiming their attorney did not inform them of the summary judgment motion.

Issue: Should a party be relieved of a default judgment entered against him on the ground that counsel's error constitutes either a mistake or excusable neglect?

Rule: A party will not be relieved of a default judgment unless he established that counsel was grossly negligent in performing his representative duties.

Edwards v. Born, Inc. (1985)

Facts: Edwards brought suit against Born, Inc. for personal injuries. Edwards' wife was later added as a party plaintiff with a loss of consortium claim. During pretrial conference, Edwards' attorney accepted a settlement offer from Born. The Edwardses later rejected the offer, claiming that their attorney had no authority to settle the claim.

Issue: In the absence of express authority, is a party bound by his attorney's settlement of a case?

Rule: A party is bound by his attorney's agreement to settle a lawsuit, even though the attorney may not have had express authority to settle, if the opposing party was unaware of any limitation on the attorney's apparent authority.

Atlas Roofing Co. v. Occupational Safety and Health Review Commission (S.Ct. 1977)

Facts: In 1970, Congress passed the Occupational Safety and Heath Act (OSHA) authorizing the Labor Department to require employers to correct unsafe working conditions, and imposing civil penalties on employers who did not comply. Any disputes were handled before an administrative law judge, and never before a jury.

Issue: May Congress create a cause of action for civil penalties that may be litigated only in an administrative agency that does not provide for a jury trial?

Rule: (White, J.) The Seventh Amendment applies to all suits "at common law." This does not prevent Congress from assigning suits of the sort normally tried by a jury before an agency instead, if the suit involves new statutes creating "public rights."

State v. Porro (1977)

Facts: Porro contested the use of voter registration lists as the sources of names in grand jury selection. He pointed out the underrepresentation of women, people between the age of eighteen and 34, students, blue-collar workers, and black people in the grand jury pool that indicted him.

Issue: Does the use of voter registration lists as a method of selecting names for grand juries violate the Constitution?

Rule: The Constitution only prohibits the systematic exclusion of a group of people. Here no group is systematically being excluded except students. However, since no common bond exists between all students, their exclusion does not deprive defendants of a grand jury comprised of a valid cross-section of the community.

People of California v. Huey P. Newton (1972)

Facts: During voir dire, a potential juror was questioned by a district attorney and defense counsel, regarding the juror's opinion with respect to the defendant's guilt or innocence. The potential juror said that he was of the "opinion" that the defendant was absolutely innocent, but did not "believe" that the defendant was absolutely innocent. Defense counsel moved to have the juror challenged for cause and excused.

Issue: May a potential juror be challenged for cause and excused if the potential juror does not believe that the defendant is innocent?

Rule: If a potential juror does not believe that the defendant is innocent, that potential juror may be challenged for cause and excused. Defendants are presumed innocent until proven guilty, and jurors must believe that the defendant is innocent before hearing any evidence. That a potential juror does not believe the defendant is guilty is not satisfactory.

Liljeberg v. Health Services Acquisition Corp. (S.Ct. 1988)

Facts: After a trial without a jury, the judge ruled for Liljeberg, the defendant. The Health Services Acquisition Corporation then learned that the judge had been on the board of trustees with which Liljeberg had been negotiating to purchase a large piece of land. The success of the negotiations turned, in large part, on Liljeberg prevailing against Health Services Acquisition. The judge did not know of any conflict of interest at the time of trial or judgment.

Issue: When may a judge be disqualified under FRCP 60(b)(6)?

Rule: (Stewart, J.) Where the judge knows that he, individually or as a fiduciary, has a financial interest in the subject matter or in a party to a proceeding, he should recuse himself. Here the judge clearly should have done so.

Dissent: (Rehnquist, C.J.) An otherwise valid judgment should not be overturned because of a conflict of interest that could not have affected the judge's decision-making ability.

People v. Rigney (1961)

Facts: Rigney, at trial, contended that his memory was impaired by alcohol and that he could not remember anything about the murder of which he was accused. The judge questioned Rigney and his medical expert extensively on this testimony and, not in the presence of the jury, said he did not believe them.

Issue: May a judge examine witnesses to elicit or clarify testimony?

Rule: The judge may question the witness when it seems that the attorneys would not clearly elicit the facts. The questions however, may not convey to the jury any sense of disbelief or ridicule.

Sitrin Bros., Inc. v. Deluxe Lines, Inc. (1962)

Facts: During trial, some of the jurors who knew about electronic equipment interrogated one of the expert witnesses about the electric motors in question.

Issue: May the jury examine the witness?

Rule: It is in the sound discretion of the court to determine whether a juror may be allowed to question a witness. As long as the questions were made in an endeavor to elicit facts, rather than express disbelief, the questioning is valid.

Committee on Professional Ethics v. Crary (1976)

Facts: Crary's mistress retained Crary's associate to represent her in her divorce proceedings. Crary assisted his associate in representing his mistress and knew that she testified falsely regarding their affair.

Issue: May an attorney allow evidence that he knows to be false to be introduced into evidence where the attorney would be forced to incriminate himself in the process?

Rule: Preventing a client from falsely testifying does not violate the attorney-client privilege. False testimony is outside the scope of the privilege. Also, self-incrimination is not material where it is obvious to the opposing attorney that the client is committing perjury.

Sioux City & Pacific Railroad Co. v. Stout (S.Ct. 1873)

Facts: At trial, the judge charged the jury with instructions on determining whether the railroad was negligent. The jury then found for Stout.

Issue: May a judge charge a jury with determining whether a party was negligent?

Rule: (Hunt, J.) The question of negligence is one properly charged to the jury, and if it is reasonable that the jury could find negligence, the decision must stand.

Newing v. Cheatham (1975)

Facts: Cheatham owned and piloted the plane in which Newing rode. When the plane crashed, both Newing and Cheatham died. Newing's representatives sued Cheatham's representatives for negligence. Although there was no direct evidence for negligence, the Newing's did try to prove that the crash could not have occurred without negligence by Newing (res ipsa loquitur). The judge directed a verdict for Newing.

Issue: What is necessary to prove negligence under a theory of res ipsa loquitur?

Rule: To find negligence under res ipsa loquitur, the accident must be of a kind which does not ordinarily occur in the absence of negligence, must be caused by an agency or instrumentality within the exclusive control of the defendant, and must not have been due to any voluntary or contributory action of the plaintiff.

Sabella v. Southern Pacific Co. (1969)

Facts: At trial Sabella's counsel characterized the railroad company as inhuman and used various derogatory epithets when speaking about it. After the jury found for Sabella, the railroad motioned for a new trial on the grounds of the counsel's misconduct.

Issue: When may a party obtain a new trial due to misconduct by opposing counsel?

Rule: Unless the conduct is extremely shocking, a party must object to any misconduct before the jury is sent to deliberate.

Evans v. Wright (1974)

Facts: While charging the jury, the judge explicitly suggested that it find for Evans, which it did.

Issue: To what extent may a judge comment on the evidence while charging the jury?

Rule: The trial judge may comment upon individual questions of fact that are strongly weighted towards one side and that are not subject to questions of credibility. The judge may not suggest a final outcome of the proceeding.

Tanner v. United States (S.Ct. 1987)

Facts: After the jury's verdict and sentencing, a juror informed Tanner's attorney that many jurors had consumed alcohol during the lunch periods and slept throughout afternoon portions of the trial.

Issue: May a juror introduce evidence impeaching the jury upon which he sits?

Rule: (O'Connor, J.) Evidence gained from juries during trial is inadmissible.

Dissent: (Marshall, J.) Every defendant is entitled to a trial by competent jurors. Evidence on that point should be admissible.

Spurlin v. General Motors Corp. (1976)

Facts: After the jury found for Spurlin, the judge granted General Motors its motions both for a judgment notwithstanding the verdict (JNOV), and alternatively, a new trial, because of insufficient evidence.

Issue: When may a trial court grant a JNOV or a new trial?

Rule: If there was substantial evidence supporting a jury's verdict, the court may not grant a JNOV. Also, the trial court should not grant a new trial motion unless the jury verdict is at least against the great weight of the evidence.

Mann v. Hunt (1953)

Facts: The judge found that the jury's verdict was against the great weight of evidence and set it aside.

Issue: When is "against the great weight of evidence" sufficient to set aside a verdict?

Rule: There is no standard by which to determine when a verdict should be set aside as against the weight of evidence. The decision depends upon the discretion of the court.

Pullman-Standard v. Swint (S.Ct. 1982)

Facts: Black employees brought suit against their employer, Pullman-Standard, alleging violations of Title VII of the Civil Rights

Act of 1964. Finding no discriminatory purpose, the trial court ruled in Pullman-Standard's favor. Making its own factual finding (i.e., determining the ultimate fact, discriminatory purpose), the appellate court reversed.

Issue: Under FRCP 52, can a federal appellate court disturb a district court's factual determination?

Rule: (White, J.) Under FRCP 52, a federal appellate court cannot set aside a district court's findings of fact unless such findings are clearly erroneous.

Dissent: (Marshall, J.) The district court's findings were clearly erroneous and should be reversed.

Jackson v. Sears, Roebuck & Co. (1957)

Facts: Sears, Roebuck sued Jackson and obtained an award. Five days before entry of the judgment, Sears, Roebuck had the sheriff levy Jackson's property to satisfy the judgment.

Issue: Is an execution issued without a judgment to support it void, even though the judgment is imminent?

Rule: A judgment is ineffective until its entry in the docket, and any executions made prior to the entry are void.

Granfinanciera, S.A. v. Nordberg (S.Ct. 1989)

Facts: Nordberg sued Granfinanciera to recover funds transferred to it by a bankruptcy debtor. Granfinanciera was denied a jury trial on the grounds that bankruptcy courts are non-Article III tribunals, which are not governed by the Seventh Amendment.

Issue: Is there a right to a jury in cases being adjudicated by non-Article III courts?

Rule: If Congress creates new causes of action involving public rights, it may assign their adjudication to tribunals that do not use juries as factfinders. However, Congress may not block application of the Seventh Amendment to private-right cases (e.g., tort, contract, property, and other suits at common law). A bankruptcy trustee's right to recover a fraudulent conveyance most nearly resembles a state-law contract claim, which carries with it a right to a jury trial.

Trezza v. Dame (1967)

Facts: In an action to recover personal injuries resulting from a car crash, the judge commented to the jury, "[I]t is rather clear in this case that the defendant is negligent and her negligence was responsible for the accident. . . ." and, "I do not think there is any issue of fact. . . ." He did, however, inform the jury that they could disagree with his opinion.

Issue: May a trial judge make comments that suggest to the jury how they should resolve factual issues?

Rule: A judge may comment on evidence and express his opinion on factual issues, but a judge may not pronounce his opinion on ultimate issues so forcefully that he usurps the function of the jury. In the instant case, the appellate court did not approve of the judge's comments, but did not find that they were sufficiently prejudicial to warrant reversal because his opinions seemed correct.

In re Beverly Hills Fire Litigation (1982)

Facts: In a suit resulting from a fire, it was alleged that a certain type of wiring had caused the fire. Concerned by an expert's characterization of the wire as "a time bomb," a juror inspected and experimented with the wiring in his house. The experiment yielded results that contradicted evidence in the case. The plaintiff moved for a mistrial.

Issue: May jurors conduct private experiments?

Rule: Jurors may not conduct experiments outside the courtroom because such experiments constitute additional evidence that is not subject to scrutiny or cross-examination. Such evidence is prejudicial and is grounds for reversal if it had any influence on the jury's deliberations or verdict. The juror's motivation for conducting the experiment is not relevant.

Lind v. Schenley Indus. (1960)

Facts: After hearing conflicting testimony as to the existence of a contract, a jury found that an oral contract existed. The trial judge did not agree and granted a new trial.

Issue: What is the standard for setting aside a jury's verdict as contrary to the weight of the evidence?

Rule: A trial judge has wide discretion to grant a new trial if a possibly erroneous verdict resulted from circumstances beyond the jury's control (e.g., improperly admitted evidence, prejudicial statements by counsel, or an improper charge). It is an abuse of discretion for a judge to set aside a jury verdict simply because he has reached a different conclusion. The degree of judicial scrutiny should vary with the subject of the litigation. Closer scrutiny of a verdict is warranted when the case deals with complex and specialized subject matter, but the jury's judgment should control on issues such as the veracity of witnesses.

Tittle v. Aldacosta (1977)

Facts: Aldacosta fell when disembarking from Tittle's boat. It was the usual practice to put down a towel to prevent disembarking passengers from slipping. The towel was not in place when Aldacosta was injured. In a bench trial, the judge found that the absent towel was not the proximate cause of Aldacosta's injuries and that the accident was not caused by negligence on the part of the owner, the crew, or the vessel. The appellate court disagreed.

Issue: What is the standard for setting aside a judge's findings of fact?

Rule: A judge's findings of fact will only be set aside if clearly erroneous. However, because a judge's factfinding role does not implicate the same Seventh Amendment concerns as jury trials, the reviewing court can be less deferential to judicial findings than jury findings.

CHAPTER 10

APPELLATE REVIEW

I. FINAL JUDGMENT RULE

A. Generally

1. For the most part, only final judgments are appealable.

2. A final judgment is reached when, on the merits, litigation ends, leaving only the execution of judgment to be completed.

3. Substance, not form, determines if a judgment is final.

B. Interlocutory Appeals Exception
Interlocutory appeals are allowed in cases involving:

1. Collateral Orders
A collateral order is one which:

   a. Raises serious legal questions;

   b. Involves a danger of irreparable harm; and

   c. Deals with an issue unrelated to the basic substantive claims asserted.

2. Multiple Claims or Parties
A final decision as to one or more, but less than all, the claims or parties before the court may be appealed before all claims of all parties have been resolved.

3. Equitable Orders
E.g., grant, denial, or modification of an injunction.

4. Questions of Great Import
If a trial judge certifies, and the appellate court agrees, that the order involves a controlling question of law over which a difference of opinion exists, and that immediate appeal may materially advance termination of the litigation, an interlocutory appeal will be allowed.

5. Possibility of Irreparable Harm

6. Courts admit interlocutory appeals of orders affecting substantial rights that will be lost if not immediately appealed.

7. Writs of Mandamus or Prohibition

    a.   When Used

    b.   Appellate courts may grant a writ only if the trial court exceeds its jurisdiction or clearly abuses its discretion.

    c.   Factors

    d.   When deciding a petition for a writ a court will consider:

    e.   Mnemonic: **PLACE**

        i. **P**rejudice
           Whether petitioner will be prejudiced in a manner not correctable on appeal;

       ii. **L**aw of First Impression
           Whether the district court's order raises important issues of law of first impression;

      iii. **A**dequate Alternate Relief
           Whether petitioner has other adequate means to obtain relief;

      iv. **C**learly Erroneous Errors
           Whether the district court's order is, as a matter of law, clearly erroneous; or

       v. **E**rror That Is Often Repeated
           Whether the district court's order is an oft-repeated error or a manifest persistent disregard of the FRCP.

II. PROCEDURES

A. Timeliness
The time period in which an appeal must be brought begins to run once judgment is entered.

B. Standing to Appeal

1. Only a party injured (or aggrieved) by the judgment of the lower court has standing to appeal.

2. It is possible for both parties to be injured by a single judgment. Simply because one party is injured less does not mean they cannot appeal.

3. Nonparties may not appeal.

C. Notice of Appeal

1. Notice of appeal must be filed within 30 days (60 days if the United States is a party) of the judgment's entry.

2. If a court finds excusable neglect or good cause, a 30-day extension to file a notice of appeal will be granted.

3. Parties to a suit cannot stipulate to alter the time within which to take an appeal.

D. Waiver
A party may expressly or impliedly waive any right to appeal.

E. Rehearing
A court (the Supreme Court, or Circuit Courts en banc), at its discretion, may order a rehearing of a case if:

1. The petition is timely filed; or

2. The strict application of the rules favoring finality of judgments would unfairly impinge on the interests of justice.

III. SCOPE OF REVIEW

A. Reviewable Issues
Generally, appellate courts only review issues of law, not factual findings.

B. Jury Trials

1. An appellate court must uphold a verdict supported by substantial evidence.

2. An appellate court cannot weigh evidence or pass on witness credibility.

3. An appellate court cannot disturb factual findings.

C. Nonjury Trials

1. If clearly erroneous, a judge's factual findings may be set aside.

2. Questions of witness credibility are solely in the trial court's province.

D. Errors
Appellate courts have jurisdiction only if an error:

1. Involves a legal issue;

2. Appears in the trial record;

3. Affects a substantial right of the aggrieved party; and

4. Is preserved by prompt objection to a court's ruling.

E. Harmless Error
When an error neither prejudices a substantial right of the aggrieved party nor has a significant effect on a case's outcome, courts will not reverse a judgment.

IV. HIGH COURTS

A. Generally
Every state has its high court, generally known as the State Supreme Court, although each state will have its own title. The federal court is of course led by the United States Supreme Court. Intermediate appellate courts generally exist to relieve the burdens of the high courts, but there are exceptions to every rule.

B. Original Jurisdiction
Every jurisdiction delineates certain areas of the law where the high court has original jurisdiction. In other words, an appeal under original jurisdiction must, as of right, go straight to the top.

C. Discretionary Review

1. Generally
According to Chief Justice Taft, there is no right to appeal all the way to the top. The Supreme Court's function is not primarily to preserve the rights of the litigants. It is to expound and stabilize principles of law. Most state systems express the same view.

2. Certiorari
The Supreme Court exercises its discretionary power by granting writs of certiorari. By requiring certification of a case before hearing it, the Court can select those cases it feels most compelled to decide.

a. Rule of Four
It takes a vote of only four of the nine justices to grant writ. In contrast, it normally requires five justices to decide a case.

b. Factors
In determining whether to grant a petition for certiorari, the justices will consider:

i. State Court Deciding Federal Law
    Where a state court is the first to interpret a federal
    law, or misinterprets it.

ii. Conflict in Court of Appeals
    The Circuits are in conflict with each other or with
    the decisions of state courts.

CASE CLIPS

Liberty Mutual Insurance Co. v. Wetzel (S.Ct. 1976)

Facts: Wetzel and others alleged that Liberty Mutual's employee insurance benefits and maternity leave regulations discriminated against women in violation of Title VII of the Civil Rights Act of 1964. The district court granted partial summary judgment for Wetzel solely on the issue of liability, without considering the issue of relief. Liberty Mutual appealed under 28 U.S.C. § 1291.

Issue 1: May an order for partial summary judgment limited to the issue of liability alone be appealed under 28 U.S.C. § 1291?

Rule 1: (Rehnquist, J.) A partial summary judgment order solely on the issue of liability is not a "final decision" as required by 28 U.S.C. § 1291.

Issue 2: May an order for partial summary judgment limited to the issue of liability be appealed under 28 U.S.C. § 1292(a)(l)?

Rule 2: Interlocutory appeals under 28 U.S.C. § 1292(a)(l) are limited to review of injunctive relief. Where, as here, no injunctive relief has been granted, a party may not appeal a district court's order under this section.

Coopers & Lybrand v. Livesay (S.Ct. 1978)

Facts: Livesay and others alleged that Coopers & Lybrand underreported the net income figures of the Punta Gorda Isles, in violation of the Securities Act of 1933 and the Securities Exchange Act of 1934. After initially certifying' the plaintiffs as a class, the district court decertified the class following additional proceedings. The plaintiffs appealed the decertification order.

Issue: Is a district court's determination that an action may not be maintained as a class action a "final decision" within the meaning of 28 U.S.C. § 1291, appealable as a matter of right?

Rule: (Stevens, J.) An order decertifying a class does not terminate the entire litigation, and thus is not a "final decision" that may be appealed under 28 U.S.C. § 1291.

La Buy v. Howes Leather Co. (S.Ct. 1957)

Facts: Judge La Buy referred a number of antitrust cases to a master for final determination. Howes Leather Company and other parties sought a writ of mandamus from the court of appeals to compel La Buy to hear the cases.

Issue: Does a court of appeals, through the issuance of writs of mandamus, have the power to review interlocutory orders?

Rule: (Clark, J.) A court of appeals has discretionary power to issue writs of mandamus to review interlocutory orders in proper circumstances.

Dissent: (Brennan, J.) Writs of mandamus may only be used to review interlocutory orders when the action of a district court frustrates the ultimate exercise of appellate jurisdiction by a court of appeals.

Atlantic City Elec. Co. v. General Elec. Co. (1964)

Facts: During pretrial discovery, General Electric submitted interrogatories to discover whether Atlantic City had passed along its alleged damages to its customers. Atlantic City successfully objected to the interrogatories. General Electric appealed the sustained objection under 28 U.S.C. § 1292(b).

Issue: Must an appellate court grant a pretrial appeal on issues the party will have full opportunity to appeal at the end of the trial?

Rule: An interlocutory appeal should only be granted if the defendant's right to an ultimate appeal would otherwise be prejudiced.

Gillespie v. United States Steel Corp. (S.Ct. 1964)

Facts: Gillespie sued the United States Steel Corporation to recover damages for the death of her son, basing her causes of action on both the Jones Act and the Ohio wrongful death statute. Holding that the Jones Act provided the exclusive remedy, the district judge struck all references to the Ohio statutes from the complaint. Gillespie immediately appealed.

Issue: May an interlocutory order be appealed as a final decision under 28 U.S.C. § 1291?

Rule: (Black, J.) Since a "final" decision does not necessarily mean the last order possible to be made in a case, interlocutory orders dealing with questions fundamental to the further conduct of a case are appealable under 28 U.S.C. § 1291.

Dissent: (Harlan, J.) The requirements of 28 U.S.C. § 1291 are intended to prevent the piecemeal litigation of the issues in a lawsuit.

Gulfstream Aerospace Corp. v. Mayacamas Corp. (S.Ct. 1988)

Facts: Gulfstream sued Mayacamas in state court for breach of contract. Soon after, Mayacamas filed a diversity action against Gulfstream in federal court, claiming breach of the same contract. Gulfstream moved to dismiss or stay the federal action pending resolution of the state court litigation. The district court denied the motion and Gulfstream appealed, citing 28 U.S.C. § 1291 and 1292(a)(l).

Issue 1: Is a district court order denying a motion to stay or dismiss an action when a similar suit is pending in state court immediately appealable under 28 U.S.C. § 1291?

Rule 1: (Marshall, J.) Since the denial of a motion to dismiss or stay is "inherently tentative" and does not terminate the litigation, it is not immediately appealable as a "final" decision under 28 U.S.C. § 1291.

Issue 2: Is a district court order denying a motion to stay or dismiss an action when a similar suit is pending in state court immediately appealable under 28 U.S.C. § 1292(a)(l)?

Rule 2: Orders granting or denying stays are not injunctions, and thus are not appealable under 28 U.S.C. § 1292(a)(l).

Concurrence: (Scalia, J.) That a decision is inherently tentative should not be enough to prevent a court order from being labeled "final." The order is still final as regards immediate appeal. This order is not appealable because the motion is likely to be renewed and reconsidered, and because the relief will be just as effective at a later date.

Note: This case overturned the *Enelow-Ettelson* doctrine, which considered motions to dismiss to be injunctions for purposes of 28 U.S.C. § 1292(a)(l) if they were made in historically legal actions on the basis of a historically equitable defense or counterclaim.

United States v. F. & M. Schaefer Brewing Co. (S.Ct. 1958)

Facts: F. & M. Schaefer Brewing Company sued the Government to recover taxes which it alleged were illegally assessed and collected. The judge granted summary judgment for Schaefer and entered the order granting the motion on April 14,1955. Formal judgment, however, was not entered until May 24, 1955. On July 21, 1955, the Government filed an appeal. Schaefer claimed that the Government's appeal was not filed within sixty days of "entry of judgment," as required by federal procedural rules.

Issue: May a filed opinion constitute final entry of formal judgment?

Rule: (Whittaker, J.) Where a judge clearly evinces the intention that an opinion shall be the final act in a case, the filed opinion constitutes final judgment from which the time to appeal runs.

J.F. White Contracting Co. v. New England Tank Industries of New Hampshire, Inc. (1968)

Facts: New England Tank Industries of New Hampshire sued J.F. White Contracting for damages suffered as a result of White's alleged defective construction of oil tanker dock facilities. On appeal, White raised an issue not previously considered at trial.

Issue 1: May an appellate court consider an issue not raised at trial?

Rule 1: An appellate court cannot consider an issue that was neither pleaded as an affirmative defense nor raised at trial.

Issue 2: When may an appellate court reverse the decision of a trial court?

Rule 2: An appellate court may only reverse a trial court's decision if it finds an error that affected the verdict or "the substantial rights of the parties."

Electrical Fittings Corp. v. Thomas & Betts Co. (S.Ct. 1939)

Facts: Thomas & Betts Company sued Electrical Fittings Corp. for patent infringement. The district court found Thomas & Betts' patent valid, but not infringed. Fearing that the judgment of the patent's validity would bind it in subsequent suits, Electrical Fittings appealed this part of the decision.

Issue: Can a party appeal from a judgment or decree in his favor for the purpose of obtaining a review of findings he deems erroneous?

Rule: (Roberts, J.) Parties may not appeal findings in an adjudication ultimately resolved in their favor. However, a party may appeal an issue actually adjudicated and specifically mentioned in a decree, even though the adjudication was immaterial to the disposition of the case.

Standard Accident Insurance Co. v. Roberts (1942)

Facts: Standard Accident Insurance Company sought a declaratory judgment that it was not liable to Roberts under a policy that it had issued. The trial court found that Roberts' policy did not cover the accident in question, but that Standard Accident was estopped from denying liability by its defense of the third party suit against Roberts. In his response to Standard Accident's appeal, Roberts raised two new issues and reasserted his claim that the policy covered the accident.

Issue 1: May appellees seek to change or add to relief accorded by a judgment in their favor?

Rule 1: An appellee may only change or add to relief accorded by a favorable judgment through a cross-appeal.

Issue 2: May an appellee challenge the reasoning of a favorable judgment?

Rule 2: An appellee may challenge the reasoning of a favorable judgment with any matter appearing in the record.

Corcoran v. City of Chicago (1940)

Facts: Corcoran sued the City of Chicago for negligence and was awarded a judgment for $5,000. The City of Chicago's motion for a new trial was denied by the trial court, but granted on appeal. Corcoran claimed that the appellate court's finding that the verdict was against the weight of the evidence denied him his right to a jury trial.

Issue: Can an appellate court set aside a verdict because the findings of fact were not supported by the evidence?

Rule: Both statutory and common law authorize appellate courts to set aside verdicts if the findings of fact are not supported by the evidence.

Orvis v. Higgins (1950)

Facts: In an action for a refund of federal estate taxes, the decision turned on whether two trusts were set up independently or by mutual agreement. Sitting as the factfinder, the trial judge heard both written and oral testimony. The government appealed a ruling that Mrs. Orvis and her deceased husband had set up their trusts independently.

Issue: May an appellate court rule that a trial judge's factual finding was "clearly erroneous" if it was based in part upon the credibility and demeanor of witnesses?

Rule: An appellate court may review the factual findings of a trial judge if they rest exclusively upon the written evidence; the evaluation of credibility must not contribute to the findings.

In Re Barnett (1943)

Facts: Cecilia Barnett (assignor), a beneficiary of her father's will, assigned her interest to Clara Essenfeld (assignee), her mother. Four years later, Cecilia filed for bankruptcy. Cecilia's father died the next day. The trustee in bankruptcy petitioned the court to direct Cecilia to assign her interest in the will to the trustee. The court granted the trustee's motion. The same attorney represented both Cecilia and Clara, and he appealed on behalf of both women.

Issue: In a suit concerning the interests of a trustee and assignee in the assignor's property, does the assignor, who is ordered to reassign by a court, have standing to appeal?

Rule: A court cannot wrongfully compel a person to do any involuntary act. When an assignment is validly executed, an assignor does have standing to appeal an order directing her to execute a new assignment.

Hoberman v. Lake of Isles (1952)

Facts: Lake of Isles sued to foreclose a mortgage against Hoberman, but Hoberman prevailed. Upon learning that Hoberman had falsified facts, Lake of Isles was granted a new trial. Hoberman appealed the order.

Issue: Is an order granting a motion for a new trial appealable as a final judgment?

Rule: An order granting a motion for a new trial is interlocutory, not final, and therefore not appealable.

Firestone Tire & Rubber Co. v. Risjord (S.Ct. 1981)

Facts: Risjord, an attorney, defended the Firestone Tire & Rubber Company in several liability suits. Firestone was insured by Home Insurance, also a client of Risjord. Firestone moved to remove Risjord as counsel in liability actions where the plaintiff was insured by Home Insurance, on the grounds of conflict of interest. The court denied Firestone's motion.

Issue: Can a party, pursuant to 28 U.S.C. § 1291, appeal a district court order denying a motion to disqualify counsel?

Rule: (Marshall, J.) Orders denying motions to disqualify counsel are not appealable as final collateral decisions under § 1291.

Mulay Plastics, Inc. v. Grand Trunk Western Railroad Co. (1984)

Facts: The district court ordered the Grand Trunk Western Railroad Company to pay Mulay Plastics $3,820.70 as a sanction for failure to produce relevant evidence. Grand Trunk appealed the order.

Issue: Is a court order imposing sanctions immediately appealable?

Rule: Since there is nothing irreparable about the harm caused by an order imposing sanctions, immediate appeal is not permitted.

Note: The doctrine of *Cohen v. Beneficial Industrial Loan Corp.* allows appeals of orders that inflict irreparable harm.

Sears, Roebuck & Co. v. Mackey (S.Ct. 1956)

Facts: Mackey sued Sears, Roebuck & Company for damages under the Sherman Antitrust Act. Mackey's complaint contained multiple claims. Some of the claims were dismissed and Mackey appealed the dismissals.

Issue: Can a district court in a multiple claim action permit an appeal on less than all claims before final judgment is entered on every claim asserted?

Rule: (Burton, J.) A district court, in a multiple claim action, may permit an appeal on less than all the claims before final judgment on every claim asserted is entered.

Rogers v. Missouri Pacific Railroad (S.Ct. 1957)

Facts: In a suit under the Federal Employers' Liability Act (FELA), evidence reasonably supported a verdict for either party. The court submitted the liability issue to the jury, who found for Rogers. Reversing, the appellate court held that, under FELA, the issue could not, as a matter of law, be submitted to the jury.

Issue: If evidence reasonably supports a verdict for either party, must the court submit the issue to the jury?

Rule: (Brennan, J.) If probative facts reasonably support a verdict favorable to either party, the decision is exclusively for the jury to make.

Dissent: (Frankfurter, J.) The Supreme Court is improperly reviewing evidence. The Supreme Court should be reviewing important issues of law, not factual determinations of a routine nature. The Court's docket is crowded enough as it is.

Sturm v. Chicago & North Western Railroad (1946)

Facts: In a negligence suit, before the case went to the jury, neither Sturm nor the railroad moved for directed verdicts, requested instructions, or objected to the jury charge. Sturm then appealed a judgment for the railroad.

Issue: When no challenge to a trial court's ruling of law is asserted, is a jury verdict appealable?

Rule: Where no ruling of the trial court is challenged, an appeal presents no question for review.

Hewlett Arcade v. Five Towns Refrigeration Corp. (1957)

Facts: Hewlett Arcade contracted with Eugene G. Brandt & Company to service Hewlett's oil burner. Eugene subcontracted with Five Towns Refrigeration Corporation, who was to perform the work. When Hewlett's burner exploded, Hewlett sued both Eugene and Five Towns. Eugene cross-claimed against Five Towns. Although the trial judge's charge to the jury was erroneous, no objection was made. Eugene appealed a verdict holding it solely liable to Five Towns.

Issue: Where, because of want of objection, an issue is not preserved for review, may an appellate court nonetheless review factual findings implicit in the verdict?

Rule: Appellate courts may review factual findings implicit in a verdict having no support in the evidence when a timely objection to a jury charge is not taken.

Miller v. Avirom (1967)

Facts: Avirom, a property owner, entered into an oral agreement with Miller, a real estate broker, to sell Avirom's property. Miller presented a buyer, but Avirom refused to accept the buyer's offer. Miller sued Avirom for a broker's commission. On appeal of an adverse judgment, Avirom raised an issue not advanced at trial.

Issue: Can an appellate court review an issue that was neither raised nor finally decided at trial?

Rule: Appellate courts cannot review an issue which was neither raised nor finally decided at trial. Review will be granted, however, in cases where denial would cause a clear miscarriage of justice.

McKelvy v. Barber (1964)

Facts: After presentation of evidence, Barber successfully moved for an instructed verdict. On appeal, McKelvy failed to assert a valid argument. Affirming, the intermediate appellate court held that McKelvy had waived his right to appeal as to the issue not urged as error.

Issue: Where an intermediate appellate court affirms without considering grounds warranting reversal, does an appellant, who had failed to raise that ground, waive his right of review?

Rule: When a holding of an intermediate appellate court is unsound, appellant's right of review is not waived, even on a ground warranting reversal but not considered by the intermediate court.

United States v. Ohio Power Co. (S.Ct. 1957)

Facts: Ohio Power sued the Internal Revenue Service for tax refunds. Ohio Power prevailed. The United States Supreme Court originally denied a petition for rehearing the case, but two and a half years later granted it.

Issue: Can the Supreme Court grant a previously denied petition?

Rule: (Per Curiam) The Supreme Court can grant a previously denied petition when the interest of justice outweighs the interest in finality of litigation.

Dissent: (Harlan, J.) If the government had petitioned the court to reconsider the case, it would have violated FRCP 58. Had this case come from Tax Court, the Court could not have reconsidered its denied writ of certiorari. By violating its own rules, the Court is throwing every case whose writ of certiorari is denied into jeopardy.

Russell v. Barnes Foundation (1943)

Facts: The Barnes Foundation appealed a summary judgment order on the issue of liability. A case to determine damages was still pending.

Issue: Is a summary judgment order "final" and therefore appealable even if it does not rule on all the issues in a case?

Rule: A summary judgment order is final only when all issues have been disposed.

Cohen v. Beneficial Industrial Loan Corp. (S.Ct. 1949)

Facts: Cohen brought a shareholder's derivative suit against the Beneficial Industrial Loan Corporation for mismanagement and fraud. Beneficial moved, under state law, for Cohen to post a bond. The district court ruled that the state statute did not apply to an action in federal court. Prior to the case's disposition on the merits, Beneficial appealed the ruling, which was reversed.

Issue: When is a trial court's ruling on law appealable prior to the case's disposition?

Rule: (Jackson, J.) An order is appealable when it is a final disposition of a claimed right that is not an ingredient of the cause of action and does not require consideration with the cause of action.

North Supply Co. v. Greater Development & Services Corp. (1984)

Facts: The North Supply Company sued the Greater Development & Services Corporation to reform their contract. Greater Development instituted arbitration proceedings, pursuant to an arbitration clause in the contract. North Supply Company moved to stay arbitration proceedings. The district court denied the motion and North Supply Company appealed.

Issue: Is a denial of a motion to stay arbitration proceedings immediately appealable?

Rule: Because of the strong federal policy favoring arbitration and disfavoring interlocutory appeals, an order denying a motion to stay arbitration proceedings is not appealable.

Carson v. American Brands, Inc. (S.Ct. 1981)

Facts: Carson and American Brands negotiated a settlement and consent decree containing injunctive relief. The district court refused to enter the decree.

Issue: When is an interlocutory order of a district court denying a joint motion of the parties to enter a consent decree an appealable order?

Rule: (Brennan, J.) An interlocutory order of a district court denying a joint motion of the parties to enter a consent decree is appealable if it contains injunctive relief. An order refusing an injunction is appealable under 28 U.S.C. § 1292(a)(1).

Kraus v. Board of County Road Commissioners (1966)

Facts: The Board of County Road Commissioners unsuccessfully moved for summary judgment on the grounds that Kraus did not give written notice of the claim within the required 60 days. The court inserted in its order a certification for immediate appeal.

Issue: When can a federal appellate court grant an interlocutory appeal?

Rule: A federal appellate court can grant an interlocutory appeal only when it materially advances the ultimate termination of the litigation.

Schlagenhauf v. Holder (S.Ct. 1964)

Facts: Holder and other bus passengers involved in a collision between a Greyhound bus and a tractor trailer sued Schlagenhauf (the bus driver), Greyhound (the bus line), Contract Carriers (the tractor owner), McCorkhill (the truck driver), and National Lead (the trailer owner). Contract Carriers and National Lead claimed the accident was due to Schlagenhauf's negligence, and requested, pursuant to FRCP 35(a), that Schlagenhauf submit to four physical and mental examinations. Schlagenhauf then went to the Court of Appeals and sought a writ of mandamus preventing any examinations.

Issue: When may a writ of mandamus, instead of an appeal, be used by a party seeking remedial action?

Rule: (Goldberg, J.) A writ of mandamus may only be used in a remedial fashion when there is a usurpation of judicial power or a clear abuse of discretion. Writs of mandamus should not be used as a substitute for appeals.

Dissent: (Harlan, J.) Once it is determined that the district court acted within its power, the writ of mandamus should have been denied. No other issues but the court's ability to act the way it did should be considered by the appellate court.

Will v. United States (S.Ct. 1967)

Facts: Judge Will ordered the government to respond to a bill of particulars submitted by a defendant in a tax-evasion case. The government refused to comply and sought mandamus to vacate Judge Will's order.

Issue: When may an appellate court grant review by means of mandamus?

Rule: (Warren, C.J.) A federal appellate court may review a lower court's order through a writ of mandamus only when the record demonstrates that the court usurped power or clearly abused its discretion.

Kerr v. United States District Court (S.Ct. 1976)

Facts: Several California inmates brought a class action against several state agencies. The agencies sought an issuance of writs of mandamus to compel the district court to vacate two discovery orders. The court of appeals refused to issue the mandamus.

Issue: When should a court issue a writ of mandamus?

Rule: (Marshall, J.) Writs of mandamus should be granted only where no other adequate remedies are available.

Cox Broadcasting Corp. v. Cohn (S.Ct. 1975)

Facts: The Cox Broadcasting Corporation (Cox) reported that Cohn's daughter was a murder victim. Cox argued that the state law permitting Cohn to sue for damages was unconstitutional. Remanding, the state's highest court held the state law to be constitutional. Without waiting for the case's resolution in lower state courts, Cox appealed to the U.S. Supreme Court.

Issue: Can the Supreme Court regard the decision of a highest state court on a federal issue as final judgment even though other issues in the same case may be pending in lower state courts?

Rule: (White, J.) When judgment is rendered on a federal issue, the Supreme Court may regard the decision of the highest court of a state as final even though there may be pending proceedings in lower state courts in the same case.

Bankers Life & Casualty Co. v. Crenshaw (S.Ct. 1988)

Facts: At trial, Bankers Life neglected to raise certain constitutional issues in its defense. Bankers Life only vaguely mentioned "constitutional principles" in its brief to the Mississippi Supreme Court, but did finally raise them in a petition for certiorari to the United States Supreme Court.

Issue: May the Supreme Court exercise certiorari jurisdiction over an issue not raised below?

Rule: (Marshall, J.) Because of comity and the need for a properly developed record for appeal, the Supreme Court will not exercise certiorari jurisdiction over an issue not pressed or passed upon below. A party may not preserve a constitutional challenge by generally invoking the Constitution and awaiting review to specify the constitutional provision it is relying upon. It is up to the prudence of the court to allow such a claim.

Concurrence 1: (White, J.) The Court is not free under "prudential standards" to hear claims not raised below. It is a matter of jurisdiction.

Concurrence 2: (O'Connor, J.) The insurer did argue a due process claim before the state supreme court which is worthy of the Supreme Court's attention.

Concurrence 3: (Scalia, J.) Justice Scalia concurs with Justice White that hearing a constitutional claim is a matter of law, not discretion. But since the majority insists that the matter be left to discretion, he agrees with Justice O'Connor that the due process claim should then be considered.

Ackermann v. United States (S.Ct. 1950)

Facts: Convicted of fraud, Ackerman faced deportation. He delayed filing an appeal on the advice of his counsel. After the time limit for appeals had expired, Ackermann sought relief from the judgment pursuant to FRCP 60(b)(6).

Issue: When will a party who fails to file a timely appeal receive relief from a judgment or an order?

Rule: (Minton, J.) Under FRCP 60(b)(6), a party failing to file a timely appeal will not receive relief from a judgment or an order when the decision to delay bringing the appeal is freely and deliberately taken.

Dissent: (Black, J.) The Court's interpretation of FRCP 60(b)(6) is inhumane. Although the rule states only five areas where an inequitable judgment should not be allowed to stand, it does not exclude other times where equity demands a decision be overturned.

Kulchar v. Kulchar (1969)

Facts: Prior to the rendering of a divorce decree, Mr. Kulchar failed to fully investigate the consequences of the proposed property settlement. Two years later, alleging extrinsic mutual mistake and fraud, Mr. Kulchar secured a modification of the decree.

Issue: May equity set aside a final judgment when the complaining party succeeds in showing only intrinsic mistake?

Rule: Equity may set aside a final judgment where extrinsic mistake or fraud is proved (i.e., others prevent a party from fully presenting his case). However, where the party himself contributed to the fraud or mistake, equity will not set aside the judgment.

Carson Products Co. v. Califano (1979)

Facts: Carson filed suit in district court too challenge an FDA determination that an ingredient in Carson's shaving powder was not entitled to trade secret protection. After judgment was rendered, it was determined in *Zotos International v. Kennedy* that FDA procedures violated due process. The FDA modified its procedures in response to the decision. Carson then brought this appeal which raised a new due process attack on FDA procedures.

Issue: May a party raise an argument for the first time on appeal?

Rule: Although parties are generally not permitted to raise issues on appeal that were not raised at trial, a court of appeals has authority to hear an issue not raised at trial in exceptional circumstances where injustice might otherwise result. A dramatic change in the legal climate that occurred subsequent to a district court decision is such an exceptional circumstance.

Massachusetts Mutual Life Insurance Co. v. Ludwig (S.Ct. 1976)

Facts: In a case for payment on an insurance policy, the district court held that under Illinois conflict-of-law rules, Michigan law applied. In an appeal brought by Ludwig, Massachusetts Mutual argued that Illinois conflict-of-law rules actually required application of Illinois law. The appeals court held that Massachusetts Mutual could not argue that Illinois law applied because it had not cross-appealed from the district court's ruling that Michigan law applied.

Issue: May an appellee who has not cross-appealed attack a ruling of the lower court?

Rule: (Per Curiam) A party who does not appeal from a final decree of a trial court may not attack the decree to correct an error or to supplement the decree with a matter not dealt with below. However, when the party only seeks to attack the reasoning of the lower court, a cross-appeal is not a necessary prerequisite. Massachusetts Mutual's argument that Illinois law applied was no more than an attack on the reasoning of the court.

Lauro Lines s.r.l. v. Chasser (S.Ct. 1989)

Facts: The plaintiffs brought suit in district court to recover damages they sustained while passengers aboard the Achille Lauro, which was hijacked by terrorists. Lauro Lines moved to dismiss, citing a forum selection clause printed on each passenger ticket that required all suits be brought in Italy. The district court declined to enforce the clause. The court of appeals would not hear Lauro Lines' appeal on the ground that the district court's order denying the motion was interlocutory (not a final judgment that ends the litigation on the merits). There is a narrow exception to the final judgment rule, the collateral order doctrine, which allows a party to appeal an interlocutory order if the asserted right would be destroyed if not vindicated before trial.

Issue: Does an order denying a motion to dismiss for improper forum fall under the collateral order exception to the final judgment rule?

Rule: (Brennan, J.) An order denying a motion to dismiss on the basis of a forum-selection clause does not fall under the collateral order exception to the final judgment rule. The potential costs associated with failure to enforce a forum selection clause (e.g., the expense of relitigating the matter in the proper forum) are not sufficient to warrant immediate appeal.

Concurrence: (Scalia, J.) The result in this case is correct because contractual forum selection is not a sufficiently important right to warrant immediate review.

Garner v. Wolfinbarger (1970)

Facts: Plaintiffs sued a corporation in which they were shareholders for a variety of violations in the Northern District of Alabama. The court transferred the case to the Southern District of Alabama under § 1404 (change of venue). The plaintiffs sought review of the transfer order by interlocutory appeal under § 1292(b). Section 1292(b) permits interlocutory appeals for the purpose of resolving a controlling issue of law as to which there is substantial ground for a difference of opinion.

Issue: Is a transfer order subject to interlocutory review under § 1292(b)?

Rule: Section 1292(b) review is inappropriate for challenges to a judge's discretion in granting or denying changes of venue under § 1404. It might be appropriate if the movants were claiming that the district judge failed to correctly construe the statute, but such is not the case here.

Anderson v. Bessemer City (S.Ct. 1985)

Facts: The district court found that Bessemer City had denied Ms. Anderson employment in favor of Mr. Kincaid because of her sex. The court's decision was based on the following subsidiary findings: Anderson was better qualified than Kincaid; male hiring committee members were biased against Anderson because she was a woman; only Anderson was asked if her spouse would object to her taking the job; and the reasons offered by the committee for choosing Kincaid were pretextual. The appellate court conducted a de novo weighing of the evidence in the record and concluded that Kincaid was indeed better qualified for the job.

Issue: When may an appellate court reverse a trial court's findings of fact?

Rule: (White, J.) An appellate court may only reverse a trial court's findings of fact when they are clearly erroneous. Where the trial court and the appellate court reach different, but equally logical, conclusions from the evidence, the interpretation of the trial court controls. Because the findings of the trial court in this case were based on reasonable inferences from the record, its findings must stand.

Gertz v. Bass (1965)

Facts: Gertz sued Bass for wrongful death and personal injuries resulting from a car crash. Without the knowledge of the court or either counsel, the bailiff gave the jury a dictionary during deliberations. This was an error because the dictionary had not been admitted into evidence and contained improper definitions of important legal terms. There was no way of knowing what actual use was made of the dictionary.

Issue: When is an error grounds for reversal?

Rule: An error is grounds for reversal only if it is prejudicial to the complaining party. However, in a situation where error is clear, the danger of prejudice is great, and proof of actual prejudice is difficult, prejudice may be inferred. Such is the case where a jury receives incompetent evidence; it is not necessary to prove that the jury gave the evidence any weight.

Bankers Trust Co. v. Mallis (S.Ct. 1978)

Facts: A district court dismissed a suit brought under the Securities Exchange Act of 1934, but did not enter judgment on a separate document. FRCP 58 stated that judgments are not effective unless set forth on a separate document. A final judgment is required for § 1291 appellate jurisdiction.

Issue: Can a district court decision be a final decision for purposes of § 1291 appellate jurisdiction if it is not set forth on a separate document?

Rule: (Per Curiam) The sole purpose of the separate document requirement is to clarify when the time for appeal begins to run. It is not a requirement for appellate jurisdiction. Thus, parties may waive the separate document requirement where a final judgment has been rendered but a separate document has accidentally not been entered.

FirsTier Mortgage Co. v. Investors Mortgage Insurance Co.
(S.Ct. 1991)

Facts: A judge announced that he intended to grant summary judgment, but he had yet to receive proposed findings of fact and conclusions of law, and he did not explicitly exclude the possibility that he would not change his mind before entering a final judgment. Following this announcement, but before judgment was entered, FirsTier filed a notice of appeal. FRAP 4(a)(2) permits notice of appeal to be filed "after the announcement of a decision or order."

Issue: Is notice of appeal premature where a court has announced that it intends to grant a final judgment, but has not yet terminated the litigation?

Rule: (Marshall, J.) FRAP 4(a)(2) permits notice of appeal following a nonfinal decision if the decision is of the type that would be appealable if immediately followed by the entry of judgment.

CHAPTER 11

PRECLUSION

I. INTRODUCTION
Preclusion of both claims and issues is a long-standing tradition of Anglo-American jurisprudence. Litigants get one opportunity to litigate their case, and if they are unsuccessful, preclusion prevents relitigation even if the first trial did not achieve the optimally just result.

A. Policies
The idea that a judgment once made is binding on all future adjudications is rooted in several policies, including:

1. Avoid multiple suits on identical issues.

2. Compel single litigation of all factually and legally related matters.

3. Achieve repose for the litigants.

4. Conservation of judicial resources.

5. Conservation of the litigants' resources.

6. Ensure uniform application of the law.

B. Stare Decisis
This doctrine is not technically one of preclusion, since neither the same claims nor litigants are involved, generally, but many of the same policy considerations hold true. Under stare decisis, courts are bound by prior decisions of law made by superior courts, and will only overturn those decisions in cases of extreme prejudice or injustice.

II. CLAIM PRECLUSION (RES JUDICATA)
After a valid and final judgment, a transactionally related claim may not be relitigated between the parties of the original suit.

A. Same Claim

1. Transactional Test
The claim to be litigated may not involve the same transaction or occurrence, or series of transactions or occurrences, as a claim litigated in a prior suit.

2. One may not "sue hand by hand or finger by finger."
For instance, a driver damaged in a car accident could not bring separate suits for damage to the driver's legs, the driver's back, the neck, etc. These are clearly transactionally related. However damage to an auto and to the driver in one accident would not be transactionally related. Similarly, if the other driver slandered the plaintiff several days later by referring to the plaintiffs poor driving abilities, that would not be transactionally related to the claims of physical injury.

B.   Same Parties

1. Generally
Parties are bound by a prior decision only when those present in the second suit, or those in privity with the parties, were present in the first suit.

2. Privity
Parties who represent others or are contractually bound to accept liabilities at issue on the case are considered to have been present at the original suit for purposes of claim preclusion. Typical examples of privity include:

   a.   Representatives
   Trustees, guardians, executors, agents, etc.

   b.   Class Action Representatives
   One of the benefits of a class action is that the claims of many plaintiffs are resolved in one action. To allow class members to relitigate their claims would disembowel the efficacy of the class action.

   c.   Co-parties Adjudicating a Finite Resource
   For claim preclusion to apply, the parties must generally have been adverse to each other in the original suit. The exception to this rule occurs with adjudications of finite

resources (water rights, in rem action, etc.). There, although the parties may nominally be on the same side of the litigation, since everybody's share depends on the legal rights of the others, everybody is essentially adverse to each other.

d.   Nonparties
In *Nevada v. United States*, parties not present in the original suit were bound under claim preclusion. However, that case was special in that it involved water rights upon which many people had relied to their detriment.

e.   Laboring Oar
A party not technically present in the original suit may be bound by claim preclusion if they had been so involved in directing the first suit that they could be said to have had a "laboring oar" in the conduct of the litigation. *Montana v. United States*.

3. Parties have no duty to join a lawsuit, and if not joined, they will generally not be bound by claim preclusion.

C.   Valid and Final Judgment

1. Validity
A judgment is valid unless procured through fraud or corruption, or where there existed a lack of personal or subject matter jurisdiction, or there had been no opportunity to be heard.

2. Finality

a.   Decision on the Merits
Defining a final judgment is no easy task. Generally, any decision on the merits of the case is final.

b.   FRCP 12(b)(1)-(5),(7)
Dismissals due to lack of subject matter jurisdiction, lack of personal jurisdiction, improper venue, or insufficient process or service of process, or failure to

join an indispensable party (FRCP 12(b)) are not final judgments.

    c.   FRCP 12(b)(6)
Dismissal for failure to state a claim upon which relief may be granted is a final judgment unless expressly dismissed without prejudice.

    d.   Unappealed Judgments
Decisions that could have been appealed, but were not, are final judgments.

    e.   Ripeness
Dismissal because a claim is not sufficiently ripe (see Justiciability) is not a final judgment.

D.   Counterclaims

1. Permissive Counterclaims
Permissive counterclaims are generally not precluded from future litigation, because they are generally not transactionally related to the case at hand.

2. Compulsory Counterclaims
By definition, compulsory counterclaims must be brought in the original suit or be barred from future litigation. Compulsory counterclaims are generally transactionally related to the case at hand. An exception exists where the court deciding the first suit decided in favor of the defendant but cannot afford that party full relief on the counterclaim.

III.   ISSUE PRECLUSION (COLLATERAL ESTOPPEL)
When an issue of fact or law is **actually litigated** and determined by a **valid and final judgment,** and the determination is **essential to the judgment,** the determination is conclusive in a subsequent action between the **parties,** whether on the same or a different claim. *Restatement, Second, Judgments* § 27.

A.   Actually Litigated

1. Similar Facts
Similar facts do not mean that the issue was actually litigated. In *Cromwell v. County of Sac*, the court held that a finding of fraud in the conveyance of one coupon of interest was not preclusive for other coupons of interest, even though the coupons all came from the same municipal bond.

2. Burdens of Proof
An issue may not have been actually litigated if the first issue had a lower burden of proof. For instance, just because a defendant was held to have committed assault in a civil case (preponderance of the evidence), does not mandate a finding of assault in a criminal case (beyond a reasonable doubt).

Likewise, a verdict of not guilty on a criminal assault charge does not preclude a finding of assault in a civil tort case, where the plaintiff's burden is much lower.

B.   Essential to the Judgment
It must be shown that the issue alleged to have preclusive effect had to be decided by the decision maker at the first trial.

1. Multiple Theories
Where a decision could have been rendered on any of several theories, without a special verdict no facts may turn out to have subsequent preclusive effect.

2. Proximate v. Ultimate Facts
In *The Evergreens v. Nunan*, Judge Hand noted that not all trivial facts should be given preclusive effect, even if they did turn out to be essential to the judgment. Although he tried to distinguish between proximate facts (no preclusion) that were mere intermediary steps and ultimate facts (preclusion), the distinction remains hazy. Some factors that could be helpful in such an analysis is whether the parties actively litigated the issue, whether the issue is "trivial," or whether the importance of the fact could have been foreseen.

C.   Same Parties

1. Traditional Rule – Mutuality
   As in claim preclusion, the traditional rule had been that in order to assert issue preclusion the same parties or their privies had to have been present at the original case. The general rule was that if you couldn't estop your adversary, they couldn't estop you.

2. Modern Rule – Nonmutuality
   The doctrine of mutuality given way to a more flexible standard of nonmutual collateral estoppel. Not all jurisdictions recognize nonmutual collateral estoppel, and some only recognize defensive nonmutual collateral estoppel.

   a. Defensive Nonmutual Collateral Estoppel
      Where a plaintiff had already received an adverse judgment on an issue, a defendant not party or privy to that first suit could use that judgment to estop the plaintiff from subsequently relitigating that claim.

   b. Offensive Nonmutual Collateral Estoppel
      Where a defendant has already litigated an issue and lost, a plaintiff not party to the first suit may use that judgment to estop the defendant from asserting the same defense.

   c. Mutuality and the United States as a Party
      Because there is only one government, requiring the United States to be bound by the first decision on an issue could result in severe public costs. Furthermore, given the limited resources of the government, the Supreme Court has been reluctant to extend the principles of nonmutual collateral estoppel against the government.

      i. Defensive Collateral Estoppel
         The government may assert defensive nonmutual collateral estoppel when sued, as any private litigant.

ii. Offensive Collateral Estoppel
In *United States v. Mendoza*, the Court refused to allow a private party to assert offensive nonmutual collateral estoppel against the government. However, mutual collateral estoppel is still available. *United States v. Stauffer Chemical Company*. It would be unfair to let the United States use its resources to get favorable legal rulings by bankrupting a single defendant through legal fees.

D. Valid and Final Judgment
The standard here is generally identical as that for claim preclusion, above.

E. Exceptions (*Restatement, Second, Judgments* § 28)

1. Party to be precluded could not by law have obtained review of the judgment in the first action.

2. There has been an intervening change in the applicable law.

3. To enforce the collateral estoppel would result in an inequitable administration of law.

4. The second court has very different procedures or rules, warranting relitigation.

5. The party to be precluded had to meet a heavier burden of persuasion in the first suit, the burden is on another party, or the party requesting preclusion has a heavier burden in the second suit.

6. The public interest warrants relitigation.

7. The effects of the preclusion were not foreseeable at the time the first action was litigated.

8. The party to be precluded did not have a full and fair opportunity to litigate the issues.

IV. INTERSYSTEM PRECLUSION

A. Interstate Preclusion

1. The Full Faith and Credit Clause
The Constitution, Art. IV, § 1, stipulates that every court in the nation must accord "full faith and credit" to the prior decisions of other courts in the country.

2. Full Faith and Credit Act (28 U.S.C. § 1738)
Enacted pursuant to the Full Faith and Credit Clause, this statute clarifies what constitutes a valid decision, and what deference it is entitled in the courts.

3. Effect
A decision of a sister state is given as much deference as it would receive in the state issued, even if not enforceable in the forum state.

4. Child Custody (28 U.S.C. § 1738A)
Even though child custody orders are not technically "final" because the issuing court generally reserves the right to modify the order to protect the needs of the child, this act prevents other courts from modifying such orders unless:

   a. The state is the home state of the child;

   b. No other state would have jurisdiction;

   c. The child was abandoned in the state, or some other emergency exists; or

   d. The state that originally issued the order has declined jurisdiction.

B. Preclusive Effect of State Judgments in Federal Courts
Although the Full Faith and Credit Clause only applies to the states, the Full Faith and Credit Statute (28 U.S.C. § 1738) extends the same requirements to the federal courts as well.

C. Preclusive Effect of Federal Judgments in State Courts
Although statutory and constitutional authority is murky, most observers agree that states must afford federal judgments the

same full faith and credit as afforded to decisions of sister states. This rule has never been seriously challenged.

D. Preclusive Effect of Foreign Judgments
    Absent a treaty, judgments of foreign nations are not given full faith and credit. However, the United States has such treaties with most countries.

CASE CLIPS

Rush v. City of Maple Heights (1958)

Facts: Rush was injured when she fell in an accident. She successfully sued for damages to personal property. Then she commenced a new action to recover for her personal injuries.

Issue: When can a plaintiff split a cause of action arising from a single act?

Rule: A plaintiff may maintain only one action arising from a single transaction or occurrence.

Mathews v. New York Racing Association, Inc. (1961)

Facts: Matthews sued two employees of the New York Racing Association, alleging assault and libel. After the conclusion of that suit, Matthews sued the Racing Association itself, alleging assault, kidnapping, false arrest, and false imprisonment. The first suit dealt with actions occurring on April 4 and 10. The second action only related to actions of April 4.

Issue: When are two claims so similar as to preclude the second claim on the grounds of res judicata?

Rule: Res judicata bars subsequent suits involving the same parties, or those in privity with them, based on a claim that once reached a judgment on the merits.

Jones v. Morris Plan Bank of Portsmouth (1937)

Facts: In a prior suit, Morris Plan Bank had obtained a judgment against Jones regarding two unpaid installments on a note secured by a conditional sales contract containing an acceleration clause. After obtaining judgment, Morris Plan brought, and won, a second action for a subsequent unpaid installment. When Morris Plan took and sold Jones's auto, Jones brought the present action.

Issue: Where an installment contract containing an acceleration clause is breached, must a party sue for all installments in a single action or can it sue for past due installments only and separately sue for payments that subsequently become past due?

Rule: If a transaction is represented by one single and indivisible contract and the breach gives rise to one single cause of action, it cannot be split into distinct parts and separate actions may not be maintained for each.

Mitchell v. Federal Intermediate Credit Bank (1932)

Facts: In a previous suit between Mitchell and Federal Intermediate Credit Bank, Mitchell's answer contained no counterclaim. After winning that suit, Mitchell brought an action against Federal Intermediate Credit Bank, asserting a counterclaim based on the subject matter of the original suit.

Issue: Is a party barred from litigating a claim that could have been asserted as a counterclaim in a previous action between the same parties?

Rule: A party may not split a cause of action by using one portion in defense of a complaint while reserving the remainder for offense in a subsequent suit.

Cromwell v. County of Sac (S.Ct. 1896)

Facts: Cromwell brought an action to cash in four bonds and four coupons for interest on those bonds. The bonds had been issued by the County of Sac. In a previous action brought by Smith, the original bondholder, other interest coupons from the same bonds had been held to be fraudulently issued, and thus null and void.

Issue: When does the doctrine of collateral estoppel preclude litigating that issue in a subsequent suit?

Rule: (Field, J.) All issues actually litigated in a previous action and all other issues that could have been litigated cannot be subsequently relitigated. If, however, a second action between the same parties is based on a different claim or demand, the judgment in the prior action operates as an estoppel only as to issues actually litigated.

Russell v. Place (S.Ct. 1876)

Facts: Russell sued Place for patent infringement and obtained a verdict for damages. Place continued to produce the product. Russell sued again and tried to estop Place from using any of the defenses raised in the first suit.

Issue: When does a prior judgment effect an estoppel in a subsequent suit between the parties?

Rule: (Field, J.) A judgment upon a question directly involved in one suit is conclusive as to that question in another suit between the same parties. It must appear, however, either on the face of the record or by extrinsic evidence, that the issue was raised and determined in the former suit.

Rios v. Davis (1963)

Facts: A car accident involved Rios, Davis and the Popular Dry Goods Company. In the first suit, the Popular Dry Goods Company sued Davis for negligence. Davis responded with a defense of contributory negligence by Popular Dry Goods and Rios, as well as a counterclaim against Rios for negligence. The jury found negligence on the part of all three litigants, thus denying recovery to Popular Dry Goods and Davis. In the second suit, Rios sued Davis for negligence. Davis's defense included an assertion that the first jury's determination of Rios's negligence precluded Rios's suit.

Issue: When does a finding in a previous trial have res judicata or collateral estoppel effect?

Rule: To have res judicata or collateral estoppel effect, a finding must serve as a basis or one of the grounds of a judgment. Since the first jury could have decided Davis's claim against Rios because of Davis's contributory negligence, Rios's negligence (or lack thereof) was irrelevant to the first suit, and cannot therefore be truly said to have been litigated.

Commissioner of Internal Revenue v. Sunnen (S.Ct. 1948)

Facts: Having won an earlier suit brought by the IRS, Sunnen, in a subsequent suit dealing with the same facts and issues, asserted collateral estoppel. During the years between the two actions, however, pertinent tax principles had changed.

Issue: Where the facts, issues, and parties are identical but applicable law changes in the time between two suits, does collateral estoppel apply?

Rule: (Murphy, J.) Collateral estoppel only applies where the matter raised in the second suit is identical in all respects with that decided in the first suit and where the controlling facts and applicable legal rules remain unchanged.

Hanover Logansport, Inc. v. Robert C. Anderson, Inc. (1987)

Facts: Hanover agreed to lease certain property to Anderson, but Hanover failed to deliver the premises on the contract date. Anderson filed suit for breach, seeking "specific performance or in the alternative money damages." Before trial, Hanover offered to convey the property to Anderson. Anderson accepted with a reservation retaining his right to recover damages from the breach. The parties consented to have their settlement entered as a judgment on the record. Subsequently, Hanover attempted to have the remaining breach action dismissed, arguing that the prior settlement constituted a judgment which prevented any further litigation.

Issue: May a plaintiff who accepts an offer of judgment which awards one type of alternative relief contained in his complaint reserve the right to additional damages from the same cause of action?

Rule: In order for a plaintiff to successfully reserve a claim, the reservation must be incorporated into the offer of judgment and must be an inherent part of the original complaint. This rule avoids protracted litigation by allowing reserved claims only after insuring that it is both parties' intention to continue litigation after a consent judgment is entered.

Griffen v. Big Spring Independent School District (1983)

Facts: Griffen, a Texas school teacher, brought suit against the school district alleging his termination was racially motivated. A two day state administrative hearing resulted in a finding for Griffen, which the school district appealed. The Board of Education took the appeal, and reversed the finding of the hearing officer based solely upon the school districts' proposal as to the findings of fact. Griffen was not given the opportunity to submit his own proposal, or respond to the district's proposal. Griffen brought a subsequent suit in federal court based on the same allegations, but the court granted summary judgment for the defendant on the grounds of collateral estoppel, relying on the finding of the Board that the discharge was not motivated by race.

Issue: Should the findings of an administrative agency always be given collateral effect in later suits concerning the same controversy?

Rule: The doctrine of collateral estoppel does not apply when the party against whom the earlier decision is asserted did not have a "full and fair opportunity" to litigate the claim or issue. If the prior litigation lacked quality, extensiveness, or fairness, relitigation is warranted.

Ralph Wolff & Sons v. New Zealand Insurance Co. (1933)

Facts: After Wolffs business was destroyed by fire, he sued a number of insurance companies. The cases were consolidated and Wolff gained judgment. Wolff subsequently sued two additional insurance companies for the same loss. The insurance companies argued that the total loss was settled in the consolidated cases, and that the amount of loss should be res judicata.

Issue: Can a party assert a prior judgment as res judicata if he was not a party to the prior suit?

Rule: In order to render a judgment res judicata there must be identity of parties or their privies, and that is so even though the judgment relied upon as a bar involved the same set of facts.

Bernhard v. Bank of America National Trust & Saving Association. (1942)

Facts: Before her death, Sather transferred money from her bank account to her executor, Cook. Bernhard, representing the beneficiaries of Sather's estate, sued Cook for the money, alleging that Cook did not have Sather's permission, and lost. Bernhard, administrator of Sather's estate, then sued the bank for wrongfully transferring the money.

Issue: Must one asserting a judgment as res judicata have been a party, or in privity with a party, to the first suit?

Rule: A party asserting res judicata need not have been a party, or in privity with a party, to the earlier action (i.e., mutuality is not required).

Parklane Hosiery Co. v. Shore (S.Ct. 1979)

Facts: Shore brought a stockholder's class action against Parklane Hosiery for damages caused by a materially false and misleading proxy statement. Before this action came to trial in state court, the SEC filed suit against Parklane Hosiery in federal district court, alleging the same violations, and won. SEC actions do not receive jury consideration. Shore moved for partial summary judgment on the issues that had been resolved in the SEC action.

Issue: Can one who was not a party to the first suit offensively assert collateral estoppel to prevent a party from relitigating issues resolved in the first suit?

Rule: (Stewart, J.) A litigant who was not a party to a prior judgment may use that judgment offensively to prevent a party from relitigating issues resolved in an earlier suit.

Dissent: (Rehnquist, J.) The Seventh Amendment requires that in order to estop a claim, it must first have been litigated before a forum where a jury trial is available.

In Re Multidistrict Civil Actions Involving Air Crash Disaster Near Dayton, Ohio, on March 9, 1967 (1972)

Facts: Humphrey, a family member of a victim of a midair collision, brought a wrongful death action against Tann Company, owner of one of the colliding airplanes. In a previous multidistrict lawsuit brought by other families of victims, the court had ruled that Tann was not liable for the midair disaster. Tann raised the defense of collateral estoppel and moved for summary judgment on the issue of liability.

Issue: May collateral estoppel be applied against a person who was not a party to the prior action?

Rule: In multilitigation arising from common disasters, collateral estoppel can preclude a nonparty from litigating identical factual and legal issues that were settled in the first suit.

Martin v. Wilks (S.Ct. 1989)

Facts: In the first suit, the National Association for the Advancement of Colored People (NAACP) and seven black firefighters received a publicly announced decree setting forth remedial schemes for the hiring of black people as firefighters. Seven white firefighters sought an injunction to intervene, but were denied relief due to the late filing of their petition to intervene. In the second suit, another group of white firefighters brought suit alleging injury due to enforcement of the decree.

Issue: When are people, not party (nor in privity) to the first suit, prohibited from contesting a judgment?

Rule: (Rehnquist, C.J.) Parties are not bound by previous litigation unless they are joined. There is no duty to intervene in the lawsuit, even if they know their rights may be affected.

Parker v. Hoeffer (1957)

Facts: Parker, a resident of Vermont, obtained a final judgment in Vermont state court against Hoeffer, a resident of New York, for both alienation of affection and criminal conversation. Since Parker could not collect damages in Vermont, she brought an action to enforce the judgment in New York. Hoeffer defended on the grounds that the New York Civil Practice Act expressed a public policy opposing claims of alienation of affection.

Issue: Must a state court give full faith and credit to a foreign judgment even though the underlying claim would not be enforceable in the forum state?

Rule: A judgment obtained in a sister state is entitled to full faith and credit in another state even if the underlying claim would not be enforced in the forum state.

Allen v. McCurry (S.Ct. 1980)

Facts: McCurry brought suit under 42 U.S.C. § 1983 against police officers, claiming violation of his Fourth Amendment right to be free from unreasonable searches and seizures. The policemen moved for summary judgment based on a previous action in state court in which the trial judge denied suppression of the evidence that was used at trial to convict McCurry.

Issue: Is a party precluded (i.e., collaterally estopped) from litigating a § 1983 claim in federal court if he previously litigated the claim in state court?

Rule: (Stewart, J.) A state court judgment or decision is binding when the state court, acting within its proper jurisdiction, has given the parties a full and fair opportunity to litigate federal claims.

Dissent: (Blackmun, J.) Section 1983 had been passed before nonmutual collateral estoppel had been established, so nonmutual estoppel should not apply. Also, the two trials are entirely different, regarding remedies, institutional pressures, and motivation to win. Finally, the decision to exclude evidence is clouded by a judge's desire to include relevant evidence, even if gained along the edges of the Fourth Amendment.

Patterson v. McLean Credit Union (S.Ct. 1989)

Facts: Patterson sued McLean Credit Union for wrongful termination, alleging racial discrimination. Previous Supreme Court decisions would have dictated a decision against McLean Credit Union.

Issue: When should a court overrule controlling precedent?

Rule: (Kennedy, J.) Precedents involving statutory interpretation should be overruled only where the decision has been undermined by subsequent changes of development in the law, where the decision is unworkable, where the decision poses a direct obstacle to important objectives defined in other laws, or where the decision has become outdated and after being tested by experience, has been found to be inconsistent with the sense of justice or with the social welfare.

Clancey v. McBride (1929)

Facts: Clancey sued for property damage when her car collided with McBride's car. The court ruled for Clancey. Subsequently, Clancey sued McBride for her personal injuries.

Issue: Must a single act giving rise to two causes of action be litigated all at once?

Rule: Where a cause of action derives from a single act, different rights are infringed and distinct causes of action exist. Recovery of a judgment on one cause of action is not a bar to a subsequent action to recover judgment on the other.

Nevada v. United States (S.Ct. 1983)

Facts: In 1913, in the first suit, the federal government, representing the Pyramid Lake Indian Reservation and the Newlands Reclamation Project, asserted a claim to water rights along the Truckee River. The defendants were named as all water users along the Truckee River in Nevada. The federal court affirmed a settlement in 1944. In 1973, the federal government instituted a second action, seeking additional rights to the Truckee River on behalf of the Pyramid Lake Indian Reservation, as well as for environmental purposes. The defendants included the successors to the defendants in the original case, and the Newlands Reclamation Project.

Issue: When is a second suit involving the same parties (or those in privity) barred where new claims are being brought?

Rule: (Rehnquist, J.) If the suit involves dividing a limited resource among claimants, the litigation is barred due to the reliance interest based on the previous decision.

Keidatz v. Albany (1952)

Facts: In the first suit between Keidatz and Albany, Albany's general demurrer was granted for failure to state a claim of action. In the second suit, Keidatz added a new allegation.

Issue: Does judgment entered on demurrer bar a subsequent suit in which an allegation absent from the former complaint is now advanced?

Rule: A general demurrer to an earlier complaint is not a bar to a subsequent suit between the same parties if new or additional facts that cure the defects in the original pleadings are alleged.

Cambria v. Jeffery (1940)

Facts: In the first action, Jeffery sued Cambria for personal injuries and property damage caused by Cambria's employee in an automobile collision. The court found that both operators were negligent, and judgment was entered for Cambria. In the second action Cambria sued to recover damages to his automobile.

Issue: When is a party barred from litigating all facts found in an earlier suit?

Rule: Res judicata only bars litigation of previously adjudicated facts only. A fact is adjudicated only when it is shown to have been a basis for relief, denial of relief, or other ultimate right established by the judgment.

Neenan v. Woodside Astoria Transportation Co. (1933)

Facts: In the first suit, Huppmann received judgment against Woodside by proving that Woodside's negligence was the sole cause of an accident between Huppmann's car and Woodside's bus. In the second suit, Neenan, a bus passenger, sued Huppman and Woodside. Neenan made an unsuccessful motion to introduce the prior judgment in order to prove his own lack of negligence.

Issue: When does a judgment in a prior lawsuit preclude trying an issue in a subsequent suit?

Rule: The judgment on the merits of a prior law suit does not preclude relitigation by a party who was neither a party nor in privity with a party of the prior action.

B.R. De Witt, Inc. v. Hall (1967)

Facts: In an earlier suit, B.R. De Witt's employee brought and won an action for damages against Hall for personal injuries sustained in a collision with B.R. De Witt's truck. Shortly thereafter, B.R. De Witt sued Hall for damage to the truck.

Issue: Can one who was not a party to a judgment assert that judgment offensively to prevent a party from relitigating issues resolved in an earlier suit?

Rule: A plaintiff may use a prior judgment rendered in a suit to which he was not a party in order to preclude the other side from asserting a defense.

United States v. Mendoza (S.Ct. 1984)

Facts: The Nationality Act provided that noncitizens who served honorably with the United States during World War II were exempt from some nationality requirements. Due to political pressure, however, the Attorney General revoked the authority of the Immigration and Naturalization Service to grant these exemptions. In the first suit, 68 Filipino war veterans challenged the Attorney General's action and prevailed. In the second suit, Mendoza, a Filipino war veteran not included in the first claim, asserted the same claim as the previous 68 veterans.

Issue: May a plaintiff suing the United States use a prior case to which the plaintiff was not a party to preclude the government from asserting the same defense asserted in the first suit?

Rule: (Rehnquist, J.) A private party may not assert offensive nonmutual collateral estoppel against the United States Government.

United States v. Stauffer Chemical Co. (S.Ct. 1984)

Facts: In the first suit, the Environmental Protection Agency (EPA) tried to inspect a chemical plant owned by Stauffer in Wyoming (Ninth Circuit). Stauffer challenged the EPA action and won. In the second suit, Stauffer challenged an attempt by the EPA to inspect Stauffer's plant in Tennessee (Sixth Circuit).

Issue: When may a party assert collateral estoppel against the federal government?

Rule: (Rehnquist, J.) Although nonmutual estoppel may not be asserted against the government (see *United States v. Mendoza,* above), mutual collateral estoppel may still be asserted, to prevent the government from using its massive resources to bankrupt a single defendant, and thus win its action.

Concurrence: (White, J.) Since the two actions occurred in different federal jurisdictions, the action might be maintained against the same defendant if the laws in the two jurisdictions differed. However, in this case, the Sixth Circuit had not decided the relevant issue, so collateral estoppel should apply.

Thompson v. Thompson (S.Ct. 1988)

Facts: Susan Clay (formerly Susan Thompson) and David Thompson had joint custody of their son, Matthew, but the California court gave Susan temporary custody until the case could be reviewed. Susan took Matthew to Louisiana, where a state court awarded her sole custody. Two months later, the California court modified its order and gave custody of Matthew to David.

Issue: What preclusive effect should one state court give to another state's custody decree, given that such decrees are normally subject to judicial modification, and thus are never "final."

Rule: (Marshall, J.) Under the Full Faith and Credit Clause of the Constitution, a state should give full preclusive effect to state custody decrees, even though they are modifiable by the state that issues them.

Marrese v. American Academy of Orthopaedic Surgeons (S.Ct. 1985)

Facts: In state court, Marrese alleged that the American Academy of Orthopaedic Surgeons violated his common law associational rights. The court dismissed the suit for failure to state a cause of action. Subsequently, in federal court, Marrese alleged that the Academy had violated the Antitrust Act, an allegation not raised in state court.

Issue: Does a state court judgment have preclusive effect on a federal claim that could not have been raised in the state suit?

Rule: (O'Connor, J.) Since state preclusion law requires that the first suit had to have been able to be brought in state court, a state court decision will not have preclusive effect on a cause of action that could only have been brought in federal court.

Concurrence: (Burger, C.J.) It is likely that state courts will not address the issue of whether exclusively federal claims should be precluded if a state suit is brought first. This may be a good reason to formulate a federal rule of preclusion.

Williamson v. Columbia Gas & Electric Corp. (1950)

Facts: Williamson claimed that Columbia Gas & Electric had conspired with others to violate antitrust laws. A few months later, Williamson brought a second action against Columbia Gas & Electric, in the same court, for the same damages, based on the same facts, but under a different theory. The court dismissed the second action because the statute of limitations had run.

Issue: When a suit begun after a pending suit results in judgment, does res judicata bar prosecution of the pending suit?

Rule: Where common operative facts are present, a judgment rendered in the second suit bars prosecution of the first suit.

Hennepin Paper Co. v. Fort Wayne Corrugated Paper Co. (1946)

Facts: Hennepin Paper brought an action against Fort Wayne Corrugated Paper to reform a written contract. Fort Wayne Corrugated Paper moved for summary judgment on the grounds that it had successfully defended an earlier judgment suit brought by Hennepin on the same contract.

Issue: Is a party barred from raising a claim he could have litigated in a previous suit against the same adversary?

Rule: A party may not maintain a second action against another if he could have joined all claims in a prior suit between the parties.

Sutcliffe Storage & Warehouse Co. v. United States (1947)

Facts: Sutcliffe Storage sued for additional rent, claiming that the United States used a greater area than was designated in the lease. The Tucker Act prevented Sutcliffe from suing for more than $10,000 in any one action. As a result, Sutcliffe Storage brought three additional separate actions against the United States for violation of the lease agreements. The district court dismissed the latter three actions on the ground they were brought for inseparable parts of the claim set forth in the first action.

Issue: When may a party split a claim?

Rule: Under the doctrine of res judicata, a claim may not be split when the resultant multiple claims arise from the same controversy.

Harrington v. Vandalia-Butler Board of Education (1981)

Facts: Harrington sued for employment discrimination under 42 U.S.C. § 2000e. As Harrington appealed an adverse decision on the first suit, the Supreme Court rendered a decision that would allow Harrington to sue under 42 U.S.C. § 1983. Harrington then brought a new suit under § 1983.

Issue: Is a claim precluded by a prior judgment when the legal theory now advanced was not available to the claimant at the time of the prior suit?

Rule: A prior judgment on the merits operates as a bar to a later suit seeking recovery for the same injury even though a different legal theory of recovery is advanced in the second suit and even if an intervening judicial decision effects a change in the law that bears directly on the legal theory advanced in the second suit.

Waterhouse v. Levine (1903)

Facts: Waterhouse's action for breach of contract was dismissed as premature, since the contract had not actually been breached even though a breach was inevitable. When Levine finally did breach, Waterhouse sued again.

Issue: Does dismissal of a premature claim have preclusive effect?

Rule: A judgment that a claim is premature is not a final judgment on the merits; consequently, it lacks preclusive effect.

Rinehart v. Locke (1971)

Facts: Rinehart sued various private detectives and police officers, alleging false arrest. The court dismissed the claim for failure to allege lack of probable cause. Rinehart subsequently brought a second action against the detectives and officers for false arrest but this time he alleged lack of probable cause.

Issue: When does the dismissal of a complaint for failure to state a claim preclude bringing a second suit on the same facts even though the complaint has been fixed?

Rule: An order dismissing a complaint for failure to state a claim which does not specify that the dismissal is without prejudice, has preclusive effect.

Schwabe v. Chantilly, Inc. (1975)

Facts: In a rental nonpayment case, the tenants interposed the affirmative defense that they were fraudulently induced to sign the lease, but did not assert any counterclaims. They then sought damages in a subsequent action based on the alleged fraud.

Issue: Is a party barred from maintaining an action that was raised as an affirmative defense in a prior action?

Rule: When a defendant prevails on an affirmative defense that could have been asserted instead as a counterclaim, he may maintain a subsequent action based upon the facts of the previously asserted defense.

Dindo v. Whitney (1971)

Facts: Whitney was a passenger while Dindo got his car into an accident. In the first suit, Whitney sued Dindo for negligent driving, and the insurance company settled the case. Dindo did not assert the compulsory counterclaim that Whitney had contributed to the accident. Dindo did raise the claim, however, in a subsequent suit against Whitney.

Issue: When does failure to raise a compulsory counterclaim not bar a subsequent action?

Rule: It is inequitable to apply FRCP 13(a) (which bars actions arising out of compulsory counterclaims) when the prior case is settled and the party did not know he had a compulsory counterclaim to assert.

Little v. Blue Goose Motor Coach Co. (1931)

Facts: Blue Goose successfully sued Little for property damage to Blue Goose's bus that occurred when Little drove his car into it. As Little appealed, he also commenced an action against Blue Goose for personal injuries. Little died before trial and his executor took over. The executor then commenced a successful wrongful death action against Blue Goose, alleging both negligence and willful and wanton negligence.

Issue: When does a judgment preclude a subsequent suit that involved the same parties and issues?

Rule: Though based on a different legal theory, preclusion arises when material issues in a subsequent lawsuit have been determined in a prior suit between the same parties or their privies.

Jacobson v. Miller (1879)

Facts: Jacobson sued Miller and obtained judgment for rent due under a lease. Subsequently, Jacobson sued for other installments due under the same lease. Miller then denied execution of the lease (which he did not do in the prior suit) and Jacobson offered the previous judgment as proof of execution.

Issue: Must a party to a lawsuit raise all his possible defenses in order not to lose them in a subsequent litigation involving the same questions, but relating to a different subject matter?

Rule: A party need not raise all his defenses in a litigation simply because of fear of losing them in a subsequent litigation relating to a different subject matter, which may involve the same questions.

Berlitz School of Language of America v. Everest House (1980)

Facts: In the first suit, Berlitz Schools sued Charles Berlitz, claiming that his "Passport" series of Spanish study guides violated the Berlitz School's trademark of the name "Berlitz." The School lost, in part because of a disclaimer on Charles Berlitz's books. Five years later, Charles Berlitz issued a new series of "Step-by-Step" Spanish study guides. Berlitz Schools then brought a new suit on the new series of books with the same disclaimer.

Issue: Are parties collaterally estopped from relitigating issues that were resolved in a previous suit?

Rule: Collateral estoppel bars parties and their privies from relitigating issues which were finally and necessarily resolved in a previous suit.

United States v. Moser (S.Ct. 1924)

Facts: One Civil War statute granted retired Civil War veterans three-quarters the salary of the rank above theirs. In the first suit, Moser, a graduate of the U.S. Naval Academy, sued the United States and received his back pay. In another suit, Jasper, also a U.S. Naval Academy cadet during the Civil War, lost because the government discovered another retirement statute that precluded recovery. The United States stopped payments to Moser, and Moser brought yet another suit to reinstate the payments.

Issue: Is a party barred from relitigating an issue where, in the prior judgment, the law had been wrongly determined?

Rule: (Sutherland, J.) Res judicata bars a party from relitigating an issue, even though the decision was based on an erroneous application of the law.

Spilker v. Hankin (1951)

Facts: Spilker gave Hankin, her attorney, a series of notes as payment for legal services. After Spilker defaulted on the second note, Hankin sued and was awarded judgment. As the remaining five notes became due, Hankin sued to collect. Spilker then raised the defense of misrepresentation.

Issue: Is a defense that is not raised in an earlier trial precluded from subsequent trials on the same issues?

Rule: Because the policies underlying the doctrine of res judicata must, at times, yield to competing policies, the doctrine will not be inflexibly applied.

Blonder-Tongue Laboratories v. University of Illinois Foundation (S.Ct. 1971)

Facts: Blonder-Tongue Labs sued a third party for patent infringement. The court declared Blonder-Tongue's patent invalid. Subsequently, Blonder-Tongue then sued The University of Illinois for patent infringement.

Issue: Where a plaintiff has fully but unsuccessfully litigated a claim in an earlier suit, is he barred from relitigating the claim against a different defendant in a subsequent suit?

Rule: (White, J.) If a plaintiff has, after fairly and fully litigating his claim, received an adverse judgment, he may not relitigate the claim against a different defendant in a subsequent suit.

Fagnan v. Great Central Insurance Co. (1978)

Facts: Two automobiles collided in Wisconsin. In the first car the driver, Robert Thompson, was killed, and the passenger, David Harness, was injured. In the second car, the driver, Duane Fagnan, was injured. In the first suit, Harness sued Thompson's estate in Minnesota. Thompson's estate sued Fagnan for contribution. Harness then sued Fagnan, and Fagnan cross-claimed against Thompson's estate. Eventually the case was settled.

In the second suit, Fagnan sued Thompson's insurer, Great Central Insurance, as well as Thompson's father in Wisconsin under a Wisconsin statute. The jury found for Fagnan against Great Central Insurance, but not against Thompson's father. Great Insurance appealed.

Issue: Is a claim precluded because of a failure to assert it in the first action, even though the claim could not have been brought in that state?

Rule: Under FRCP 13(a), a counterclaim arising out of the same transaction or occurrence that is the subject of a suit not requiring for its adjudication the presence of third parties is compulsory and, if not advanced, extinguished by a judgment. Consequently, a compulsory counterclaim not asserted against an insured is barred as against an insurer whose liability is derivative.

Fauntleroy v. Lum (S.Ct. 1908)

Facts: In Mississippi, Fauntleroy brought suit to enforce a Missouri judgment involving a gambling transaction. Lum claimed that the transaction was illegal under Mississippi state law. Lum further claimed that he had not been allowed to show in the Missouri trial that the transaction was illegal under Mississippi law. Nevertheless, the court ordered judgment for Fauntleroy.

Issue: Is a foreign state court judgment entitled to full faith and credit when the decision is based on a mistake of law?

Rule: (Holmes, J.) A foreign state court judgment is conclusive, entitled to full faith and credit and cannot be impeached by showing it was based upon a mistake of law.

Dissent: (White, J.) No state is obligated to give effect to a judgment of a sister state that would contravene the state's own public policy. The rule of comity (deference and voluntary respect) governs the relations between and among the states.

Hart v. American Airlines; Landano v. American Airlines; Kirchstein v. American Airlines (1969)

Facts: A number of wrongful death actions were brought in various courts. The first case to be tried resulted in a verdict for Creary. Subsequently, in the present action, American Airlines moved for a joint trial and all the plaintiffs crossmoved for summary judgment on the issue of liability, alleging the judgment in the Creary case was conclusive on the issue of American's liability.

Issue: Is a party precluded from relitigating the issue of liability that was decided against him in a previous suit in another state brought by a party not present here?

Rule: A party is estopped from relitigating issues decided in a prior suit in another state, if he had a full and fair opportunity to defend and the issue in the previous suit is decisive of the issue in the present suit.

Hilton v. Guyot (S.Ct. 1895)

Facts: Guyot, a Frenchman sued Hilton, an American, in a United States circuit court to recover judgment rendered by a French court. Hilton unsuccessfully contended that the merits of the case should be re-examined.

Issue: Is a judgment of a foreign nation's court entitled to full credit and conclusive effect when sued upon in the U.S.?

Rule: (Gray, J.) A foreign judgment is not entitled to full faith and credit when sued upon in the United States, but is prima facie evidence only of the justice of plaintiff's claim.

Bank of Montreal v. Olafsson (1981)

Facts: Olafsson sued to recover payments due on promissory notes. The district court granted Olafsson a default judgment, but subsequently discovered that it lacked jurisdiction over the subject matter. The Bank of Montreal successfully moved to have the judgment set aside.

Issue: Must a court vacate an invalid judgment?

Rule: The granting of a motion under FRCP 60(b) is a matter of discretion for the district court, whose order will be set aside only if it constitutes an abuse of discretion.

Marshall v. Lockhead (1952)

Facts: Lockhead sued Marshall to set aside a prior judgment that divested Lockhead of title to realty because of delinquent taxes. Lockhead argued the judgment was invalid because he had not been served with process and did not enter an appearance. Marshall contended that the judgment was not subject to collateral attack, because Lockhead accepted the benefits of the judgment.

Issue 1: Can a plaintiff introduce evidence outside the record (i.e., collaterally attack a judgment) to show that judgment was rendered against him without effective service of process?

Rule 1: Where a personal judgment that resulted in the seizure and sale of property has been rendered against a party, he may not introduce evidence outside the record to show that the judgment was rendered without any service of process on him.

Issue 2: Is one who accepts and retains the fruits of a judgment estopped from later asserting the judgment's invalidity?

Rule 2: One who accepts and retains the benefits of a judgment is estopped from thereafter asserting the judgment's invalidity.

Britton v. Gannon (1955)

Facts: Gannon sued Britton in Illinois and won. Gannon then sued to recover the judgment in Oklahoma. Britton argued that the judgment was fraudulently obtained. The court held it was compelled to enforce the judgment under the Full Faith and Credit Clause of the United States Constitution and would not hear any evidence of fraud.

Issue: Must a state enforce a judgment, rendered in another state, that may have been fraudulently obtained?

Rule: A state court is not required to recognize the judgment of a another state court if the judgment was obtained by extrinsic fraud.

Baldwin v. Iowa State Traveling Men's Association (S.Ct. 1931)

Facts: Baldwin sued the Iowa State Traveling Men's Association in a Missouri state court. The Men's Association removed the case to the district court, made a special appearance, and moved both to quash service and to dismiss for lack of personal jurisdiction. The court quashed service, but refused to dismiss the suit. The Men's Association took no further steps to defend the suit, and judgment was rendered against them. Baldwin subsequently sued the Men's Association in a federal district court in Iowa to recover the judgment. The Men's Association contended that the original judgment had been obtained without personal jurisdiction.

Issue: When a defendant specially appears and fully litigates the issue of personal jurisdiction, is the issue of jurisdiction precluded from relitigation?

Rule: (Roberts, J.) Res judicata bars relitigation of a defense of lack of personal jurisdiction when the defendant specially appears to litigate the jurisdictional issue and that issue is fully litigated.

Chicot County Drainage District v. Baxter State Park (S.Ct. 1940)

Facts: Because the statute on which judgment was grounded was later found unconstitutional, Baxter collaterally attacked the judgment, contending it void and, hence, not res judicata. Baxter had failed to challenge the statute's validity in the prior suit.

Issue 1: Is a court's ruling on jurisdiction open to collateral attack?

Rule 1: (Hughes, CJ.) A court's determination that it has jurisdiction, while open to direct review, may not be assailed collaterally.

Issue 2: Does the res judicata doctrine apply to issues that could have been, but were not raised in a prior suit?

Rule 2: Res judicata bars relitigation of all issues that were actually raised, as well as those issues that could have been raised, in a prior suit.

Federated Department Stores v. Moitie(S.Ct. 1981)

Facts: Moitie and others all lost in separate suits against the Federated Department Stores. The other independent plaintiffs gained reversal on appeal. Without appealing, Moitie brought the present action, alleging the same injury and facts. The Federated Department Stores asserted res judicata.

Issue: Does res judicata bar relitigation of an unappealed adverse judgment when other plaintiffs in similar suits against the same defendants successfully appealed the judgments?

Rule: (Rehnquist, J.) Res judicata bars the relitigation of an unappealed adverse judgment, even though other plaintiffs in similar suits against common defendants successfully appealed the judgments against them.

Concurrence: (Blackmun, J.) Sometimes, but not here, the doctrine of res judicata must give way to "overriding concerns of public policy and simple justice." Second, res judicata applies not only to those claims that were actually litigated, but to all claims that could have been litigated.

Sawyer v. First City Financial Corp. (1981)

Facts: In the first suit, Sawyer sued First City Financial Corporation on a contract claim and judgment was entered for First City. In the second suit, Sawyer sued First City on a tort claim. Although each action rested on a completely separate set of facts, First City's claim of res judicata was granted.

Issue: Does res judicata bar a party who has separate and severable actions arising from a single transaction from separately litigating each claim?

Rule: Where a plaintiff has several causes of action, even though they may arise from the same factual setting, and even though they may be joined, the plaintiff is privileged to bring separate actions based on each separate cause.

Antrim Mining, Inc. v. Davis (1991)

Facts: Antrim polluted a watershed and was sued by a citizens' group under a citizens' suit provision of the Federal Clean Water Act. The dispute was resolved in a consent decree drafted by the parties and approved by a federal court. The consent decree purported to bind "all parties or potential parties who had notice of the instant claims and this Consent Decree." The Pennsylvania Department of Environmental Resources subsequently brought a new suit against Antrim, based on the same facts and the same law. Antrim argued that the Department's suit was barred by either the consent decree or by res judicata.

Issue 1: Can parties bind non-parties by entering into a consent decree that contains language purporting to bind the non-parties?

Rule 1: Parties cannot bind non-parties by entering into consent decrees that contain language purporting to bind the non-parties. Non-parties are entitled to their "day in court."

Issue 2: Is a non-party bound by a judgment or settlement if a party to the suit has the same interest as the non-party?

Rule 2: A non-party may be bound by a judgment or settlement if one of the parties to the suit is so closely aligned with the non-party's interests as to be his "virtual representative." However, as a matter of law, private citizens cannot act as the virtual representative of the government. Therefore, the Department in this case could not be bound by the citizens' group consent decree under a theory of virtual representation.

Parsons Steel, Inc. v. First Alabama Bank (S.Ct. 1986)

Facts: Parsons Steel sued First Alabama Bank in both federal and state court. The actions were simultaneously prosecuted. First Alabama prevailed in the federal suit. The Alabama state court refused to dismiss the state suit on the grounds of res judicata, and First Alabama appealed that decision. Without considering the state court's resolution of the res judicata issue, the federal court, on First

Alabama's motion, enjoined Parsons Steel from further prosecuting the state action.

Issue: Before enjoining a state court proceeding as res judicata, must a federal court with concurrent jurisdiction review the state court's resolution of the res judicata issue?

Rule: (Rehnquist, J.) The Full Faith and Credit Clause requires that federal courts give a state court judgment, particularly a state court's resolution of a res judicata issue, the same preclusive effect it would have had in another court of the same state. A federal court, before enjoining a state proceeding under res judicata, must consider the preclusive effect of the state court's determination that an earlier federal court judgment does not bar the state action.

Csohan v. United Benefit Life Insurance Co. (1964)

Facts: In the first suit, Csohan sued United Benefit in Ohio to recover the proceeds of her recently deceased father's life insurance policy. Two months later, United Benefit filed an interpleader action in California on the same policy. Csohan successfully moved to enjoin United Benefit from proceeding with the California action.

Issue: When may a court enjoin a party from continuing with a related suit already pending in another jurisdiction?

Rule: The court may enjoin a suit already pending in another jurisdiction if it will completely settle all the issues brought in the enjoined suit. If some issues will remain unsettled, the court must let the other jurisdiction handle them.

Frier v. City of Vandalia (1985)

Facts: Vandalia towed four of Frier's cars because they were blocking traffic. He brought an action for replevin in Illinois state court and lost, the court having determined that the City had the right to tow the cars. Frier then brought an action in federal court, alleging violation of his Fourteenth Amendment Due Process rights and 42 U.S.C. § 1983.

Issue: Does claim preclusion bar a suit that is based on the same facts as a prior suit, but propounds a different legal theory?

Rule: A suit is barred by claim preclusion if it arises out of the same core of operative facts or the same transaction that gave rise to the original suit, even if the first suit was decided on different grounds than those advanced in the second suit.

Concurrence: In determining whether disposition of a claim in state court precludes a subsequent claim in federal court, the federal court should apply the state's res judicata law. Here, Illinois adheres to the traditional "common core of operative facts" standard. The court should not apply the more expansive "transaction" test.

Martino v. McDonald's System, Inc. (1979)

Facts: McDonald's sued Martino because Martino breached a provision in their franchise agreement that provided he would not acquire a financial interest in a competing self-service food business. The suit was terminated in favor of McDonald's by a consent judgment (on the merits) before an answer was filed. Martino brought the present action, alleging that enforcement of the franchise restriction violated the Sherman Act. McDonald's asserted that the new action was barred by FRCP 13(a), which provided that a *pleading* must state as a counterclaim any claim the *pleader* has against the opposing party arising out of the same transaction. McDonald's also asserted that the suit was barred by common law principles of res judicata.

Issue 1: When does FRCP 13(a) bar a claim arising out of a transaction that was the subject of a prior suit?

Rule 1: FRCP 13(a) bars claims that are not raised during pleading. It does not bar claims asserted by one who filed no pleadings in a prior suit. Because Martino's first action was terminated before he filed an answer, FRCP 13(a) does not bar him from bringing a claim arising out of the same transaction.

Issue 2: Does res judicata bar a claim that arose out of a transaction that was the subject of a prior suit, but was not litigated in the prior suit?

Rule 2: Res judicata treats a judgment on the merits as an absolute bar to relitigation between the parties of every matter that was offered or could have been offered to sustain or defeat a prior claim. Similarly, precedent and policy require that res judicata bar a counterclaim when its prosecution would nullify rights established by a prior action. Martino's antitrust claim would have been an appropriate defense in his first suit, and its successful prosecution might have nullified rights established in the prior action. Thus, Martino was not permitted to bring the antitrust claim in a second action.

Searle Bros. v. Searle (1978)

Facts: In a divorce suit, a court determined that the Slaugh House property was part of the marital property and awarded it all to Mrs. Searle. Searle Brothers, a partnership comprised of Searle's sons, brought this action to claim that they had a one-half interest in the property, having purchased it with partnership funds. The trial court ruled that their claim was precluded, even though they were not parties to the original action.

Issue: May collateral estoppel be applied against a party who was not a party to the original action?

Rule: Because a party is only subject to judgments or decrees of courts if their interests were legally represented, collateral estoppel can only be asserted against a party in a subsequent suit who was a party or in privity with a party in the prior suit. A person is in privity with another if their interests are so closely identified that they represent the same legal right. Collateral estoppel was not properly applied to Searle Brothers because it was not a party to the first suit and there was not sufficient evidence to show that its interest in the property was ever litigated.

Illinois Central Gulf R.R. v. Parks (1979)

Facts: Mr. & Mrs. Parks brought a suit against Illinois Central following a collision between their car and a train. Mrs. Parks successfully sought damages for personal injuries. Mr. Parks unsuccessfully sought damages for loss of Mrs. Parks' services, consortium, etc. Thereafter, he brought a second suit seeking damages for his own personal injuries. Illinois Central argued that the new action was barred by claim preclusion.

Issue: When does estoppel by judgment (claim preclusion) apply?

Rule: Estoppel by judgment precludes the relitigation of a cause of action finally determined between two parties, and decrees that a judgment rendered is a complete bar to any subsequent action on the *same* claim or cause of action. Here, the court held that Mr. Parks could proceed with his suit because his claim for personal injuries required adjudication of certain issues, such as contributory negligence, that were not necessarily resolved in conjunction with his claim for loss of consortium.

Halpern v. Schwartz (1970)

Facts: A court found that Halpern committed "an act of bankruptcy" after a creditor alleged that she had committed three such acts, one of which was transferring property with the intent to hinder, delay or defraud. Any or all of them would have been grounds for the court's finding. A creditor brought a second action to prevent Halpern from receiving a bankruptcy discharge, also on the grounds that she transferred property with the intent to hinder, defraud or delay.

Issue: When a prior judgment is based on more than one independent, alternative ground, is a party precluded from relitigating any of those grounds?

Rule: Although an issue may have been fully litigated in a prior action, the prior judgment will not preclude reconsideration of the same issue if that issue did not necessarily determine the prior judgment. This is because an issue that was not essential to the prior judgment may not have been subject to the careful deliberation and analysis normally applied to essential issues, since a different disposition would not have affected the judgment. Also, a decision on an inessential issue is not subject to the safeguard of appellate review.

Winters v. Lavine (1978)

Facts: Winters was denied Medicaid compensation for Christian Science treatment. She brought a claim in state court, which was denied because (1) the statute that denied her claim was constitutional; or (2) she did not present sufficient proof of illness and treatment. She brought a second suit in federal court, alleging that the statute violated her constitutional rights.

Issue: When a prior judgment is based on more than one independent, alternative ground, is a party precluded from relitigating all of those grounds?

Rule: A party is barred from litigating any alternative grounds that were litigated in a prior action, so long as the plaintiff could fully anticipate the potential barring effect of the earlier judgment. Such is the situation in the instant case, where both grounds were fully briefed and discussed at length in the first court's decision.

State Farm Fire & Casualty Co. v. Century Home Components (1976)

Facts: A fire started in Century Home Components' (Century) shed and damaged many nearby properties. Century won the first two actions that reached judgment, but it was found negligent in the third. State Farm sought to use the third judgment to collaterally estop Century Home from denying liability in the instant action.

Issue: Can issue preclusion apply if prior suits have reached inconsistent verdicts regarding the issue in question?

Rule: Where there have been several lawsuits with varying verdicts, issue preclusion will not apply, even if the identical-issue and fully-and-fairly-litigated requirements are satisfied.

Durfee v. Duke (S.Ct. 1963)

Facts: Durfee brought a suit in Nebraska state court to quiet title to land beneath the Missouri river. There was a question of fact as to whether the land was in Nebraska or Missouri. If the land was in Missouri, Nebraska would not have subject matter jurisdiction. The Nebraska court determined that the land was in Nebraska. Two months later, Duke filed a suit to quiet title in Missouri state court, which was subsequently removed to federal court on the basis of diversity. An appellate court held that the district court did not need to give full faith and credit to the Nebraska judgment.

Issue: Must courts give full faith and credit to decisions rendered in other jurisdictions?

Rule: (Stewart, J.) Full faith and credit requires every state to give a judgment at least the res judicata effect that the judgment would be accorded in the state that rendered it. This even applies to challenges to the other court's jurisdiction, so long as the question was fully and fairly litigated and finally decided in the court that rendered the original judgment. Thus, the District Court must enforce the Nebraska judgment because Nebraska would enforce the Nebraska judgment.

Rozier v. Ford Motor Co. (1978)

Facts: Mr. Rozier was killed because the gas tank of his Ford exploded when struck from behind. In a wrongful death action brought by Mrs. Rozier, Ford was served with an interrogatory requesting any cost/benefit analyses about gas tank designs. Ford replied that it had no such information. They found the information shortly before trial, but they never disclosed it. Mrs. Rozier moved for a new trial on grounds of fraud, pursuant to FRCP 60(b)(3).

Issue: Is it proper to grant a new trial after judgment because of party's misconduct?

Rule: A party is entitled to a new trial upon proof that misrepresentation and other misconduct by their adversary prevented them from fully and fairly presenting their case.

CHAPTER 12

ALTERNATIVE SYSTEMS

I.   ANALYSIS

A.   Characteristics of the Traditional System

1. Adversarial Method
The traditional civil proceeding involves a plaintiff and defendant whose interests are adverse. The proceedings are thus designed to use that natural animosity to encourage each side to get at the truth. However, sometimes parties do not want the truth, but a fair resolution of their dispute. Furthermore, an adversarial tack can be very damaging to a longstanding relationship that the parties may want to preserve beyond the resolution of the one dispute.

2. Advocacy
Professional advocates (attorneys) represent the parties in court to help them get through the often complicated legal maze. As a result, however, a client's concerns may become subordinated to the legal issues relevant to the case.

3. Adjudication
Although a judge-mandated resolution of disputes may be useful for adverse parties, in some instances it might be better to encourage parties to resolve their differences voluntarily to both parties' satisfaction. In adjudication, more often than not, one party leaves satisfied, while the other does not. In close relationships (neighbors, family, etc.) this may not be a desired result.

B.   Need for Alternative System

1. Delay
With the massive increase in litigation in recent years, courts have been overwhelmingly backed up. Given their time constraints, many courts focus on triage-type scheduling. Criminal cases are prioritized, then cases involving the court's power of injunctive relief. As a result, many civil

suits involving traditional damages may not be resolved for months, or even years.

2. Economics
Litigation gets more and more expensive every year. Although delay is responsible for much of the cost, many would-be litigants simply cannot afford the attorneys' fees.

3. Complex Litigation
Multiplicity of parties, issues, jurisdictions, and laws all present unique situations that are not readily translatable into the adversarial relationship. As such, several alternative dispute resolution methods have been generated to deal with these issues.

II. ALTERNATIVES

A. Arbitration

1. Court-Ordered Arbitration
Although most arbitration is voluntary, some states have experimented with mandated arbitration as a means of freeing much of the court docket. However, since arbitration does not grant many of the procedural protections of litigation (especially the right to a jury), it is not a widespread or favored practice of states.

2. Arbitrability

a. By Agreement
When looking at whether a given contractual dispute is arbitrable, courts will look first at the arbitration agreement in the contract, and construe it as broadly as possible. Almost everything relating to the contract is arbitrable, including the validity of the arbitration clause itself.

b. Subject Matter
Some specific matters are not generally arbitrable. These include:

i. Family Matters
Including child custody, alimony, guardianship, etc.

ii. Punitive Damages
Some, but not all, courts have decided that punitive damages are not arbitrable on policy grounds.

iii. Antitrust Claims
The Supreme Court reasoned that private antitrust suits are an important part of the enforcement of antitrust policy that would be hindered through allowing arbitration of the claim. Interestingly, the Court did not extend this reasoning to RICO claims or Securities Exchange Act violations.

iv. Fraud in the Arbitration Agreement
Although a claim of fraud in the contract itself is arbitrable, courts will hear claims that the arbitration clause itself was fraudulently entered.

3. Procedure
Although specific arbitration associations supply their own arbitration procedure, state and federal law does not require any specific procedure.

a. Evidence
Arbitrators are free to hear or exclude any evidence they like.

b. Witnesses
They may hear from witnesses orally, in writing only, or not at all.

c. Examination
They may allow attorneys to perform all questioning, or they may participate. Cross-examinations are discretionary.

d. Opinions
They need not even write an opinion explaining their decision (and some associations discourage such opinions to prevent a court from overturning).

e. Arbitrator
One arbitrator may decide, or a panel. Dissenting and concurring opinions are neither promoted nor discouraged by law.

4. Judicial Review
Judicial review of awards are very limited, and occur only after the rendering of an arbitral award. A court will only overturn a decision where enforcement would violate basic notions of morality and justice. However, very few situations survive this standard.

5. Enforcement
Courts will enforce the award as long as there was some possible basis for an arbitrator to have reached that decision. There need not be an arbitral opinion.

B. Family Courts
These courts attempt to bring about a mutually acceptable resolution of family issues, so as to lessen the adverse affects of divorce and separation on children. If mediation fails, the case may be adjudicated.

C. Small Claims
To lessen costs to litigants, these informal courts serve to resolve disputes of less than a statutorily specified amount. The amount varies from jurisdiction to jurisdiction, depending on the state's acceptance of this form of dispute resolution (which often varies proportionally to the backlog in civil courts).

D. Negotiations
Many courts have rules designed to encourage settlement of disputes before trial. However, a judge must be careful not to favor one side too heavily, thus impinging on rules regarding impartiality.

E. Local Resolution
    Some jurisdictions have set up neighborhood courts that informally mediate disputes between neighbors, spouses, and local merchants in close neighborhoods. This serves to maintain a sense of community and stability, as well as offer individualized remedies. Mediators are given wide discretion in arriving at a mutually acceptable solution. If a solution cannot be found, the dispute may then be litigated in court.

F. Rent-A-Judge
    A favorite of complex litigation, all parties split the cost of hiring a retired judge to act as a more formal arbitrator of their dispute. Often, but not always, the proceedings are held with many of the rules of civil procedure and evidence, hybridized from the various jurisdictions.

G. Other Countries
    Foreign nations have different philosophies of jurisprudence. Civil law countries, for instance, are governed almost entirely by statute, with little or no common law. Many countries do not have trials, judges take an active role in questioning parties, and witnesses may appear seldom or only in writing. Some commentators have advocated that certain of these rules or approaches be transplanted into the American system.

CASE CLIPS

Prima Paint Corp. v. Flood & Conklin Manufacturing Co. (S.Ct. 1967)

Facts: Prima Paint Corporation and Flood & Conklin Manufacturing Company had executed a contract containing a broad arbitration clause, requiring arbitration of all claims arising out of or relating to the contract. After Flood & Conklin served Prima Paint with notice to arbitrate, Prima Paint sought to enjoin arbitration and rescission of the contract in district court. Prirna Paint alleged fraudulent inducement in the making of the contract. The court granted Flood & Conklin's motion to stay Prima Paint's action pending arbitration.

Issue: Under the United States Arbitration Act, is a claim of fraud in the inducement of the contract to be resolved by the courts or an arbitrator?

Rule: (Fortas, J.) A claim of fraud in the inducement of the contract – as opposed to the arbitration clause itself – is for the arbitrators and not the courts to decide.

Perry v. Thomas (S.Ct. 1987)

Facts: In his application for employment, Thomas agreed to arbitrate any claim against Kidder, Peabody & Co., his employer. The Federal Arbitration Act controlled enforcement of arbitration agreements, but the California Labor Code provided that actions for collection of wages may be maintained without regard to the existence of any private agreement to arbitrate. Thomas brought suit, claiming Kidder, Peabody had not given him his proper commission.

Issue: Does the Federal Arbitration Act preempt state laws that expressly forbid arbitration of an issue?

Rule: (Marshall, J.) The Federal Arbitration Act enforces arbitration clauses regardless of any contrary state statute or public policy.

Dissent 1: (Stevens, J.) The states may except certain areas from alternative dispute resolution unless Congress expressly declares otherwise.

Dissent 2: (O'Connor, J.) The state law states important public policy that the federal system should accord respect.

Mitsubishi Motors Corp. v. Soler Chrysler-Plymouth, Inc. (1983)

Facts: Mitsubishi initiated arbitration proceedings against Soler Chrysler-Plymouth for breach of its dealership agreement, and subsequently filed a complaint with the federal district court to compel Soler to arbitrate. Soler counterclaimed that Mitsubishi's sales agreement violated antitrust laws, that Soler was entitled to terminate the dealership agreement, and requested damages. The district court ordered arbitration of the antitrust defense and counterclaim. Soler appealed.

Issue: May a federal district court compel the arbitration of antitrust claims?

Rule: Since federal private antitrust claims serve to enforce important public policy that may not be furthered in arbitration, antitrust claims are not arbitrable.

Parsons & Whittemore Overseas Co., Inc. v. Societe Generale De L'Industrie Du Papier (Rakta) (1974)

Facts: Parsons & Whittemore, an American corporation, entered into a contract with Rakta, an Egyptian Corporation, to manage Rakta's business, located in Egypt, for one year. The contract terms included an arbitration clause as a means of settling disputes that arose from the contract, and a "force majeure" clause, which excused performance due to causes beyond Parsons & Whittemore's reasonable capacity to control. In 1967, as a result of the Six Day War in the Middle East, the Egyptian government broke diplomatic ties with the United States and expelled all Americans. Parsons & Whittemore then stopped work and claimed force majeure. A foreign arbitral board granted an award. Parsons & Whittemore subsequently brought an action to prevent Rakta from collecting the award. Rakta counterclaimed to affirm the award, and the court granted summary judgment for Rakta.

Issue: When may a United States court (federal or state) refuse to enforce a foreign arbitral award rendered under the New York Convention?

Rule: A court may refuse to enforce a foreign arbitral award only where enforcement would violate the forum state's most basic notions of morality and justice. However, acting in accordance with the prevailing diplomatic winds is not within the realm of basic notions of morality and justice.

Lassiter v. Department of Social Services (S.Ct. 1981)

Facts: Lassiter, an indigent, did not receive counsel at custody hearings that terminated with the loss of custody over her child.

Issue: When does due process require that indigents be provided with counsel?

Rule: (Stewart, J.) Due process requires that judicial proceedings be fundamentally fair. Here, the proceedings were fair despite the absence of counsel.

Concurrence: (Burger, C.J.) The purpose of the proceedings here was not punitive. Its purpose was protective of the child's best interests.

Dissent 1: (Blackmun, J.) The court seems to be deciding the case on its personal distaste for the plaintiff, not on whether she had an opportunity to be heard before termination of a commanding right.

Dissent 2: (Stevens, J.) The reasons for supplying counsel in criminal cases apply with equal force in a case involving the loss of one's child.

Webster Eisenlohr, Inc. v. Kalodner (1945)

Facts: Speese brought a class action on behalf of preferred stockholders of Webster Eisenlohr. One part of the trial revolved about the definition of "full voting rights." However, that provision only became relevant where certain preconditions were met. They had not been met at the time of the trial.

Issue: May courts interpret contractual clauses where certain triggering preconditions had not been met?

Rule: Where mandatory preconditions have not been met, no present case or controversy exists.

Vincent v. Hughes Air West, Inc. (1977)

Facts: Relatives of victims of a midair collision brought several lawsuits against Hughes Air West and the United States, owners of the respective airplanes. The federal district court ordered and approved the election of lead counsel. Lead counsel were to be paid from a common fund to which the plaintiffs were to contribute a portion of their settlement or recovery. Nonlead counsel questioned the court's power to appoint lead counsel.

Issue: What authority does a federal district court have regarding the activities of counsel in multiparty litigation?

Rule: The court has the power to appoint lead counsel to supervise and coordinate multiparty litigation, set reasonable compensation, and restrict the activity of nonlead counsel.

Carlstrom v. United States (1960)

Facts: The United States brought condemnation proceedings that involved the taking of Carlstrom's "estate for years." The United States subsequently amended its complaint to add the taking of a fee from Carlstrom. The district court allowed one jury to hear both suits. On appeal, Carlstrom argued that the cases were too complex for one jury and that the court abused its discretionary powers in permitting the amendment.

Issue: Does a trial court abuse its discretion when it allows a claimant to litigate two complex issues in one lawsuit before one jury at one time?

Rule: It is within the discretion of the trial court whether addition to the original issues in a lawsuit makes the case too complex for one trial.

Gilmer v. Interstate/Johnson Lane Corp. (S.Ct. 1991)

Facts: As a prerequisite to employment with Interstate, Gilmer registered as a securities representative with the New York Stock Exchange. The NYSE registration application required Gilmer to arbitrate any dispute arising from his employment with or termination by Interstate. At age 62, Gilmer was fired by Interstate, and Gilmer sued under the Age Discrimination in Employment Act (ADEA). Interstate moved to have the matter arbitrated, based on Gilmer's NYSE registration application and the Federal Arbitration Act, which required courts to enforce arbitration agreements.

Issue: Are agreements to arbitrate statutory claims enforceable under the FAA?

Rule: Agreements to arbitrate statutory claims are presumptively enforceable under the FAA. However the agreement may not be enforceable if a party can show that Congress intended to preclude a waiver of a judicial forum for the statutory claim at issue. In this case, the Court found no such waiver in the ADEA and held the arbitration agreement to be enforceable.

Dissent: Arbitration clauses contained in employment agreements are specifically exempt from coverage of the FAA, pursuant to § 1 of the Act. The arbitration agreement in this case, the dissent argues, should not be enforced because it arose from Gilmer's employment agreement with Interstate.

Ferguson v. Writers Guild of America, West (1991)

Facts: Ferguson was hired to write the screenplay for Beverly Hills Cop II. Members of the Writers Guild agreed that the task of determining the relative contributions of the various writers would be handled by Writers Guild committees. When the picture was completed, the Writers Guild determined that Ferguson should share credit for the screenplay; credit for the story was given to two others. The Writers Guild had elaborate rules for making such determinations and arbitrating subsequent disputes. After Ferguson was unsuccessful in the arbitration proceedings, he brought suit in state court.

Issue: What is the scope of judicial review of arbitration proceedings?

Rule: Where parties have agreed among themselves to bring a matter before a specially skilled arbitration committee and not to litigate the matter, judicial review is limited to whether the arbitrators exceeded their powers and whether the procedures employed deprived the objecting party of a fair opportunity to be heard.

Lockhart v. Patel (1987)

Facts: A teenager who lost an eye brought a medical malpractice action. After several formal and informal pretrial conferences, the judge ordered the defense counsel to bring a representative, "not some flunky" from the insurance company who was authorized to enter into a settlement. They sent a flunky. Consequently, the court struck the defendant's pleadings and declared him in default.

Issue: May a court order parties and their insurers to attend settlement conferences?

Rule: FRCP 16 authorizes courts to order parties and their liability insurers to attend settlement conferences, and to impose sanctions for disregarding such orders.

TABLE OF AUTHORITIES

TABLE OF CASES

Free Software!
and full electronic version of this book.

Thank you for purchasing Blond's Law Guides COMPREHENSIVE & CONCISE...JUST RIGHT!

Not only have you purchased the absolute best course preparation and study aid on the market, but you are now entitled to a **FREE ELECTRONIC VERSION** of this book delivered through the **ULTIMATE organization and study software** designed specifically for law students – FREE!

This powerful software allows you to organize your law outlines, case clips, class notes and more.

- Search, customize, and annotate in electronic format.
- Generate instant custom study outlines.
- Save hours of prep time!
- Electronic version of this title includes the full law outline and ALL the case clips – more than any other study aid!

TO DOWNLOAD YOUR FREE SOFTWARE AND ELECTRONIC OUTLINE VISIT:

www.blondslaw.com/freesoftware

626774C538B72013

4EA6A546C1942725

Printed in the United States
21041LVS00004B/39